THE RELATIVE HILLS OF BRITAIN

Dunkery Beacon
Photo: John Earle

THE RELATIVE HILLS OF BRITAIN

by

Alan Dawson

CICERONE PRESS
MILNTHORPE, CUMBRIA

ISBN 1-85284-068-4

Hill walking is true mountaineering, however the hard-bitten rock climber may regard it. Walking is the head and corner stone of all mountain climbing, whether we are dealing with the little 1000-foot hill near our homes or taking part in an assault on an unclimbed 20000-foot giant of the Himalaya. In certain kinds of weather and atmospheric lighting the one can look almost as beautiful and impressive as the other.

J. H. B. Bell

All photos by the author except where stated

Cover: Approaching the summit of a Lakeland Marilyn on the ridge of High Stile

Photo: Walt Unsworth

Contents

Chapter 1

Mountains, Munros and Marilyns

There's not much doubt that Britain is not a particularly mountainous country. Although the *Hackenthorpe Book of Lies* maintains that the highest point in the world is only eight feet, most sources of information agree that Mount Everest is over 29000 feet high, with Ben Nevis only 4400 feet. By global standards Britain's mountains are quite insignificant. Many other countries not only have higher mountains, they also have roads, railways, hotels, restaurants, towns and even capital cities that are far higher than any mountain in Britain.

Height isn't everything though. British hills and mountains have many other qualities, which is one reason why there is a long tradition of writing about them and making lists of the highest ones. These lists have been based on the assumption that hills must be a certain height above sea level - usually at least 2000 feet.

This book takes a different approach. It concentrates on hills that are ***relatively high,*** compared to the surrounding area, rather than compared to sea level. The main feature of the book is a comprehensive list of every hill in Britain that is at least 500 feet (roughly 150 metres) higher than the land around it. In practice this means at least 500 feet above sea level, as none of these hills start below sea level. Five hundred feet is a completely arbitrary figure of course, just as arbitrary as 2000 or 3000 feet, but I will make some attempt to justify it. To do this requires a brief summary of the existing literature.

In the beginning there was Sir Hugh Munro. He saw that there were lots of mountains in Scotland over 3000 feet high, he saw that they were good, and he set about compiling a list of them. No-one seems to known why he chose 3000 feet, but no-one questions his choice. Most hill walkers are well aware of the result - a book of *Munro's Tables* that has evolved through several editions. This has led to the increasingly popular sport of Munro-bagging, which involves attempting to climb all the 277 separate mountains over 3000 feet that are listed in *Munro's Tables,* and are commonly known as 'Munros'. This can be a highly addictive pursuit.

Many of us who enjoy hill walking for its own sake find that the enjoyment of walking is enhanced by having a list to help guide where we go and a long-term target to achieve. There are however a number of reasons why Munro's tables are not satisfactory as a list of British hills:

- Munro ignored England and Wales.

- Munro did not define what criteria he used for including a hill on his list. He divided the summits into two categories - separate mountains and mere 'tops' - but did not define either.
- Munro's tables have been revised several times since they were first published. Some revisions have simply reflected more accurate and up-to-date maps, but some appear to be arbitrary modifications to the original list.
- There are many fine hills in Scotland, England and Wales that are less than 3000 feet high.

Next on the scene was J.Rooke Corbett (the fourth person to complete the ascent of all the Munros), who took some of these points into account by compiling a list of all the Scottish mountains between 2500 and 3000 feet high that have a drop of at least 500 feet on all sides. This list is a lot less fun than Munro's, as it leave no scope for arguments about which summits should be promoted to separate mountain status or relegated to being only 'tops.' Corbett's list was passed on to the editors of *Munro's Tables* after his death, and there is no record of why he chose 500 feet as the amount required to separate one hill from another. Like Munro, Corbett was concerned only with Scotland.

There are very few summits over 3000 feet high in England and Wales (none at all in Southern Scotland), and relatively few over 2500 feet, and so the subsequent list compilers had to include hills as low as 2000 feet in order to produce worthwhile lists. There have been various efforts published in recent years.

- Percy Donald compiled a list of all the hills over 2000 feet in Southern Scotland that have a drop of one hundred feet on all sides, together with several further tops that have a drop of between fifty and one hundred feet. This list is also published in the book of *Munro's Tables.*
- George Bridge published a book listing all the summits of England and Wales over 2000 feet high, using a formula based on a combination of height difference and distance apart to decide which summits to include. This list was published in 1973, based on one-inch-to-the-mile maps. Recent maps show that it is now well out of date.
- More recently John and Anne Nuttall have produced the two-volume comprehensive *Mountains of England and Wales* (Vol 1:Wales, Vol 2: England). These books list summits over 2000 feet (610m) that have a drop of fifty feet (fifteen metres) on all sides, with walking routes to cover them all.
- Terry Marsh has produced guides to the mountains of Wales, the Lake District and the Pennines that are over 600 metres high (about 1968 feet). These are useful as guidebooks, but the lists of summits are not

very satisfactory as they are not strictly defined - most of them have at least thirty metres (one hundred feet) drop on all sides, but Marsh includes numerous other summits of 'topographical merit', which is an arbitrary and subjective concept.

- A small booklet published by Chris Buxton and Gwyn Lewis in 1986 lists all the summits in England and Wales over 2000 feet high with a minimum of only ten metres drop all round. This list is accurate, up-to-date and consistent, but includes a large number of insignificant summits of little intrinsic interest.
- Writers of guidebooks such as the renowned Alfred Wainwright and Walter Poucher have included lists of prominent and well-known summits based on no particular criteria. These are excellent and worthwhile guidebooks, but are not intended to be definitive references. A separate booklet listing all the summits named in Wainwright's book was published by John Turner, but this is intended as an index and does not attempt to rationalise any of the details.
- In 1989 Eric Yeaman produced a handbook listing all the Scottish hills that have a drop of one hundred or more metres on all sides, together with others qualifying by distance instead of relative height. This is an interesting and up-to-date publication, though in my opinion it is awful to look at and appears complicated to use. It has several odd features, such as the listing of hills in reverse order (lowest first), the use of four-figure grid references, and the duplication of hills that happen to appear on more than one map. However, I cannot be too critical of it as it comes closest to this book in its concept and content. Apart from its poor presentation its main drawback is that, like all the other lists, it does not cover the whole country, as it ignores hills outside Scotland.

Why then do we need yet another list of British hills? Perhaps the honest answer is that no-one actually needs a new list, but a lot of walkers would probably like one. It is sometimes claimed that an attraction to lists is a sign of arrested personal development. If this is the case then I will try to cover up my own psychological deficiencies by suggesting a list(!) of reasons why publishing this new list of hills is eminently desirable:

- None of the existing publications are fully satisfactory or comprehensive. They use different definitions for hills and do not cover the whole of Britain.
- There has been a major change in recent years to the maps used by most walkers. In 1988 the Ordnance Survey completed publication of the Second Series of 1:50000 scale maps. Although publication of these maps began in the early 1970s, the changeover to metric contours at ten-metre intervals only occurred with the Second Series.

The contouring on the new maps is much more detailed than on the older ones, and shows that much of the data in previous lists of hills is in need of revision.

- The encouragement of walkers to explore a wider range of hills in different regions of the country might relieve the pressure of feet on well-known summits in the popular areas. This may not prevent any erosion, but it might distribute it more evenly.
- The lower hills can provide more attractive walks in poor weather, especially when the higher summits are obscured by clouds. A low-level walk with views is usually more enjoyable than a high-level one in mist. The smaller hills are also ideal for filling in an odd hour or half day, or for exploring during busy holiday periods when the bigger hills and popular routes tend to get somewhat crowded.
- In mountainous areas the lesser hills often make excellent viewpoints for higher ones. For example, some walkers reckon that the finest view of the Cuillin Hills on Skye is from the top of Sgurr na Stri, which is a mere 1630 feet high.
- The listing of some hills in Southern England gives walkers unfortunate enough to live in that part of the country some constructive walking to do when they're not away in the northern hills. At the same time the list convincingly demonstrates how few hills there are in England and Wales compared to Scotland.
- The new list gives those fanatics who have completed all the Munros, Corbetts, Bridges, etc a renewed purpose in life. It also provides a good alternative, if used selectively, for those walkers getting too old to think of completing the Munros.

These are all good reasons for publishing a new list, yet there is another consideration that is possibly more important than any of them. It arises from the uncomfortable feeling that a lot of the minor summits which have appeared in previous lists are really a bit on the boring side. The more distinct hills usually provide enjoyable walks and good viewpoints, and it is very satisfying to plan and follow a long continuous route taking in as many tops as possible. But after walking an extra two or three miles just to stand on top of a flattish rounded hump that happens to be a few metres higher than the surrounding bog, then even the most obsessive of summit baggers begin to ask questions.

I think it was in the Lake District that I first became aware of these nagging doubts, as a natural traverse over Skiddaw from Ullock Pike to Lonscale Fell was interrupted by a lengthy trudge to take in Sale How, which is a prime example of the sort of featureless summit that occurs in lists of the 2000-foot hills of England and Wales. In fact, most of the summits in the Lake District are well worth a visit - it is the Pennines and parts of Wales that contain most of the really tedious tops. I have spent a full day in both the Berwyn Hills and the Northern Pennines driving round to different spots and doing three or four different 'walks' to bag relatively accessible but thoroughly unmemorable summits, usually via thigh-deep heather or shin-deep sludge.

Even the Munros, and particularly some of the Munro Tops, are not exempt from this problem. Carn Sgulain, for example, in the Monadh Liath Hills, is a Munro almost entirely lacking in distinctive features. It rises only sixty metres from the col separating it from Carn Dearg, and although it is a few miles away, the distance and re-ascent fail to give it any character or appearance of being a separate mountain. Some other summits have even less to offer. Irvine Butterfield, in his book *The High Mountains of Britain and Ireland,* describes the Munro Top called Tom Dubh, which is near Braeriach in the Cairngorms, as being:

> one for the real enthusiast, the most meaningless 3000 foot 'top' in all Britain, for here lies the ultimate in desolate wilderness, a landscape so featureless that it almost defies man's ability to use map and compass. Devoid of landmarks, in mist only the oozy drains of the plateau's few streams offer guides of any consequence.

The ascent of Tom Dubh involves a considerable detour from any reasonable route, and its remote austerity has made it into a prized collector's piece.

It seems that only Corbett's list offers a guarantee of satisfaction. All of the Corbetts are summits of some significance, and of course this is because they all have a relative height of at least 500 feet. In his book, *Climbing the Corbetts,* Hamish Brown agrees that 'by definition Corbetts are much more solitary and individualistic' than the Munros, and claims that 'there are fewer "dull" Corbetts than there are "dull" Munros'.

In the Andes or Himalaya most summits with a drop of only 500 feet would hardly warrant a second glance. In Britain 500 feet is significant, and seems a good measure of what makes a separate hill or mountain - it feels right. Well, almost right. Now that Ordnance Survey maps have metric contours it is impossible to work in feet. Five hundred feet is equal to 152.4 metres, so to make matters easier the metric measure of 150 metres (492 feet) has been used to compile the new list.

Having settled on the type of hills to be included in the new list, it is of course vitally necessary to find a name for them. A flippant item in a recent Scottish Mountaineering Club Journal suggested using the term 'Mungo' for the millions of hills over 300 feet high. I have decided to use the more distinguished and appropriate term 'Marilyn', and I therefore officially define a Marilyn as any hill that has a drop of at least 150 metres on all sides, regardless of distance, absolute height or topographical merit. At the last count there were 1542 of them, and they are all listed in Chapters 3 and 4.

In essence Marilyns are similar to Corbetts, but whereas Corbetts are only between 2500 and 3000 feet high and are only found in Scotland, Marilyns may be from 500 to 4500 feet high and are found throughout Scotland, England and Wales. It must be admitted that not every single one of the Marilyns is terrifically interesting, but a high proportion of them are significant summits or local landmarks, whereas the list excludes many of the more tedious summits that have been included in other lists.

A good example of the measure of 150 metres is found between the highest two peaks in England. The drop in height from the top of Scafell Pike to the col which separates it from Scafell is just about 150 metres, though it looks much greater from some vantage points. The re-ascent to the summit of Scafell is slightly less, but Scafell has been included in the list of Marilyns because most walkers traversing the two summits will descend well over 150 metres in order to avoid the direct route over Broad Stand. This route is more of a rock climb than a walk and is usually treated as such. Scafell is the only summit to receive this preferential treatment - elsewhere the 150-metre rule has been rigorously applied.

Examples of prominent small hills which just exceed a relative height of 150 metres are Whitbarrow and Hutton Roof Crags, which may not be well-known names but are familiar sights as they rise up on either side of the M6 motorway near Milnthorpe in Southern Cumbria. Many other distinctive small hills, such as Glastonbury Tor and Arnside Knott, just fail to make the grade. This is hardly likely to lessen their popularity as viewpoints and tourist attractions. Fortunately, major sea stacks such as the Old Man of Hoy and the Great Stack of Handa are also under 150 metres high. Unfortunately there are two sea stacks in the St Kilda group of islands that do make the grade, and these are likely to test the commitment of even the most dedicated summit bagger.

The existence of a number of Marilyns in an area may be seen as a measure of the ***peakedness*** or undulating nature of the land, as opposed to its altitude. Statisticians have a word for this notion of peakedness - they call it ***kurtosis.*** So we can say that although the Cape Wrath peninsula reaches no great height, it clearly has positive kurtosis as it contains eight Marilyns. By contrast, large areas of land that are well above sea level can be fairly flat; some of the major uplands of England such as Dartmoor and the Peak District have very few Marilyns.

The concept of relative height seems to make more sense the more you think about it, yet some walkers may feel that it would be preferable to use the 500-foot limit in order to identify the most important hills over a certain height, such as 2000 feet. For those who feel this way the solution is simple - ignore the lower hills. The existence of the list does not compel anyone to use it. But I am sure that if I had drawn the line at 2000 feet, then sooner or later someone else would have extended this down to 1500 feet, then 1000 feet, so we may as well get it all over with now. The lower hills will always be there for anyone who wishes to finish the 2000-footers first!

Chapter 2

The Challenge of the Marilyns

For hundreds of years small groups of Britons have travelled all over the world looking for adventure, discovering new continents, scaling unclimbed peaks, boldly going where no-one has gone before, and so on. Now that all the major mountain ranges of the world have been explored and the highest summits climbed, it may seem strange to suggest that there is still a significant challenge provided by the British hills that is awaiting its first conquest. Yet the fact is that no-one has ever climbed all the relative hills of Britain. This is largely because no-one has ever known where they all are. The publication of this book changes all that. The listing of the relative hills for the first time naturally raises the question of who will be the first person to stand on top of them all. This is part of the challenge of the Marilyns.

Although several hundred people are known to have completed the ascent of all the Munros, it is unlikely that many will attempt the Marilyns. The scale of the task is daunting. It requires the equivalent of one ascent per week for almost thirty years. Of course anyone who has already climbed all the Munros and Corbetts has a good start, but it still leaves a vast number of hills outstanding. There are several problems likely to be faced by anyone contemplating the challenge:

Commitment

This is the key factor, as no-one is going to complete the Marilyns by accident. It will require dedicated commitment and perseverance. Even being a very keen hill walker will not be sufficient, as a small number of Marilyns can hardly be regarded as hills in the usual sense. For example, the tops of Bishop Wilton Wold (Humberside) and Grendon Green (Hereford & Worcester) are just next to a main road, Crowborough (East Sussex) is a town, while Arthur's Seat (Lothian) is in the middle of a large city. It requires a particular type of mentality to be bothered with this type of summit bagging. It's not the sort of thing that is likely to appeal to Reinhold Messner or Chris Bonington but, let's face it, not many of us come into that category.

Time and Money

Walking is one of the few leisure activities that costs nothing, but transport, accommodation and outdoor clothing can all be expensive. Anyone wealthy enough to not have to work for a living should have both the time and the money to consider attempting the challenge of the Marilyns, but few of these people seem to be interested in hill walking. Unemployed walkers may have the time but not the resources, whereas the retired may have enough money but not the time or the health. Those in full-time employment would need to set aside a substantial chunk of leisure time each year, which is likely to rule out anyone with family responsibilities. Probably those best placed to make a serious attempt on the Marilyns will be fairly solitary characters with a job that allows them generous amounts of free time. It is surely no coincidence that the first two men to complete the Munros were both ministers of the church.

Credibility

Perhaps another reason why vicars were the first recorded Munroists was that they were the first to be believed! What proof is there? The same problem applies to the Marilyns. Even a photograph from each summit is unlikely to suffice, given the frequency of mist on the Scottish hills and the similarity of most cairns. So an important quality is credibility - it is not just a question of completing the Marilyns, but also of being known as an honest and reliable character.

Access

The fact that a summit is listed in this book gives no guarantee that access to it is possible. Most summits are on privately-owned land, and it is of course up to the individual walker to abide by any restrictions that may be imposed or to ask permission for access. Hundreds of hills in the Scottish highlands are virtually closed to walkers for several weeks each year so that deer and grouse can be safely shot without disturbance. Some summits are on Ministry of Defence land and subject to severely restricted access (Ben Clach in Central Scotland is a notable example). Look out for the red 'Danger Area' lettering on Ordnance Survey maps. Access to hills on the island of Rhum is also restricted, though for different reasons, as it is a national nature reserve, and all visitors must obtain advance permission.

Terrain

The great majority of summits can be attained by anyone with a degree of stamina and the ability to put one foot in front of the other. However, there are a few significant exceptions. On the British mainland perhaps the most awkward summit is The Cobbler, which has a dramatic outline overlooking Arrochar and Loch Long. On its summit are three rocky peaks, the highest of which is undoubtedly a climb rather than a walk. In the Cuillin Hills of Skye both Sgurr nan Gillean and Sgurr Alasdair require liberal use of hands as well as feet, but the main problem is the Inaccessible Pinnacle of Sgurr Dearg. This has proved a thorn in the side of many aspiring Munro baggers, as it requires reasonable athleticism and proficient ropework to successfully complete the rock climb and abseil.

These difficulties are relatively trivial compared to those posed by St Kilda. For a start you have to get there. There are some summer sailings for tourists to Hirta, the main island, but there are difficult Marilyns on three other islands and two sea stacks - Stac Lee and Stac an Armin. These stacks will look absolutely frightening to most walkers. They have been climbed on several occasions, by some of the inhabitants of St Kilda before its evacuation in 1930, and by a few rock climbers since then, but there is no easy route up either of them. Even landing is a problem, as the stacks have no beach or cove, and calm seas are a rarity in this part of the world. Once on the stacks the multitude of seabirds on the narrow ledges are likely to pose an additional hazard.

Rock is not the only natural hazard to be encountered on the Marilyns. Trees and water can cause problems on some hills. As an increasing proportion of British uplands are becoming coated in forestry plantations, it can be awkward to find a route through to some of the summits. Tracks or fire-breaks can usually be found somewhere among all the gloomy conifers, but they rarely run for long in a convenient direction, and the map may offer little help. Rivers and streams are less of a problem near the summits, but in wet weather they can make the approach to some of the remote Scottish hills difficult and dangerous. It is generally possible to plan a route to avoid river crossings, but after heavy rain even a minor stream can become an impassable barrier, and force a long detour or an unscheduled encampment.

Ethics

It may seem silly to raise ethical questions in an activity as essentially simple as walking, but anyone contemplating the ascent of all the Marilyns must make some decisions about what are acceptable means of reaching the summits. Does a trip on the Snowdon mountain railway and a fifty-yard stroll to the top count as an ascent of Snowdon? Most walkers would say certainly not. But the mainline railway across Rannoch Moor to Corrour Station is usually considered a valid means of access to the remote hills of the Ben Alder area. Everyone uses public roads to reach the start of a walk, but in some places they come very close to the summit of a hill. No-one seriously argues against using these, as the only ethical alternative is to start every walk from sea level, which even the purest of purists would regard as excessively silly.

Yet once off a public road any form of motorised transport is likely to be frowned upon by those on foot. The off-road use of man-powered devices is less controversial, but it's a tricky question to decide whether an ascent assisted by skis or mountain bike is as valid as an ascent on foot. Personally I would say it isn't, but I have no intention of laying down rules for valid means of reaching a summit. The only techniques I would definitely outlaw are those that involve landing on or near a summit from the air, so any 'ascents' by helicopter, chair-lift, parachute, balloon etc definitely do not count!

The Real Challenge

Despite the difficulties outlined above, there will no doubt be some poor fools out there who can not resist a challenge, and will probably have reached the top of all the Marilyns before the end of the century. However, the challenge of the Marilyns is not just the race to be first. There are lots of other challenges - the first winter ascent, the first to complete the Marilyns in one calendar year or one continuous journey, the first to complete them in alphabetical order or height order, the first ascent by a disabled dog, and so on.

But of course the real challenge is for each individual to set his or her own target and try to achieve it, by being selective and choosing to concentrate on the hills in a particular area of interest. There are numerous possibilities, such as the British mainland, England or Wales, a particular region or regions, summits above or below a certain height, and so on. For example, you might decide to tackle the 110 Marilyns that are over 1000 metres high, which might seem feasible to those who regard the 277 Munros as too many for one lifetime, or you could choose to concentrate on the Marilyns in England over 1000 feet high, and be surprised to discover that there are only 136 of them.

My recommendation is to use the list to give some extra purpose and enjoyment to your walking, and to encourage you to visit new areas and see new views, but do not let it dominate your thoughts so much that the bagging of summits blinds you to the character of the countryside. Lists can offer a tremendous incentive to actually go out walking more often, and you'll find that it's almost always worthwhile and enjoyable wherever you go.

Chapter 3

The Marilyns by Region

One of the most difficult decisions to make when compiling a list of hills is how to divide the country into different regions. It is an essential task, so that readers can conveniently look up all the hills in a given area. For this chapter the regions defined in *Munro's Tables* have been used as the starting point, so that Regions 1 to 17 are almost identical to those used for the Munros, with some regions enlarged where necessary to include hills under 3000 feet. The other 25 regions have been arrived at by using an appropriate combination of coastline, rivers, roads and county boundaries. Most of the regions have been further divided into smaller more manageable sections.

Each region is given a descriptive heading to provide a general idea of its location, and a detailed specification of its boundaries. Similarly, each section is given a brief heading followed by details of its boundary within the larger region.

In this chapter the hills are listed in height order within each section. The information is laid out in the following columns:

Height: The first two columns give the height of the hill in metres and feet. All of the Ordnance Survey 1:50000 scale maps (Landranger), and most of the 1:25000 scale maps (Pathfinder or Outdoor Leisure) are now available with metric contours and heights given in metres. Unfortunately the Ordnance Survey has the infuriating habit of giving some hills different heights on the two different scales of map, and it cannot be assumed that the most recently published map is always the more accurate. The guidance offered by the Ordnance Survey is that 'the Pathfinder series should as a general rule prove to be the most reliable source of heighting information'. However, it is not possible to rely solely on the 1:25000 maps, as metric versions are not available for all areas, and also because numerous spot heights are shown on 1:50000 maps but omitted from the 1:25000 maps (and vice-versa). There also appear to be cases where heights have been updated on the 1:50000 map but not on the 1:25000. The heights listed below are therefore taken from both sets of maps, and in cases where a different height in metres is given on the two scales of map, then the higher figure is given here.

Name: Most names have been taken from the relevant Landranger map, but if a hill is not named on this then the name given on the Pathfinder map has been used. A star in front of a name indicates that the name is not shown on the latest Landranger map. In a few cases a different name is given on the Pathfinder map, but this has only been used if it clearly indicates that the name given on the Landranger map does not apply to the summit. Where a hill has a general name and a summit name, the general name is given first followed by a hyphen, e.g. 'Snowdon - Yr Wyddfa'. Where a hill has two alternative names given on the Landranger map, the second name is included in brackets. Accents have been omitted from the Scottish names, but great care has been taken to get the spelling correct (or as correct as the Ordnance Survey has managed).

Map Number: This column gives the number of the Landranger (1:50000 scale) map on which the summit of the hill is to be found. Note that a different map may be required for the start of the walk. Where a summit appears on two or three overlapping maps then each of them is listed.

Grid Reference: This is essential information for all walkers, as it pinpoints the location of the summit of the hill (to within 100 metres). Details of how to use the grid reference are given on all Landranger maps. Summit baggers should take particular note of the grid reference, as it does not always coincide with the position of the spot height or triangulation point on the map. The grid reference can be used to identify the Pathfinder map on which the summit appears, by taking the two letters followed by the first and fourth numbers. For example, Schiehallion has grid reference NN714548 and so appears on Pathfinder map NN75.

Date: This column is left blank so that you can enter the date on which you ascend each hill. With over 1500 hills to choose from it would take quite a feat of memory to remember exactly where you've been and when. If you're going to keep some sort of record it might as well be here.

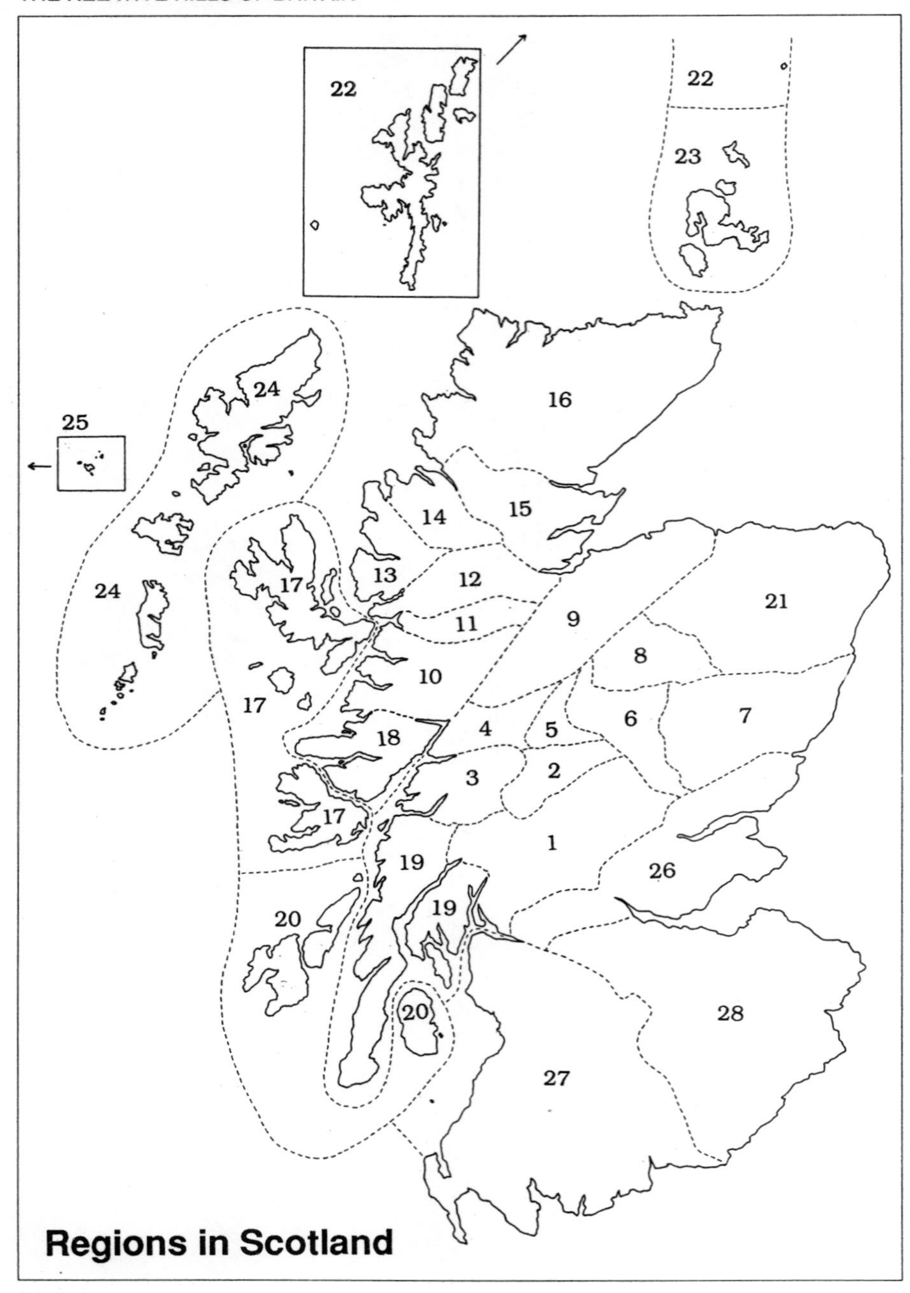
22
22
23
25
24
24
16
15
14
13
12
17
11
9
21
8
10
17
6
7
4
5
18
3
2
17
1
19
26
20
19
20
28
27
Regions in Scotland

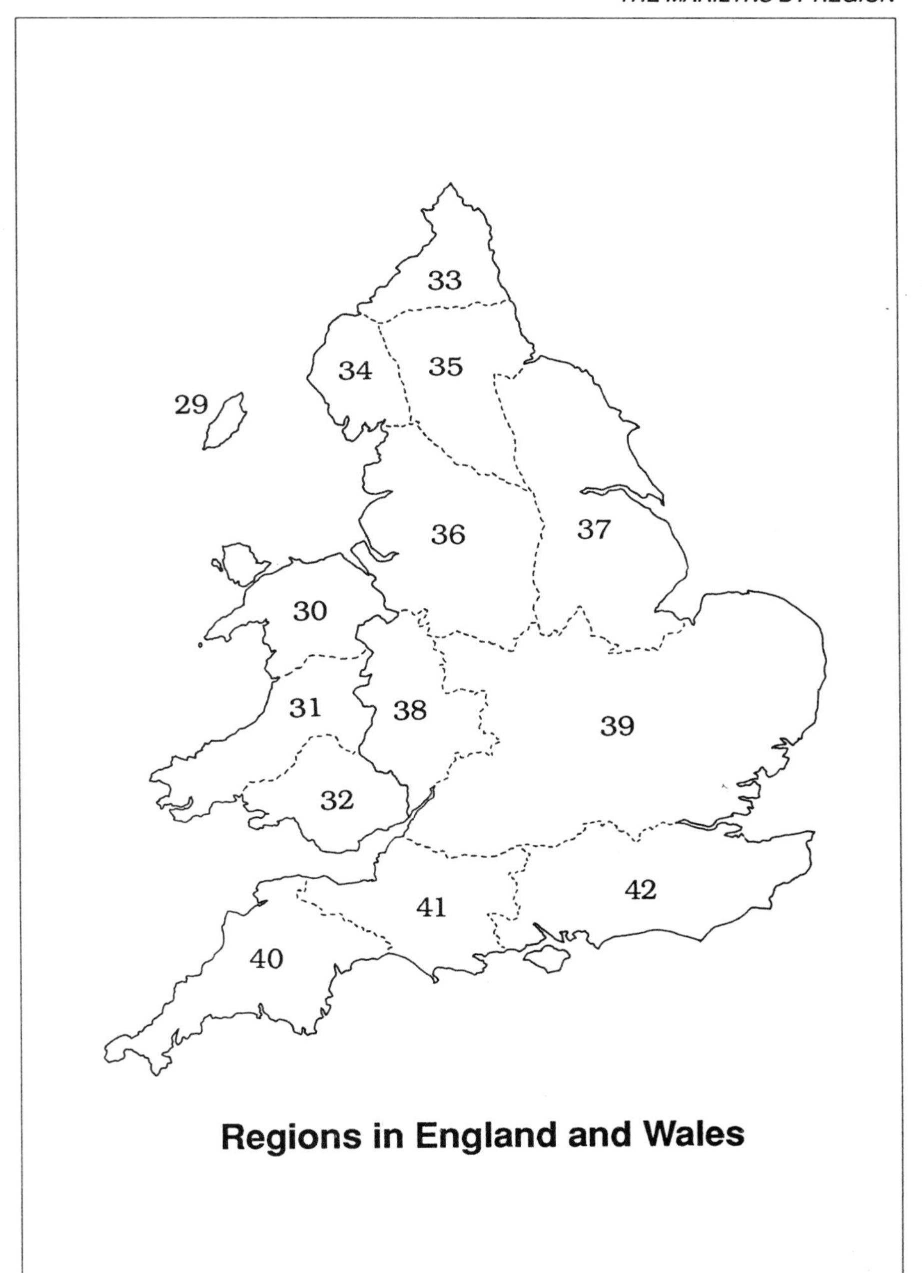

Regions in England and Wales

REGION 1
Firth of Clyde to Strath Tay

Crianlarich; A85 and A827 to Killin; Loch Tay and River Tay to Perth; A9 to Stirling; A811 to Drymen; Endrick Water, Loch Lomond and River Leven to Dumbarton; coast to Arrochar; A83 to Inveraray; A819 and A85 to Crianlarich.

Section 1A Loch Tay to Perth

North of Loch Earn and River Earn from Lochearnhead to the A9

Metres	*Feet*	*Name*	*Map*	*Grid Ref*	*Date*
931	3054	Ben Chonzie	51/52	NN 773309	______
888	2913	Creagan na Beinne	51/52	NN 744369	______
879	2883	Creag Uchdag	51/52	NN 708323	______
789	2589	Auchnafree Hill	52	NN 809308	______
759	2490	Ciste Buide a'Claidheimh *	51/52	NN 729352	______
730	2395	Beinn na Gainimh	52	NN 837345	______
719	2359	Meall Buidhe	51	NN 577276	______
712	2335	Creag Ruadh *	51	NN 674292	______

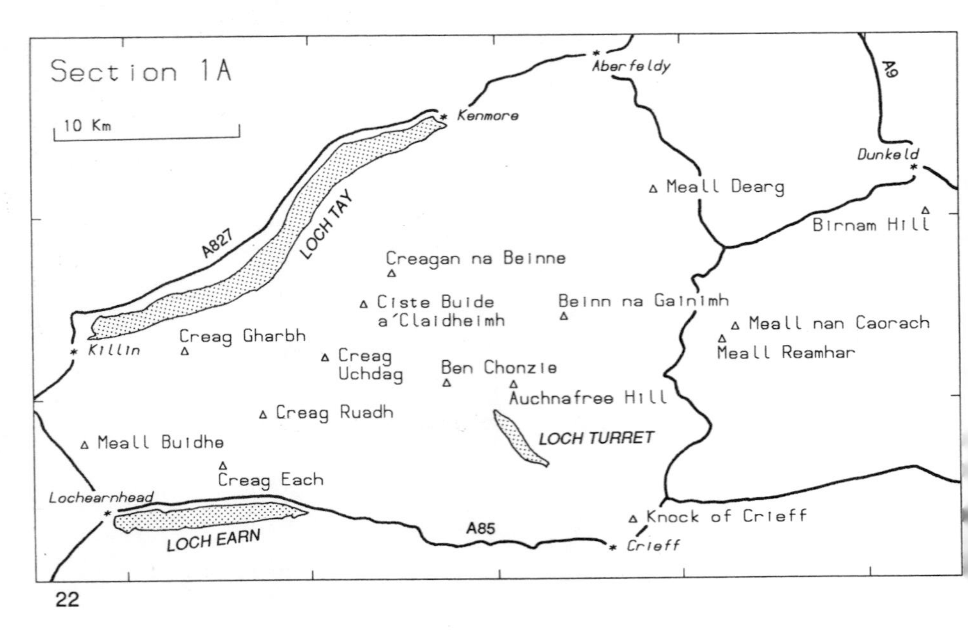

Metres	Feet	Name	Map	Grid Ref	Date
690	2264	Meall Dearg	52	NN 886415	______
672	2204	Creag Each *	51	NN 652264	______
637	2091	Creag Gharbh	51	NN 632327	______
623	2045	Meall nan Caorach	52	NN 929339	______
620	2035	Meall Reamhar	52	NN 922332	______
404	1324	Birnam Hill - King's Seat	52/53	NO 032402	______
279	915	Knock of Crieff	52/58	NN 873233	______

Section 1B Strathyre to Strathallan
East of A84 from Lochearnhead to Stirling

Metres	Feet	Name	Map	Grid Ref	Date
985	3231	Ben Vorlich	57	NN 629189	______
975	3199	Stuc a'Chroin	57	NN 617175	______
813	2667	Beinn Each	57	NN 602158	______
809	2654	Meall na Fearna	57	NN 651186	______
706	2316	Beinn Dearg	57	NN 697197	______
665	2181	Uamh Bheag	57	NN 691119	______
645	2116	Sgiath a'Chaise	57	NN 583169	______
640	2100	Mor Bheinn	51/52/57	NN 716212	______
533	1748	Ben Clach	57	NN 759152	______
393	1290	Torlum	57	NN 819192	______

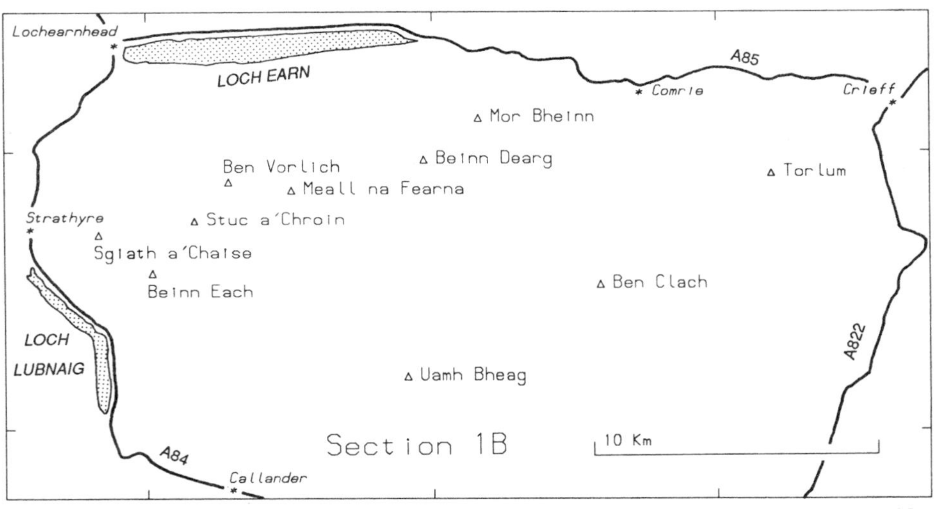

Section 1C Loch Lomond to Strathyre

East of A82 and Loch Lomond from Crianlarich to Drymen

Metres	*Feet*	*Name*	*Map*	*Grid Ref*	*Date*
1174	3852	Ben More	51	NN 432244	______
1165	3821	Stob Binnein	51	NN 434226	______
1046	3432	Cruach Ardrain	51/56	NN 409211	______
995	3264	An Caisteal	50/56	NN 379193	______
974	3194	Ben Lomond	56	NN 367029	______
933	3061	Beinn Chabhair	50/56	NN 367179	______
879	2883	Ben Ledi	57	NN 562098	______
869	2850	Stob a'Choin	56	NN 416160	______
852	2794	Meall an t-Seallaidh	51	NN 542234	______
821	2694	Benvane	57	NN 535137	______
809	2654	Creag MacRanaich	51	NN 546256	______
771	2531	Ceann na Baintighearna	57	NN 474163	______
770	2525	Beinn a'Choin	50/56	NN 354130	______
753	2470	The Stob	51	NN 491231	______
747	2451	Meall Mor	50/56	NN 384152	______
729	2391	Ben Venue	57	NN 474063	______
688	2257	Stob Breac	57	NN 447166	______
658	2160	Creag Mhor	57	NN 510185	______
633	2077	Cruinn a'Bheinn	56	NN 365052	______
598	1962	Beinn Uamha	56	NN 386069	______
597	1957	Beinn Uird	56	NS 399985	______
586	1923	Binnean nan Gobhar	56	NS 419968	______
572	1877	Beinn an t-Sidhein	57	NN 547179	______
566	1856	Meall Gainmheich	57	NN 509095	______
511	1675	Beinn Dubh	56	NN 404045	______
427	1400	Beinn Dearg	57	NN 589038	______
400	1312	Craig of Monievreckie *	57	NN 547020	______
361	1185	Conic Hill	56	NS 432923	______

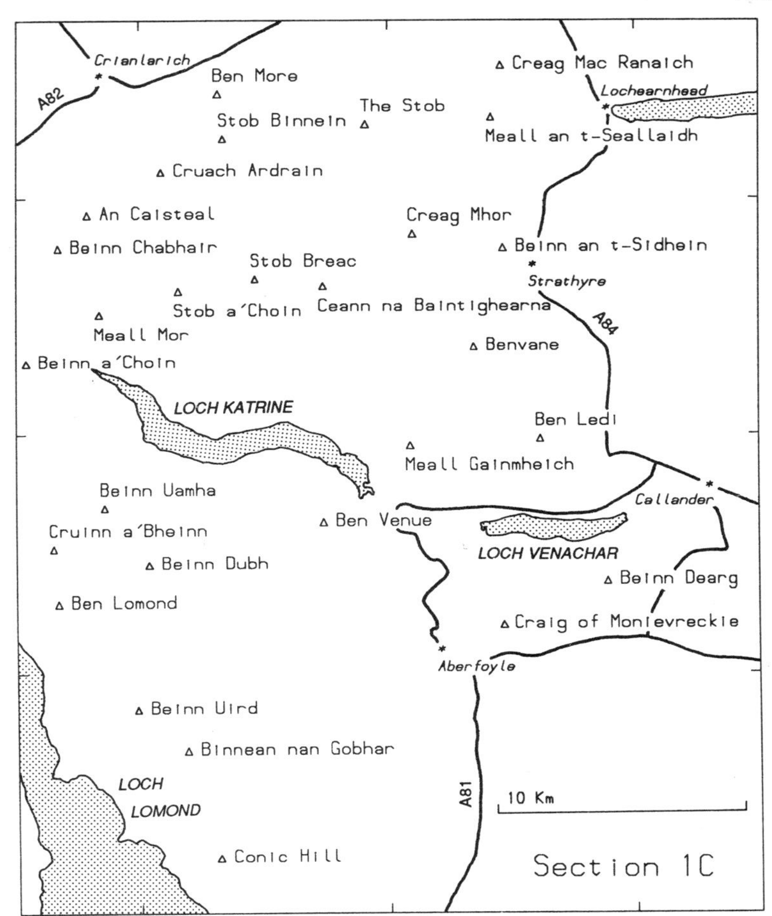

Section 1D Inveraray to Crianlarich

North of A83 from Inveraray to Arrochar

Metres	*Feet*	*Name*	*Map*	*Grid Ref*	*Date*
1130	3708	Ben Lui	50	NN 266263	______
1029	3376	Ben Oss	50	NN 287253	______
1011	3318	Beinn Ime	56	NN 255085	______
978	3209	Beinn Dubhchraig	50	NN 308255	______
948	3111	Beinn Bhuidhe	50/56	NN 204187	______

Metres	Feet	Name	Map	Grid Ref	Date
943	3093	Ben Vorlich	50/56	NN 295124	______
926	3038	Beinn Narnain	56	NN 272067	______
916	3004	Ben Vane	56	NN 278098	______
884	2899	The Cobbler (Ben Arthur)	56	NN 259058	______
880	2887	Beinn Chuirn	50	NN 281292	______
858	2815	Beinn Luibhean	56	NN 243079	______
817	2680	Binnein an Fhidhleir	50/56	NN 230109	______
764	2508	Meall an Fhudair	50/56	NN 271192	______

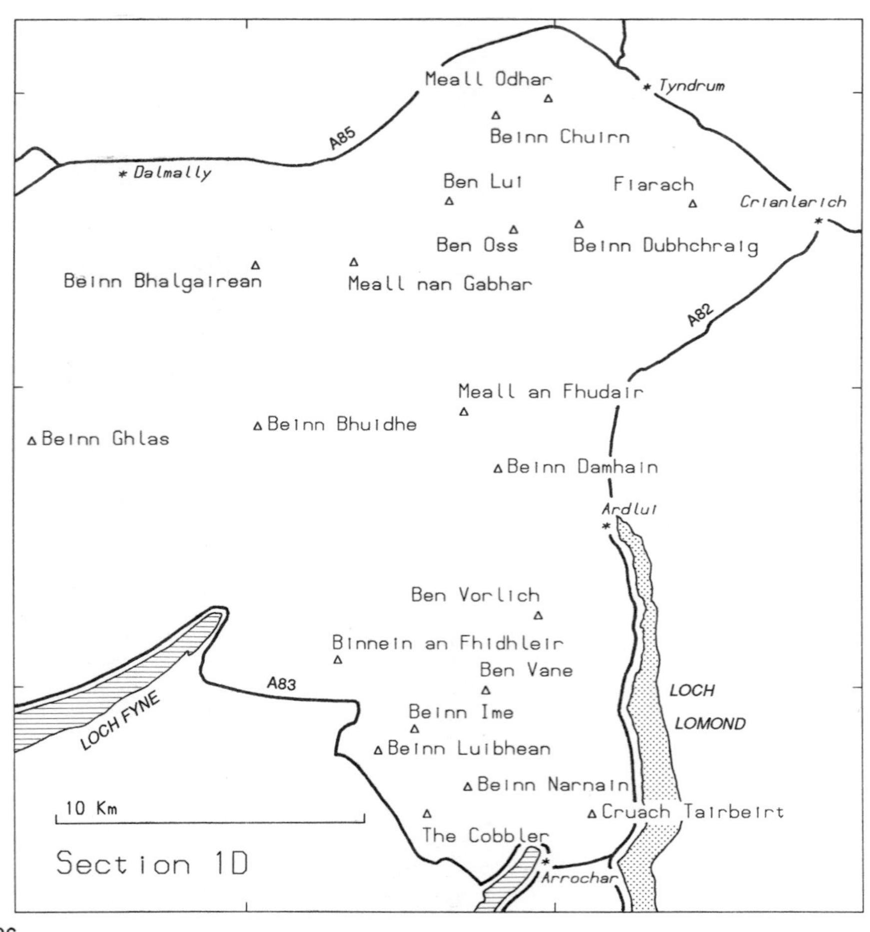

Metres	Feet	Name	Map	Grid Ref	Date
743	2438	Meall nan Gabhar	50	NN 235242	______
684	2243	Beinn Damhain	50/56	NN 282173	______
656	2152	Meall Odhar	50	NN 298298	______
652	2139	Fiarach	50	NN 345262	______
636	2085	Beinn Bhalgairean	50	NN 203241	______
550	1804	Beinn Ghlas	50/56	NN 131182	______
415	1362	Cruach Tairbeirt	56	NN 312058	______

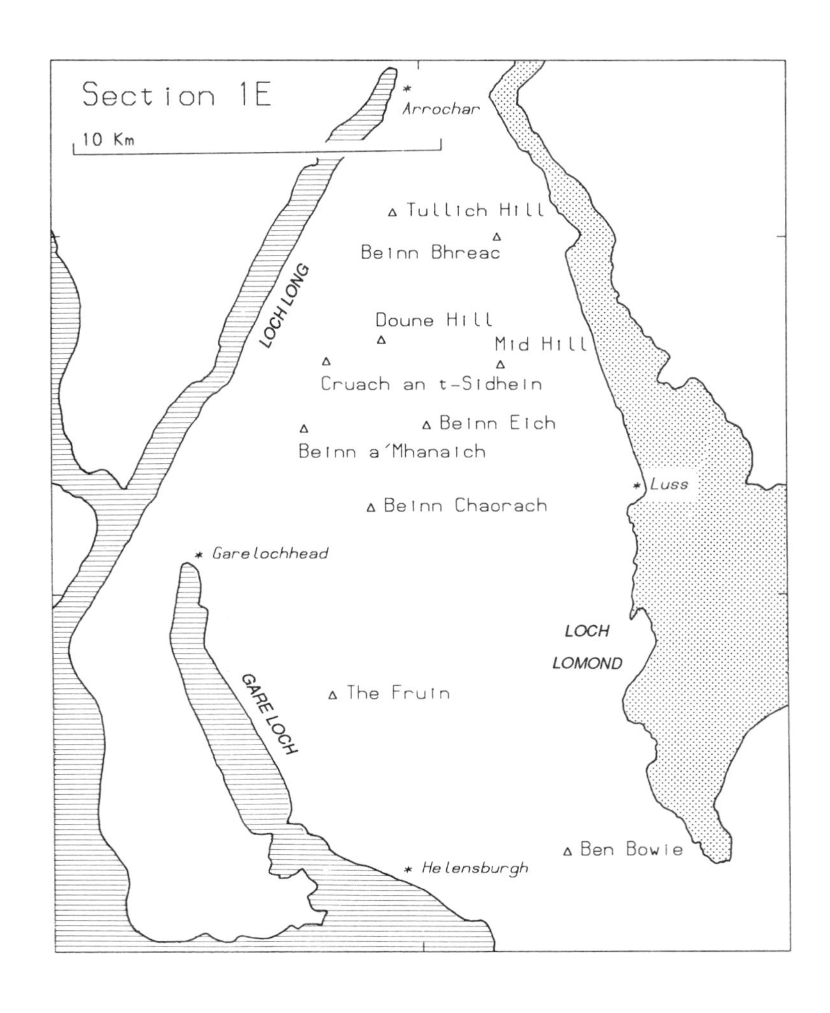

Section 1E Loch Long to Loch Lomond

West of Loch Lomond and River Leven from Tarbet to Dumbarton

Metres	Feet	Name	Map	Grid Ref	Date
734	2408	Doune Hill	56	NS 290971	______
713	2339	Beinn Chaorach	56	NS 287924	______
710	2328	Beinn a'Mhanaich	56	NS 269946	______
703	2305	Beinn Eich	56	NS 302947	______
684	2244	Cruach an t-Sidhein	56	NS 275965	______
681	2233	Beinn Bhreac	56	NN 321000	______
657	2155	Mid Hill	56	NS 322964	______
632	2075	Tullich Hill	56	NN 293007	______
361	1183	The Fruin *	56	NS 276872	______
314	1029	Ben Bowie	56	NS 339828	______

REGION 2
Loch Rannoch to Loch Tay

Rannoch Station; B846 and Loch Rannoch to Kinloch Rannoch; River Tummel, River Tay and Loch Tay to Killin; A827 and A85 to Tyndrum; railway to Rannoch Station.

Section 2A Loch Rannoch to Glen Lyon
North of Loch Lyon and Glen Lyon

Metres	*Feet*	*Name*	*Map*	*Grid Ref*	*Date*
1083	3554	Schiehallion	42/51/52	NN 714548	______
1081	3547	Beinn a'Chreachain	50	NN 373441	______
1076	3530	Beinn Dorain	50	NN 326378	______
1042	3419	Carn Mairg	42/51	NN 684513	______
1038	3404	Beinn Achaladair	50	NN 344432	______
1029	3377	Carn Gorm	42/51	NN 635501	______
1004	3294	Beinn an Dothaidh	50	NN 332408	______
960	3150	Stuchd an Lochain	51	NN 483449	______
953	3125	Beinn Mhanach	50	NN 373412	______
932	3057	Meall Buidhe	51	NN 498499	______
910	2985	Meall Buidhe	51	NN 426449	______

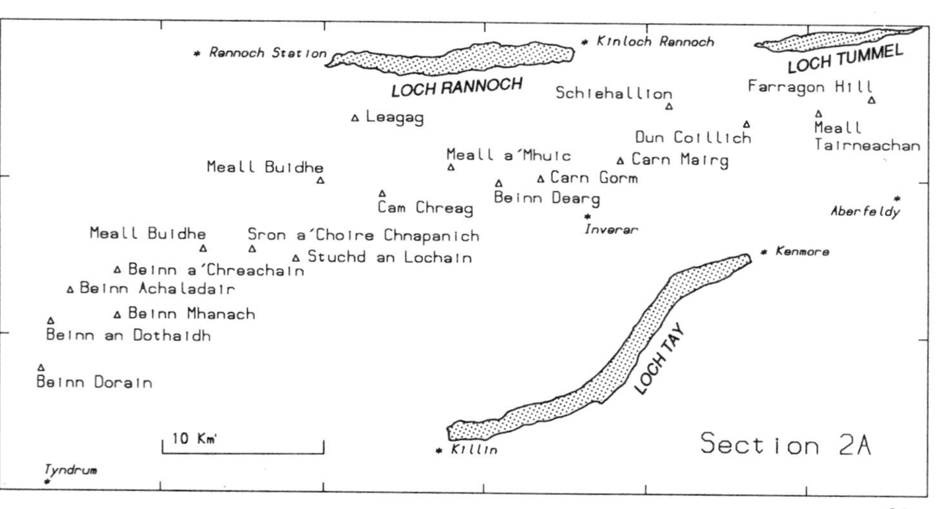

Metres	Feet	Name	Map	Grid Ref	Date
862	2828	Cam Chreag	51	NN 536491	______
837	2746	Sron a'Choire Chnapanich *	51	NN 456453	______
830	2723	Beinn Dearg	51	NN 609497	______
787	2582	Meall Tairneachan	52	NN 807544	______
783	2569	Farragon Hill	52	NN 840553	______
745	2444	Meall a'Mhuic	42/51	NN 579508	______
601	1972	Leagag	42/51	NN 519539	______
572	1877	Dun Coillich	42/51	NN 762537	______

Section 2B Glen Lyon to Glen Dochart and Loch Tay

South of Loch Lyon and Glen Lyon

Metres	Feet	Name	Map	Grid Ref	Date
1214	3984	Ben Lawers	51	NN 636414	______
1118	3668	Meall Garbh	51	NN 644437	______
1078	3536	Beinn Heasgarnich	51	NN 413383	______
1069	3507	Meall Corranaich	51	NN 616410	______
1047	3435	Creag Mhor	50	NN 391361	______
1044	3425	Meall nan Tarmachan	51	NN 585390	______
1039	3410	Meall Ghaordaidh	51	NN 514397	______
1025	3363	Ben Challum	50	NN 387322	______
1001	3284	Meall Greigh	51	NN 674438	______
959	3145	Meall Glas	51	NN 431322	______

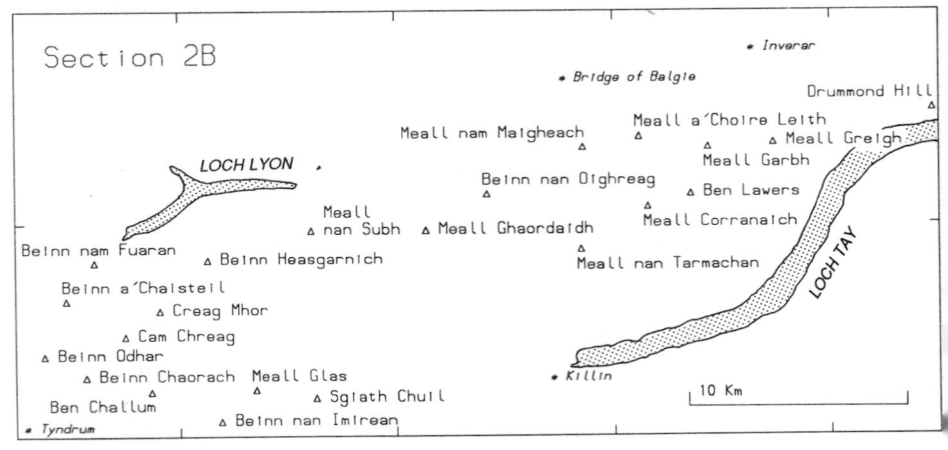

926	3038	Meall a'Choire Leith	51	NN 612439	______
921	3021	Sgiath Chuil	51	NN 463318	______
909	2982	Beinn nan Oighreag	51	NN 542412	______
901	2955	Beinn Odhar	50	NN 338338	______
886	2907	Beinn a'Chaisteil	50	NN 348364	______
884	2900	Cam Chreag	50	NN 375346	______
849	2785	Beinn nan Imirean	51	NN 419309	______
818	2685	Beinn Chaorach	50	NN 359328	______
806	2645	Beinn nam Fuaran	50	NN 361382	______
806	2645	Meall nan Subh	51	NN 461397	______
780	2558	Meall nam Maigheach	51	NN 586436	______
460	1509	Drummond Hill	51/52	NN 749454	______

REGION 3
Loch Leven to Connel Bridge and Glen Lochy

Kinlochleven; River Leven, Blackwater Reservoir, Black Water and railway to Rannoch Station; railway to Tyndrum; A85 to Taynuilt; Loch Etive and coast to Kinlochleven.

Section 3A Loch Leven to Rannoch Station
North of A82 from Glencoe to Bridge of Orchy

Metres	*Feet*	*Name*	*Map*	*Grid Ref*	*Date*
967	3173	Aonach Eagach - Sgorr nam Fiannaidh	41	NN 141583	______
867	2844	Garbh Bheinn	41	NN 169601	______
857	2811	Beinn a'Chrulaiste	41	NN 246567	______
742	2433	Sgorr na Ciche (Pap of Glencoe)	41	NN 125594	______
739	2423	Stob na Cruaiche	41	NN 363571	______
548	1798	Leathad Mor	41	NN 378510	______
501	1645	Glas Bheinn	50	NN 327473	______

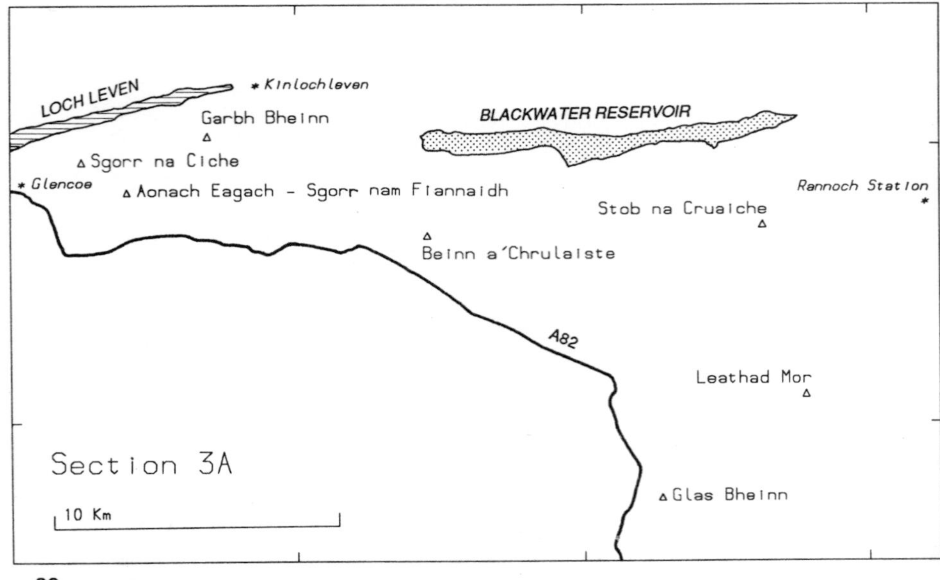

Section 3B Loch Linnhe to Loch Etive

West of Glen Etive and Loch Etive

Metres	Feet	Name	Map	Grid Ref	Date
1150	3773	Bidean nam Bian	41	NN 143542	______
1024	3361	Beinn a'Bheithir - Sgorr Dhearg	41	NN 056558	______
1022	3353	Buachaille Etive Mor - Stob Dearg	41	NN 223543	______
1001	3284	Beinn a'Bheithir - Sgorr Dhonuill	41	NN 040555	______
994	3260	Sgor na h-Ulaidh	41	NN 111518	______
959	3145	Beinn Fhionnlaidh	50	NN 095498	______
958	3143	Buachaille Etive Beag - Stob Dubh	41	NN 179535	______
937	3074	Beinn Sgulaird	50	NN 053461	______
925	3035	Buachaille Etive Beag - Stob Coire Raineach	41	NN 191548	______
907	2975	Beinn Maol Chaluim	41	NN 135526	______
879	2883	Fraochaidh	41	NN 029517	______
840	2755	Beinn Trilleachan	50	NN 086439	______

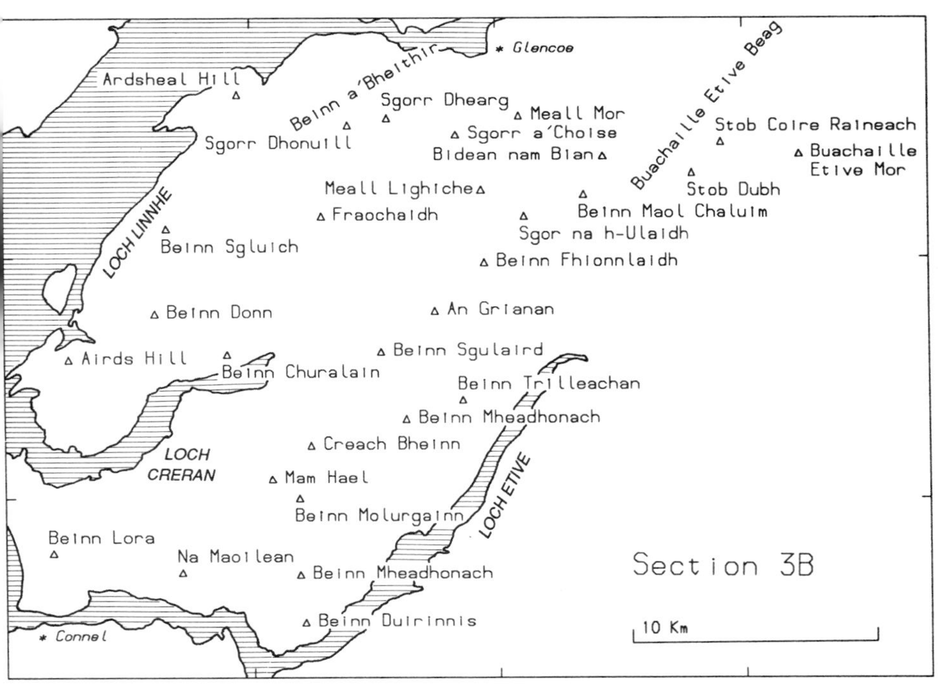

Metres	Feet	Name	Map	Grid Ref	Date
810	2656	Creach Bheinn	50	NN 024422	______
772	2533	Meall Lighiche	41	NN 094528	______
726	2382	Mam Hael	50	NN 008408	______
715	2345	Beinn Mheadhonach	50	NN 019368	______
690	2264	Beinn Molurgainn	50	NN 019401	______
676	2218	Meall Mor	41	NN 106559	______
663	2175	Sgorr a'Choise	41	NN 084551	______
589	1932	Beinn Mheadhonach	50	NN 063435	______
555	1821	Beinn Duirinnis	50	NN 021348	______
549	1800	An Grianan	50	NN 075478	______
549	1800	Beinn Churalain	49	NM 990461	______
473	1553	Beinn Donn	49	NM 961477	______
466	1529	Beinn Sgluich	49	NM 966512	______
350	1147	Na Maoilean	49	NM 971369	______
308	1010	Beinn Lora	49	NM 919377	______
263	864	Ardsheal Hill	49	NM 995568	______
181	593	Airds Hill	49	NM 926458	______

Section 3C Glen Etive to Glen Lochy

East of Glen Etive and Loch Etive

Metres	Feet	Name	Map	Grid Ref	Date
1126	3695	Ben Cruachan	50	NN 069304	______
1108	3636	Meall a'Bhuiridh	41	NN 251503	______
1100	3609	Creise *	41	NN 238507	______
1090	3575	Stob Ghabhar	50	NN 230455	______
1078	3538	Ben Starav	50	NN 126427	______
1044	3425	Stob Coir'an Albannaich	50	NN 169442	______
997	3271	Glas Bheinn Mhor	50	NN 153429	______
989	3245	Beinn Eunaich	50	NN 136328	______
980	3215	Beinn a'Chochuill	50	NN 110328	______
960	3150	Beinn nan Aighenan	50	NN 149405	______
947	3107	Stob a'Choire Odhair	50	NN 257460	______
928	3045	Meall nan Eun	50	NN 192449	______
897	2942	Beinn a'Bhuiridh	50	NN 094283	______
883	2897	Stob Dubh	50	NN 166488	______

Metres	Feet	Name	Map	Grid Ref	Date
864	2835	Beinn Mhic Chasgaig	41	NN 221502	______
840	2755	Beinn Udlaidh	50	NN 280333	______
803	2633	Beinn Bhreac-liath	50	NN 304339	______
796	2610	Beinn Mhic-Mhonaidh	50	NN 209350	______
709	2327	Beinn nan Lus	50	NN 130375	______
701	2300	Meall Garbh	50	NN 168367	______
676	2218	Beinn Suidhe	50	NN 211400	______
665	2181	Meall Tairbh	50	NN 251376	______
649	2128	Beinn Donachain	50	NN 198316	______
636	2085	Beinn na Sroine	50	NN 234289	______
569	1866	Beinn a'Chuirn	50	NN 217373	______
492	1615	Meall Mor *	50	NN 304471	______

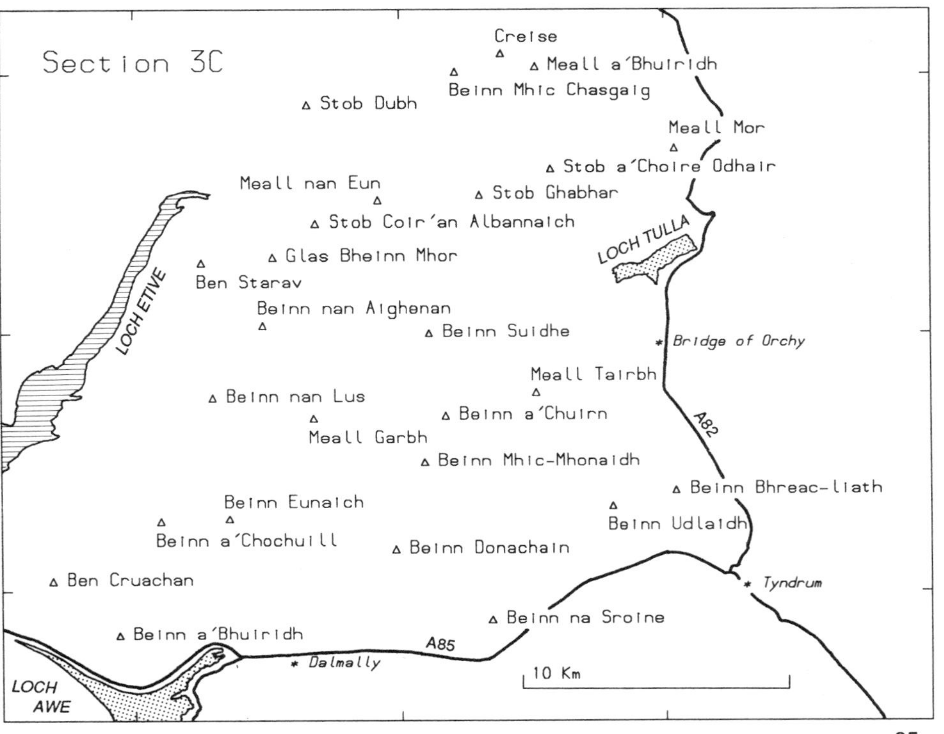

REGION 4

Fort William to Loch Ericht

Fort William; River Lochy to Gairlochy; River Spean to Spean Bridge; A86 to Kingussie; A9 to Dalwhinnie; Loch Ericht and River Ericht to Loch Rannoch; B846 to Rannoch Station; railway, Black Water, Blackwater Reservoir and River Leven to Kinlochleven; Loch Leven and Loch Linnhe to Fort William.

Section 4A Fort William to Loch Treig and Loch Leven

West of Loch Treig and railway from Tulloch Station to Rannoch Station

Metres	*Feet*	*Name*	*Map*	*Grid Ref*	*Date*
1344	4408	Ben Nevis	41	NN 166713	______
1236	4055	Aonach Beag	41	NN 196715	______
1223	4012	Carn Mor Dearg	41	NN 177722	______
1177	3862	Stob Choire Claurigh	41	NN 262739	______
1130	3706	Binnein Mor	41	NN 212663	______
1116	3660	Stob Coire Easain	41	NN 308730	______
1099	3606	Sgurr a'Mhaim	41	NN 165667	______
1095	3592	Sgurr Choinnich Mor	41	NN 227714	______
1034	3391	Am Bodach	41	NN 176651	______
1010	3313	Sgurr Eilde Mor	41	NN 231658	______
999	3278	Stob Ban	41	NN 148654	______
985	3230	An Gearanach *	41	NN 187670	______
977	3205	Stob Ban	41	NN 266724	______
943	3093	Binnein Beag	41	NN 222677	______
906	2972	Leum Uilleim	41	NN 331641	______
857	2812	Cruach Innsé	41	NN 280763	______
809	2654	Sgurr Innse	41	NN 290748	______
796	2611	Mam na Gualainn	41	NN 115625	______
792	2597	Glas Bheinn	41	NN 259641	______
742	2434	Cnap Cruinn *	41	NN 303775	______
646	2120	Beinn na Cloiche	41	NN 285649	______
621	2037	Tom Meadhoin	41	NN 087621	______
618	2028	Creag Ghuanach	41	NN 300691	______

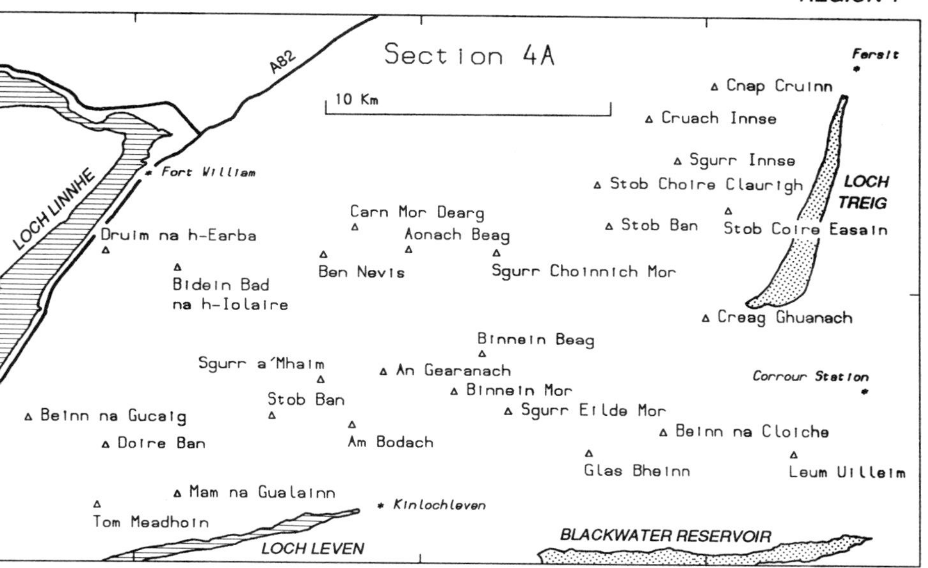

Metres	Feet	Name	Map	Grid Ref	Date
616	2022	Beinn na Gucaig	41	NN 063653	______
566	1857	Doire Ban	41	NN 090643	______
528	1732	Bidein Bad na h-Iolaire	41	NN 115708	______
288	944	Druim na h-Earba *	41	NN 090713	______

Section 4B Loch Treig to Loch Ericht

East of Loch Treig and railway from Tulloch Station to Rannoch Station

Metres	Feet	Name	Map	Grid Ref	Date
1148	3765	Ben Alder	42	NN 496718	______
1132	3714	Geal-Charn *	42	NN 470746	______
1087	3566	Beinn a'Chlachair	42	NN 471781	______
1049	3443	Geal Charn	42	NN 504812	______
1047	3435	Chno Dearg	41	NN 377741	______
1034	3391	Carn Dearg	42	NN 504764	______
1019	3343	Beinn Bheoil	42	NN 517717	______
955	3133	Stob Gaibhre	42	NN 444674	______
941	3087	Carn Dearg	42	NN 418661	______
937	3074	Beinn na Lap	41	NN 376696	______

Metres	Feet	Name	Map	Grid Ref	Date
911	2989	The Fara	42	NN 598844	______
868	2848	Beinn Pharlagain - Meall na Meoig	42	NN 448642	______
746	2447	Binnein Shuas	34/42	NN 463827	______
667	2188	Binnein Shios	34/42	NN 492857	______
658	2159	Meall nan Eagan	42	NN 597875	______
590	1935	Cruban Beag	35	NN 668924	______
574	1883	Creag na Doire Duibhe	35	NN 615906	______
514	1686	Meall Luidh Mor	42	NN 416797	______
511	1676	Sron Smeur	42	NN 452602	______

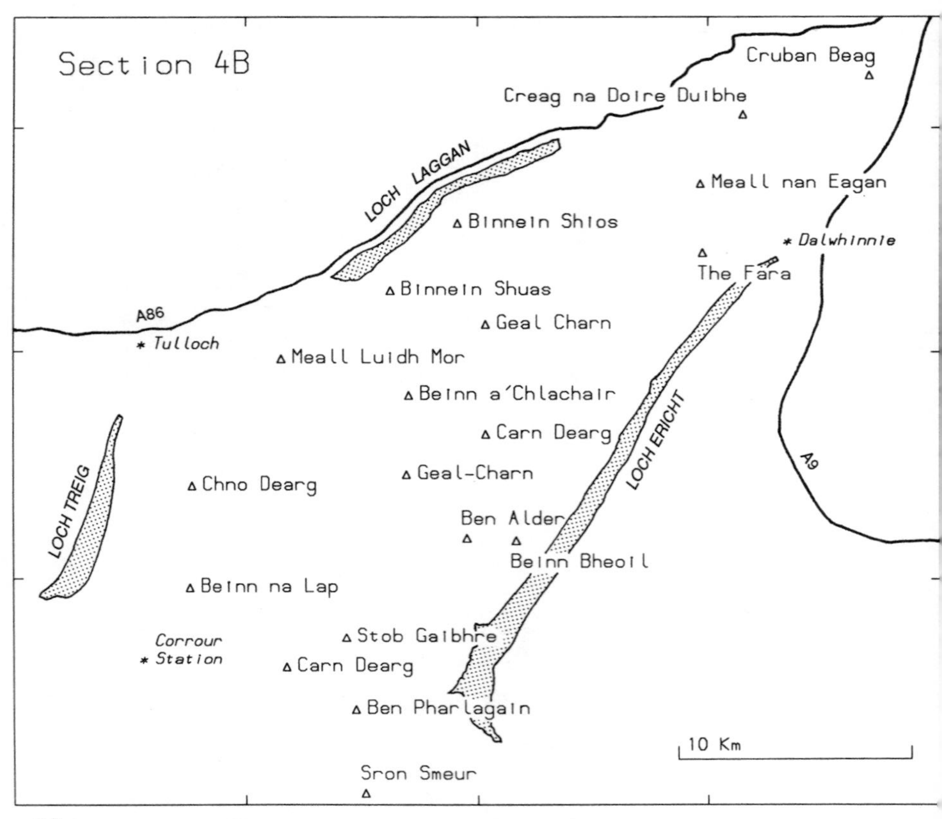

REGION 5

Loch Ericht to Glen Tromie and Glen Garry

Kingussie; Glen Tromie to Gaick Lodge; Gaick pass and Edendon Water to Dalnacardoch Lodge; River Garry and River Tummel to Loch Rannoch; River Ericht, Loch Ericht and A9 to Kingussie.

Metres	*Feet*	*Name*	*Map*	*Grid Ref*	*Date*
1010	3314	Beinn Udlamain	42	NN 579739	______
991	3251	Sgairneach Mhor	42	NN 599731	______
951	3120	Meall Chuaich	42	NN 716879	______
941	3087	Carn na Caim	42	NN 677822	______
917	3008	Geal-charn	42	NN 598783	______
892	2926	Beinn a'Chuallaich	42	NN 684618	______
855	2805	Stob an Aonaich Mhoir	42	NN 537694	______
841	2759	Beinn Mholach	42	NN 587655	______
827	2713	An Dun	42	NN 716802	______
803	2634	The Sow of Atholl	42	NN 624741	______
775	2544	Meall na Leitreach	42	NN 639703	______
658	2159	Creag Ruadh	42	NN 685882	______
612	2008	Creag a'Mhadaidh	42	NN 634650	______
512	1680	Drumcroy Hill	42	NN 741629	______

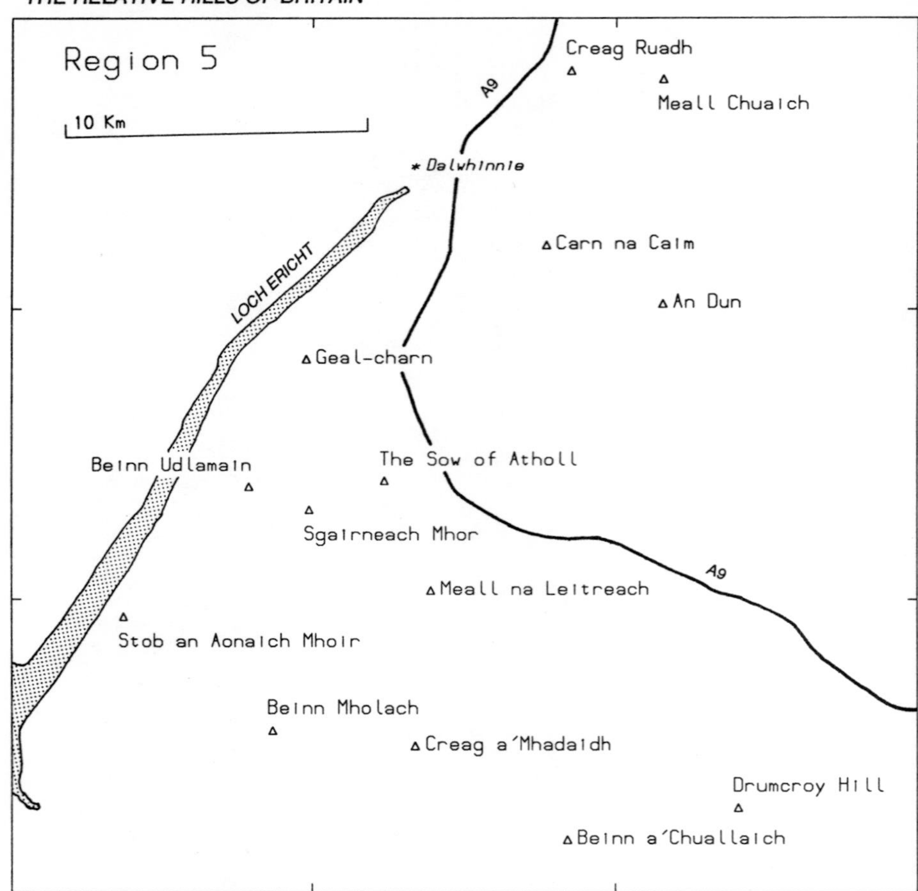
Region 5
10 Km
A9
Creag Ruadh
Meall Chuaich
Dalwhinnie
LOCH ERICHT
Carn na Caim
An Dun
Geal-charn
Beinn Udlamain
The Sow of Atholl
Sgairneach Mhor
A9
Meall na Leitreach
Stob an Aonaich Mhoir
Beinn Mholach
Creag a'Mhadaidh
Drumcroy Hill
Beinn a'Chuallaich

REGION 6

Forest of Atholl to Braemar and Blairgowrie

Braemar; A93 to Blairgowrie; River Ardle, River Isla, River Tay, River Tummel and River Garry to Dalnacardoch Lodge; Edendon Water, Gaick pass and Glen Tromie to Kingussie; River Spey, River Feshie, Geldie Burn and River Dee to Braemar.

Section 6A Glen Tromie to Glen Tilt

North and west of River Tilt and Allt Garbh Buidhe

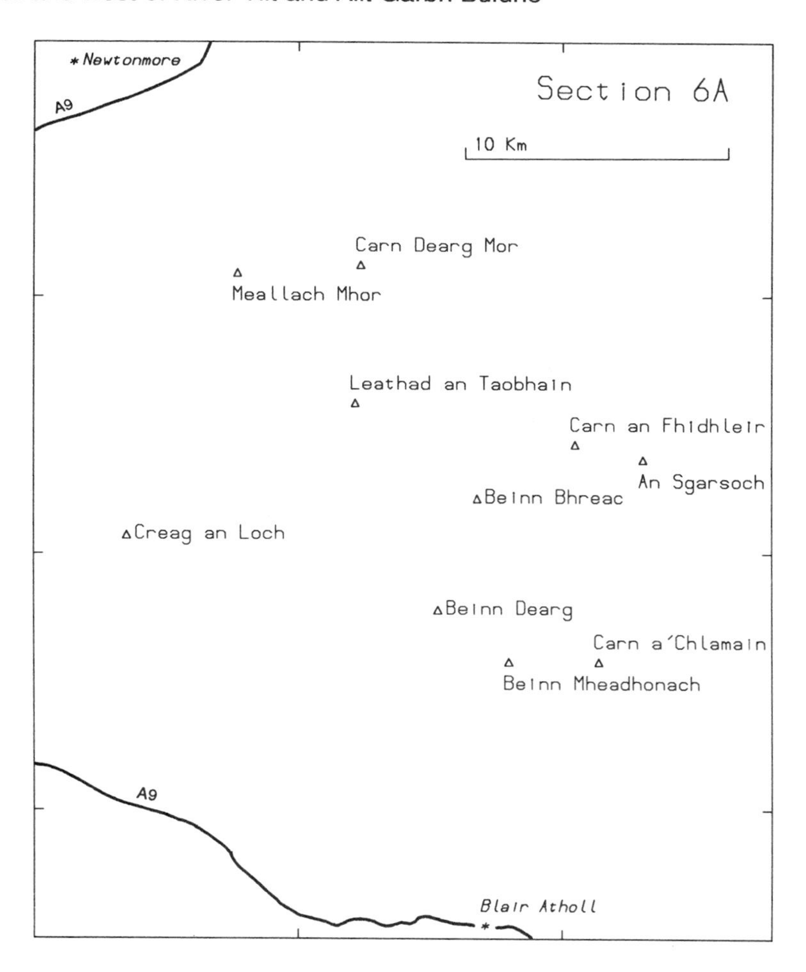

Metres	Feet	Name	Map	Grid Ref	Date
1008	3307	Beinn Dearg	43	NN 853778	______
1006	3300	An Sgarsoch	43	NN 933836	______
994	3261	Carn an Fhidhleir (Carn Ealar)	43	NN 905842	______
963	3159	Carn a'Chlamain	43	NN 916758	______
912	2992	Beinn Bhreac	43	NN 868821	______
912	2991	Leathad an Taobhain	43	NN 822858	______
901	2956	Beinn Mheadhonach	43	NN 880758	______
876	2874	Creag an Loch	42	NN 735807	______
857	2813	Carn Dearg Mor	35/43	NN 824912	______
769	2522	Meallach Mhor	35	NN 777909	______

Section 6B Pitlochry to Braemar and Blairgowrie
East of River Tilt and Allt Garbh Buidhe

Metres	Feet	Name	Map	Grid Ref	Date
1129	3704	Beinn a'Ghlo - Carn nan Gabhar	43	NN 971733	______
1070	3510	Braigh Coire Chruinn-bhalgain	43	NN 946724	______
1051	3449	Glas Tulaichean	43	NO 051760	______
1045	3427	Beinn Iutharn Mhor	43	NO 045792	______
1029	3377	Carn an Righ	43	NO 028772	______
975	3200	Carn Liath	43	NN 936698	______
975	3198	Carn a'Gheoidh	43	NO 107767	______
946	3104	Carn Bhac	43	NO 051832	______
944	3097	An Socach	43	NO 079799	______
903	2962	Ben Vuirich	43	NN 997700	______
859	2819	Morrone	43	NO 132886	______
841	2759	Ben Vrackie	43	NN 951632	______
806	2645	Ben Gulabin	43	NO 101722	______
641	2102	Blath Bhalg	43	NO 019611	______
563	1846	Creag nam Mial	52/53	NO 054541	______
511	1676	Deuchary Hill	52/53	NO 037485	______
447	1466	Hill of Persie	53	NO 122560	______
317	1041	Newtyle Hill	52/53	NO 050419	______

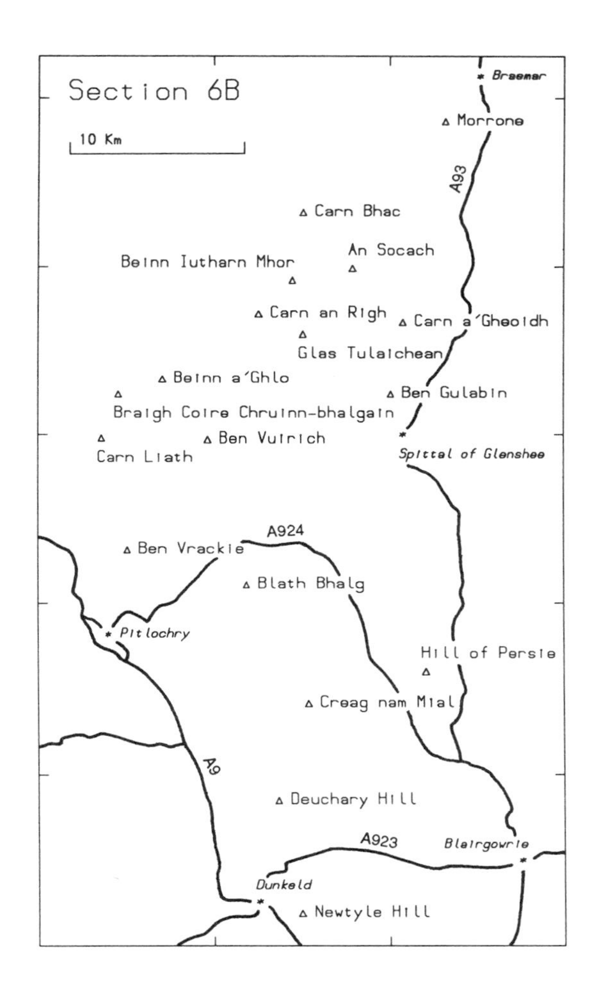
Section 6B
10 Km
Braemar
Morrone
A93
Carn Bhac
An Socach
Beinn Iutharn Mhor
Carn an Righ
Carn a'Gheoidh
Glas Tulaichean
Beinn a'Ghlo
Ben Gulabin
Braigh Coire Chruinn-bhalgain
Ben Vuirich
Carn Liath
Spittal of Glenshee
A924
Ben Vrackie
Blath Bhalg
Pitlochry
Hill of Persie
Creag nam Mial
A9
Deuchary Hill
A923
Blairgowrie
Dunkeld
Newtyle Hill

REGION 7
Braemar to Montrose

Braemar; River Dee to Aberdeen; coast to Montrose; River South Esk to Brechin; Strathmore and River Ardle to Blairgowrie; A93 to Braemar.

Metres	*Feet*	*Name*	*Map*	*Grid Ref*	*Date*
1155	3790	Lochnagar - Cac Carn Beag	44	NO 244861	______
1068	3504	Glas Maol	43	NO 166765	______
939	3080	Mount Keen	44	NO 409869	______
896	2941	Ben Tirran	44	NO 373746	______
865	2838	Conachcraig	44	NO 280865	______
834	2736	Creag nan Gabhar	43	NO 154841	______
807	2648	Monamenach	43	NO 176707	______
778	2554	Mount Battock	44	NO 549844	______
744	2442	Mount Blair	43	NO 167629	______
740	2428	Badandun Hill	44	NO 207678	______
705	2313	Hunt Hill	44	NO 379806	______
702	2302	Mealna Letter (Duchray Hill)	43	NO 161672	______
678	2224	Cat Law	44	NO 319611	______
678	2224	Hill of Wirren	44	NO 523739	______
611	2005	Corwharn	44	NO 288651	______
601	1972	The Coyles of Muick	44	NO 329910	______
555	1820	Crock	44	NO 226633	______
551	1808	Meall Mor	43	NO 173602	______
534	1753	Kerloch	45	NO 696879	______
516	1693	Hare Cairn	44	NO 242623	______
498	1635	Creigh Hill	53	NO 271594	______
486	1594	Creag Ghiubhais	37/44	NO 312955	______
414	1358	Strathfinella Hill	45	NO 693787	______
410	1345	Mile Hill	53	NO 311571	______
378	1241	Cairn-mon-earn	38/45	NO 782919	______
277	910	Hill of Garvock	45	NO 726692	______

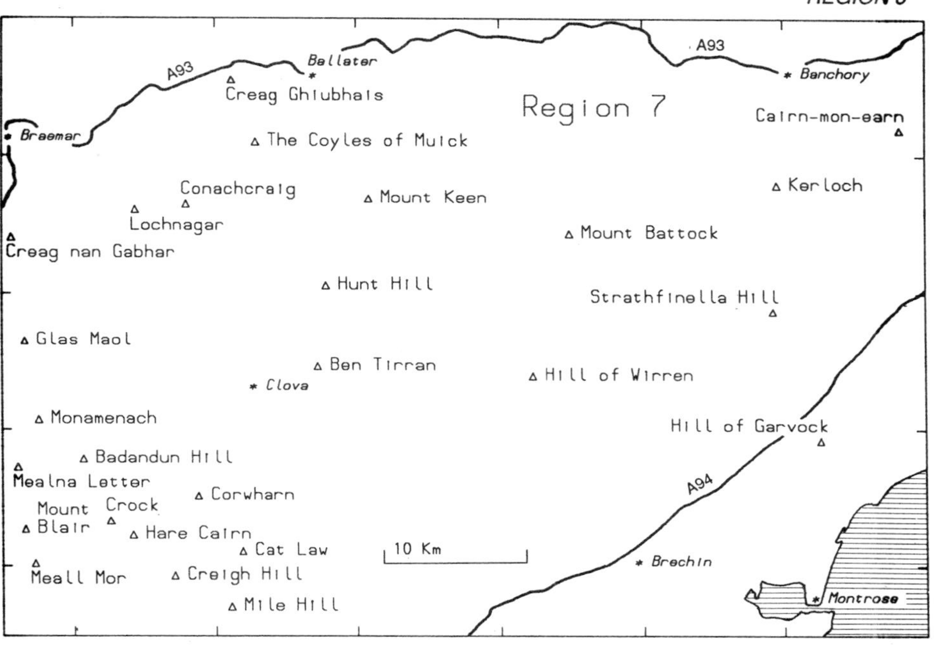

REGION 8
The Cairngorms

Aviemore; River Spey to Grantown-on-Spey; A939 to Ballater; River Dee to Braemar and Linn of Dee; Geldie Burn, River Feshie and River Spey to Aviemore.

Metres	*Feet*	*Name*	*Map*	*Grid Ref*	*Date*
1309	4296	Ben Macdui	36/43	NN 989989	______
1296	4252	Braeriach	36/43	NN 953999	______
1293	4242	Cairn Toul	36/43	NN 963972	______
1197	3927	Beinn a'Bhuird - North Top	36	NJ 092006	______
1182	3878	Beinn Mheadhoin	36	NJ 024016	______
1171	3843	Ben Åvon - Leabaidh an Daimh Bhuidhe	36	NJ 132019	______
1157	3795	Beinn Bhrotain	43	NN 954923	______
1118	3668	Sgor Gaoith	36/43	NN 903989	______
1090	3575	Bynack More	36	NJ 042063	______
1082	3550	Beinn a'Chaorainn	36	NJ 045013	______

Metres	Feet	Name	Map	Grid Ref	Date
1037	3402	Carn a'Mhaim	36/43	NN 994952	______
900	2953	Culardoch	36/43	NO 193988	______
895	2936	Creag Mhor	36	NJ 057048	______
862	2829	Carn Liath	36/43	NO 165977	______
829	2721	Brown Cow Hill	36	NJ 221044	______
821	2692	Geal Charn	36	NJ 090127	______
818	2685	Carn na Drochaide	36/43	NO 127938	______
813	2667	Sgor Mor	43	NO 006914	______
810	2657	Meall a'Bhuachaille	36	NH 991115	______
792	2600	Carn Ealasaid	36	NJ 228118	______
743	2438	Geallaig Hill	37/44	NO 298981	______
715	2345	Cnap Chaochan Aitinn	36	NJ 146099	______
668	2192	Creag Bhalg	43	NO 091912	______
560	1837	Meall Alvie	44	NO 203919	______
428	1404	Ord Ban	35/36	NH 892085	______

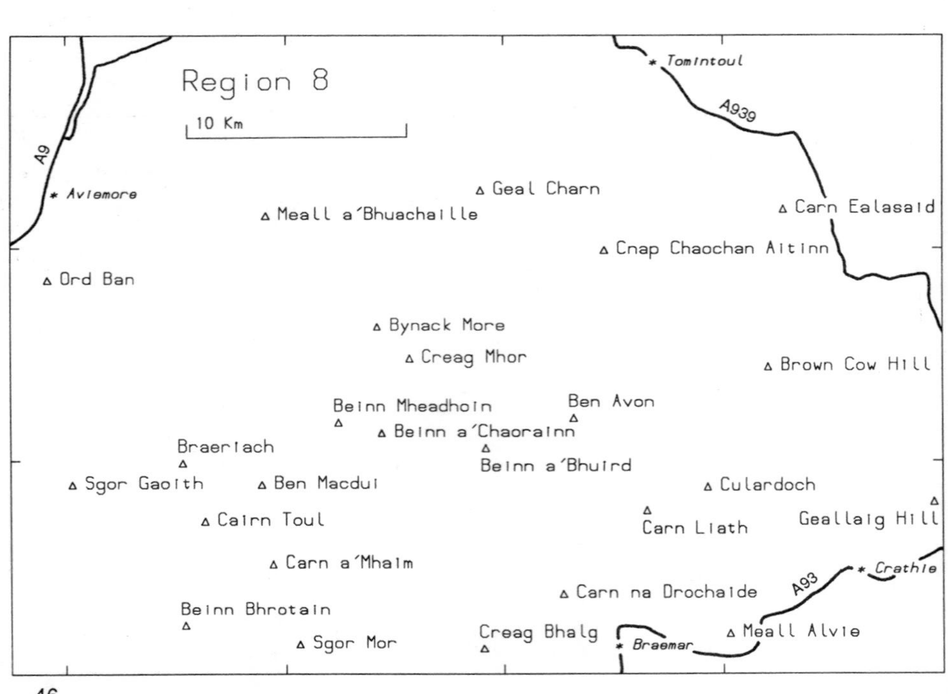

REGION 9

Spean Bridge to Elgin

Inverness; coast to Spey Bay; River Spey to Kingussie; A86 to Spean Bridge; River Spean to Gairlochy; Great Glen to Inverness.

Section 9A Inverness to Strathspey

North and east of A9 from Inverness to Aviemore

Metres	*Feet*	*Name*	*Map*	*Grid Ref*	*Date*
659	2162	Carn Glas-choire	35/36	NH 892292	______
615	2017	Carn nan Tri-tighearnan	27	NH 823390	______
549	1800	Carn na Loine	27	NJ 070361	______
492	1615	Meall Mor	27	NH 737356	______
471	1545	Beinn Mhor	36	NH 993281	______
456	1495	Knock of Braemoray	27	NJ 011418	______
339	1111	Brown Muir	28	NJ 258548	______
319	1046	Hill of the Wangie	28	NJ 137537	______
254	832	Burgiehill	27	NJ 097559	______

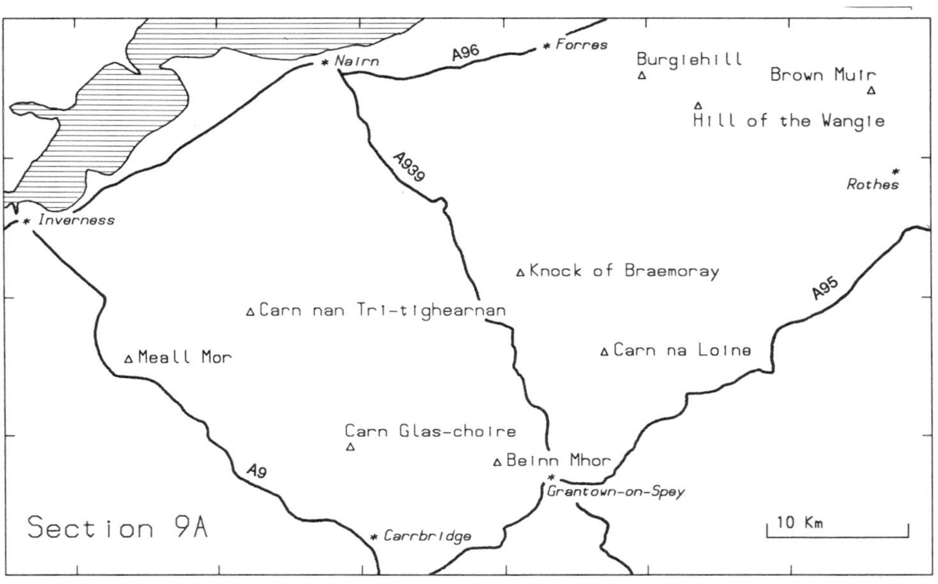

Section 9B Glen Albyn and the Monadh Liath

North of River Turret and River Spey from Laggan to Laggan

Metres	*Feet*	*Name*	*Map*	*Grid Ref*	*Date*
945	3100	Carn Dearg	35	NH 635024	______
896	2940	Gairbeinn	34	NN 460985	______
878	2879	Carn an Fhreiceadain	35	NH 726071	______
862	2828	Meall na h-Aisre	35	NH 515000	______
824	2703	Geal-charn Mor	35	NH 837124	______
816	2677	Carn a'Chuilinn	34	NH 416034	______
815	2675	Carn Dearg	34	NN 349967	______
811	2660	Carn na Saobhaidhe	35	NH 600145	______
768	2520	Carn Dearg	34	NN 357948	______
756	2479	Creag Dhubh	35	NN 677972	______
745	2444	Creag Liath	35	NH 663008	______
618	2027	Carn na h-Easgainn	27	NH 743321	______
556	1824	Beinn Mheadhoin	26/35	NH 604215	______

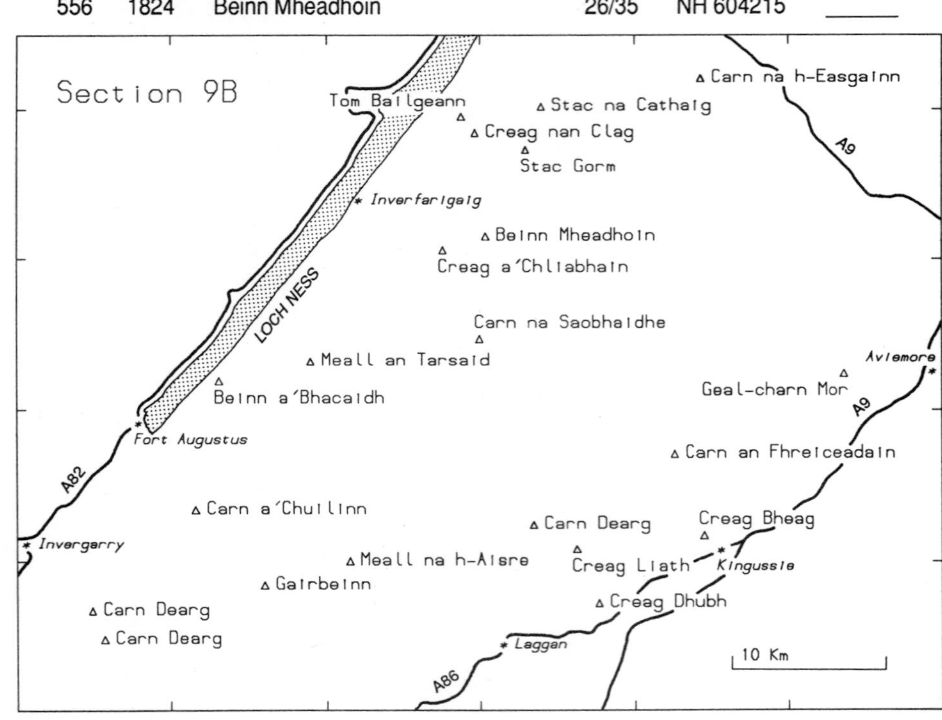

Metres	Feet	Name	Map	Grid Ref	Date
555	1821	Beinn a'Bhacaidh	34	NH 431119	______
520	1706	Creag a'Chliabhain *	26/35	NH 576206	______
492	1614	Meall an Tarsaid	34	NH 490132	______
487	1597	Creag Bheag	35	NH 745017	______
464	1522	Tom Bailgeann	26/35	NH 588295	______
446	1463	Stac na Cathaig	26	NH 640302	______
430	1411	Stac Gorm	26/35	NH 630273	______
407	1336	Creag nan Clag	26/35	NH 597283	______

Section 9C Loch Lochy to Loch Laggan
South of River Turret and River Spey from Laggan to Laggan

Metres	Feet	Name	Map	Grid Ref	Date
1130	3707	Creag Meagaidh	34/42	NN 418875	______
1050	3445	Beinn a'Chaorainn	34/41	NN 386851	______
915	3002	Beinn Teallach	34/41	NN 361859	______
834	2736	Carn Dearg	34/41	NN 345887	______
800	2625	Beinn Iaruinn	34	NN 296900	______
685	2247	Leana Mhor	34/41	NN 284879	______
678	2224	Leana Mhor	34/41	NN 317879	______
658	2160	Creag Dhubh	34/41	NN 322824	______
622	2041	Creag Ruadh	35	NN 558914	______
568	1863	Beinn a'Mhonicag	34/41	NN 287854	______

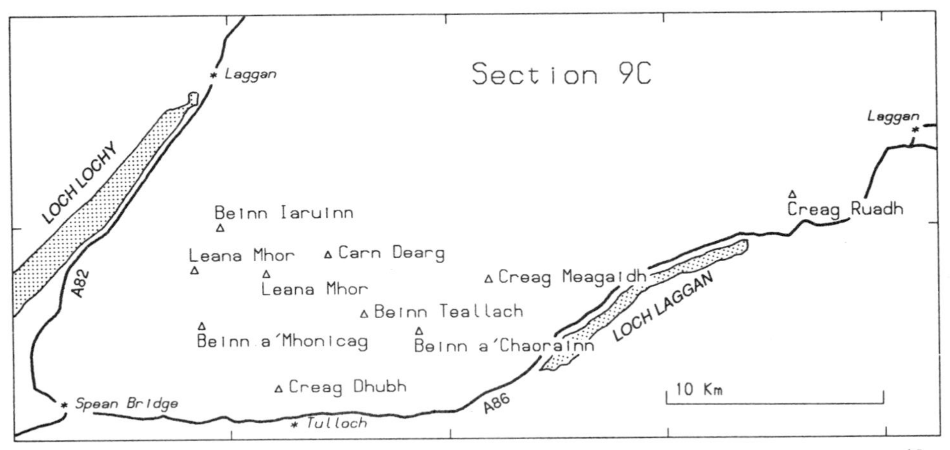

REGION 10

Glen Shiel to Glenfinnan

Shiel Bridge; Glen Shiel and Glen Moriston to Invermoriston; Great Glen to Fort William; Loch Eil and A830 to Lochailort; coast to Shiel Bridge.

Section 10A Glen Shiel to Loch Hourn and Loch Quoich

North of Loch Hourn and the Kinloch Hourn road, and west of A87 from Loch Cluanie to Loch Garry

Metres	*Feet*	*Name*	*Map*	*Grid Ref*	*Date*
1035	3394	Gleouraich	33	NH 039054	______
1027	3369	Sgurr a'Mhaoraich	33	NG 984065	______
1021	3350	Aonach air Chrith	33	NH 051083	______
1010	3314	Sgurr an Doire Leathain	33	NH 015099	______
1010	3314	The Saddle	33	NG 934131	______
996	3268	Spidean Mialach	33	NH 066043	______
974	3194	Beinn Sgritheall	33	NG 836126	______
946	3104	Sgurr na Sgine	33	NG 946113	______
918	3012	Creag nan Damh	33	NG 983112	______

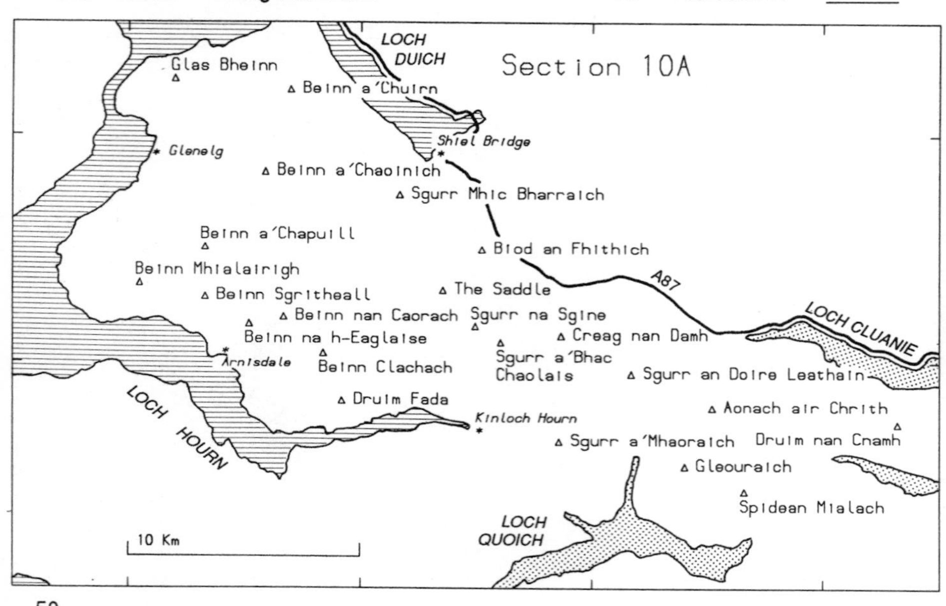

Metres	Feet	Name	Map	Grid Ref	Date
885	2904	Sgurr a'Bhac Chaolais	33	NG 958110	______
805	2641	Beinn na h-Eaglaise	33	NG 854120	______
790	2592	Druim nan Cnamh	34	NH 131077	______
781	2561	Sgurr Mhic Bharraich	33	NG 917174	______
774	2539	Beinn nan Caorach	33	NG 871122	______
759	2490	Beinn a'Chapuill	33	NG 835149	______
713	2339	Druim Fada	33	NG 894084	______
644	2113	Biod an Fhithich	33	NG 951148	______
643	2109	Beinn Clachach	33	NG 886109	______
603	1977	Beinn a'Chuirn	33	NG 870220	______
548	1798	Beinn Mhialairigh	33	NG 800129	______
410	1345	Beinn a'Chaoinich	33	NG 859184	______
397	1301	Glas Bheinn	33	NG 821227	______

Section 10B Knoydart to Glen Kingie

North of Loch Nevis, Glen Dessary and Glen Kingie

Metres	Feet	Name	Map	Grid Ref	Date
1040	3412	Sgurr na Ciche	33/40	NM 902966	______
1020	3345	Ladhar Bheinn	33	NG 824040	______
1013	3323	Garbh Chioch Mhor	33/40	NM 909961	______

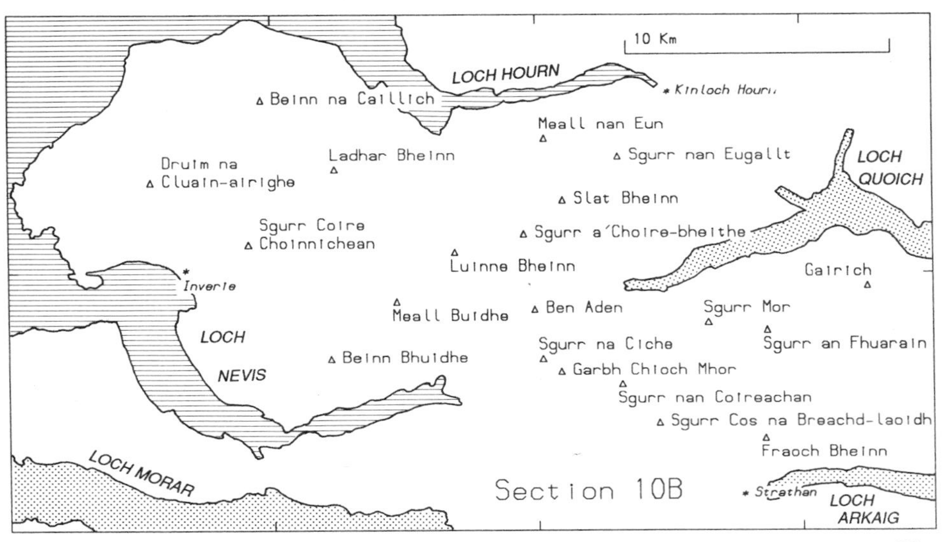

Metres	Feet	Name	Map	Grid Ref	Date
1003	3290	Sgurr Mor	33/40	NM 965980	______
953	3125	Sgurr nan Coireachan	33/40	NM 933958	______
946	3105	Meall Buidhe	33/40	NM 849989	______
939	3082	Luinne Bheinn	33	NG 869008	______
919	3015	Gairich	33	NN 025995	______
913	2994	Sgurr a'Choire-bheithe	33	NG 895015	______
901	2956	Sgurr an Fhuarain	33/40	NM 987980	______
894	2933	Sgurr nan Eugallt	33	NG 931045	______
887	2910	Ben Aden	33/40	NM 899986	______
858	2815	Fraoch Bheinn	33/40	NM 986940	______
855	2805	Beinn Bhuidhe	33/40	NM 822967	______
835	2739	Sgurr Cos na Breachd-laoidh	33/40	NM 948947	______
796	2612	Sgurr Coire Choinnichean	33	NG 791011	______
785	2575	Beinn na Caillich	33	NG 796067	______
700	2297	Slat Bheinn	33	NG 910028	______
667	2188	Meall nan Eun	33	NG 903052	______
518	1699	Druim na Cluain-airighe	33	NG 752035	______

Section 10C Loch Arkaig to Glen Moriston
North of Loch Arkaig and east of A87 from Loch Cluanie to Loch Garry

Metres	Feet	Name	Map	Grid Ref	Date
935	3066	Sron a'Choire Ghairbh	34	NN 222945	______
917	3008	Meall na Teanga	34	NN 220925	______
901	2957	Ben Tee	34	NN 241972	______
880	2886	Sgurr Mhurlagain	33	NN 012944	______
838	2749	Meall na h-Eilde	34	NN 185946	______
804	2638	Geal Charn	34	NN 156943	______
788	2585	Meall Dubh	34	NH 245078	______
749	2457	Sgurr Choinich	34	NN 128949	______
732	2402	Glas Bheinn	34	NN 172919	______
656	2152	Meall Blair	33	NN 077950	______
607	1991	Burach	34	NH 383142	______

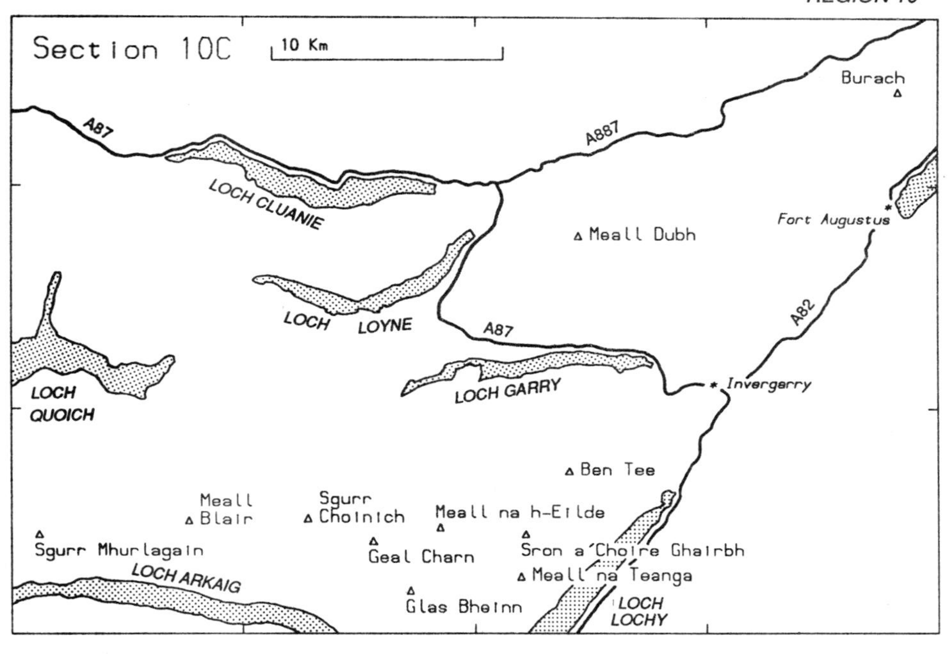

Section 10D Mallaig to Fort William

South of Loch Nevis, Glen Dessary and Loch Arkaig

Metres	Feet	Name	Map	Grid Ref	Date
987	3238	Gaor Bheinn (Gulvain)	41	NN 002876	______
963	3160	Sgurr Thuilm	40	NM 939879	______
956	3136	Sgurr nan Coireachan	40	NM 903880	______
909	2982	Streap	40	NM 946863	______
867	2844	Bidein a'Chabair	33/40	NM 889931	______
829	2719	Carn Mor	33/40	NM 903909	______
796	2612	Beinn Bhan	34/41	NN 140857	______
796	2610	Sgurr an Utha	40	NM 885839	______
774	2540	Meall a'Phubuill	41	NN 029854	______
765	2510	Braigh nan Uamhachan	40	NM 975867	______
744	2441	Druim Fada - Stob a'Ghrianain	41	NN 087823	______
727	2385	Mullach Coire nan Geur-oirean	41	NN 049892	______
718	2355	An Stác	40	NM 866889	______

Metres	Feet	Name	Map	Grid Ref	Date
710	2328	Meith Bheinn	40	NM 821872	______
681	2234	Meall Onfhaidh	41	NN 010840	______
663	2175	Aodann Chleireig	40	NM 994825	______
633	2076	Glas-charn	40	NM 846837	______
601	1972	Sidhean Mor	40	NM 729866	______
584	1916	Druim a'Chuirn	40	NM 827887	______
574	1883	Beinn nan Cabar	40	NM 765866	______
548	1797	Carn a'Ghobhair	33/40	NM 716964	______
510	1673	Creag Bhan	40	NM 782847	______
440	1444	Sgurr Bhuidhe	33/40	NM 722946	______
292	958	Cruach Doir'an Raoigh *	40	NM 735826	______
197	646	Sgurr na Dubh-chreige *	40	NM 691938	______

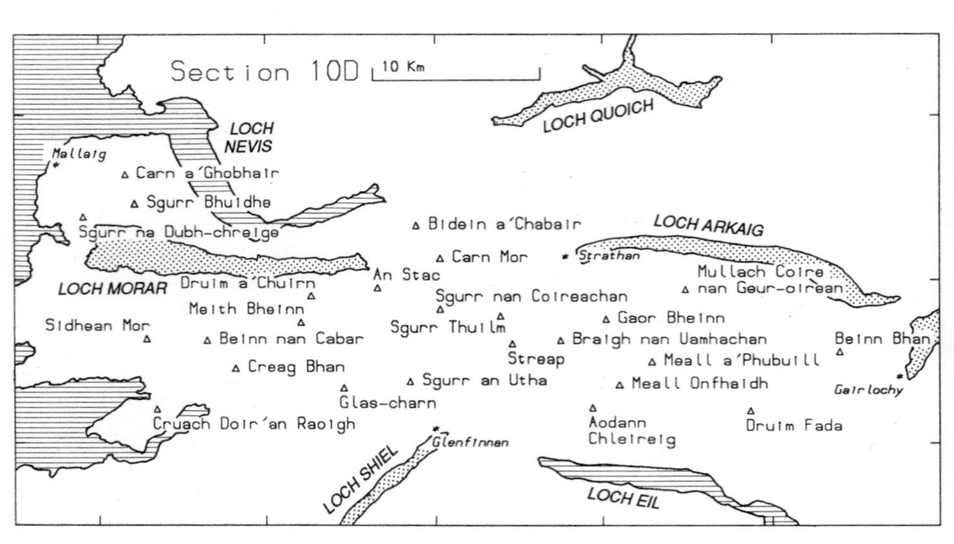

REGION 11
Loch Duich to Loch Ness, South of Loch Mullardoch

Shiel Bridge; Loch Duich, Loch Long and Glen Elchaig to Carnach; pass to Loch Mullardoch; Glen Cannich and A831 to Drumnadrochit; Loch Ness to Invermoriston; Glen Moriston and Glen Shiel to Shiel Bridge.

Section 11A Loch Duich to Cannich

North of Glen Affric and west of pass from Alltbeithe to Loch Cluanie

Metres	*Feet*	*Name*	*Map*	*Grid Ref*	*Date*
1183	3880	Carn Eige	25	NH 123262	______
1151	3776	Sgurr nan Ceathreamhnan	25/33	NH 057228	______
1068	3505	Sgurr Fhuaran	33	NG 978167	______
1054	3458	Toll Creagach	25	NH 194283	______
1036	3399	Sgurr a'Bhealaich Dheirg	33	NH 035143	______
1032	3385	Beinn Fhada	33	NH 018192	______
1027	3370	Sgurr na Ciste Duibhe	33	NG 984149	______
1005	3298	Beinn Fhionnlaidh	25	NH 115282	______

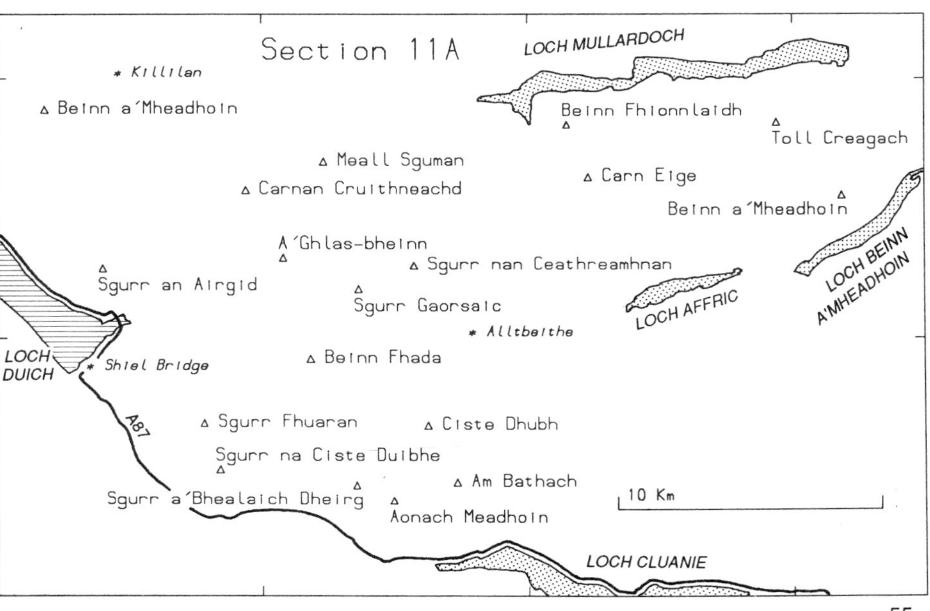

Metres	Feet	Name	Map	Grid Ref	Date
1001	3284	Aonach Meadhoin *	33	NH 049137	______
982	3222	Ciste Dhubh	33	NH 062166	______
918	3012	A'Ghlas-bheinn	25/33	NH 008231	______
841	2759	Sgurr an Airgid	25/33	NG 940227	______
839	2752	Sgurr Gaorsaic	25/33	NH 036219	______
798	2618	Am Bathach	33	NH 073144	______
730	2395	Carnan Cruithneachd	25/33	NG 994258	______
610	2002	Beinn a'Mheadhoin	25	NH 219255	______
544	1785	Meall Sguman	25/33	NH 023267	______
414	1358	Beinn a'Mheadhoin	25/33	NG 918288	______

Section 11B Glen Affric to Glen Moriston

South of Glen Affric and east of pass from Alltbeithe to Loch Cluanie

Metres	Feet	Name	Map	Grid Ref	Date
1120	3673	A'Chralaig	33	NH 094148	______
1109	3639	Sgurr nan Conbhairean	34	NH 129139	______
1102	3614	Mullach Fraoch-choire	33	NH 095171	______
889	2917	Aonach Shasuinn	34	NH 173180	______

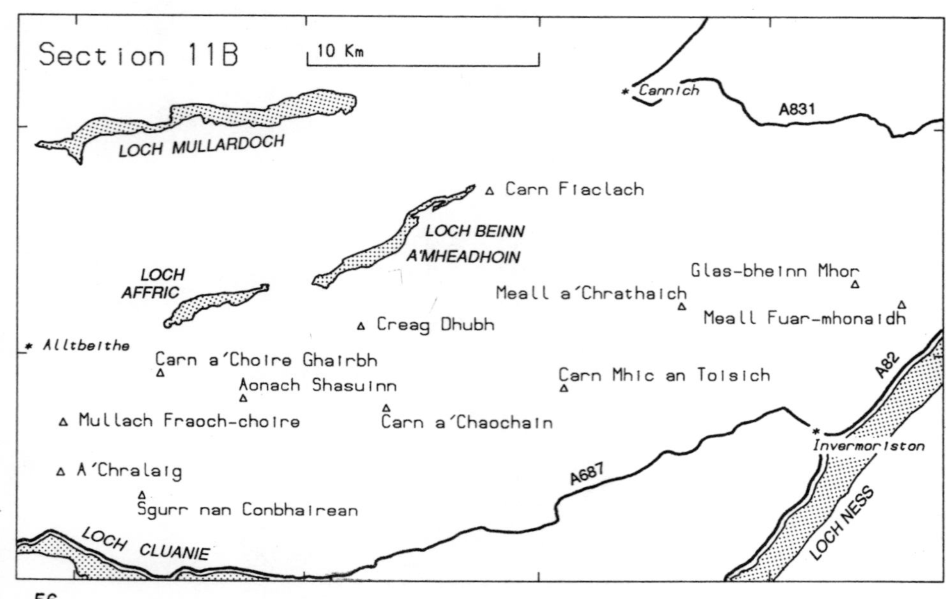

Metres	Feet	Name	Map	Grid Ref	Date
865	2837	Carn a'Choire Ghairbh	34	NH 137189	______
706	2315	Carn a'Chaochain	34	NH 235178	______
699	2293	Meall Fuar-mhonaidh	26	NH 457223	______
680	2231	Carn Mhic an Toisich	34	NH 311186	______
679	2227	Meall a'Chrathaich	26	NH 361221	______
651	2136	Glas-bheinn Mhor	26	NH 437232	______
539	1769	Creag Dhubh	25	NH 225217	______
457	1499	Carn Fiaclach	25	NH 279273	______

REGION 12
Kyle of Lochalsh to Inverness, North of Loch Mullardoch

Kyle of Lochalsh; coast to Strathcarron; railway to Garve; A832 to Beauly; Beauly Firth to Inverness; Great Glen to Drumnadrochit; A831 to Cannich; Glen Cannich, Loch Mullardoch and pass to Carnach; Glen Elchaig, Loch Long and Loch Alsh to Kyle of Lochalsh.

Section 12A Kyle of Lochalsh to Garve

North of River Ling, Loch Cruoshie, Loch Monar, Glen Strathfarrar and River Beauly

Metres	*Feet*	*Name*	*Map*	*Grid Ref*	*Date*
1083	3554	Sgurr a'Choire Ghlais	25	NH 259430	______
1053	3455	Sgurr a'Chaorachain	25	NH 087447	______
1007	3304	Maoile Lunndaidh	25	NH 135458	______
993	3258	Sgurr na Ruaidhe	25	NH 289425	______
986	3234	Lurg Mhor	25	NH 065404	______
945	3100	Bidein a'Choire Sheasgaich	25	NH 049412	______
928	3045	Moruisg	25	NH 101499	______
915	3002	Sgurr nan Ceannaichean	25	NH 087480	______
879	2883	Sgurr a'Mhuilinn	25	NH 265558	______
863	2831	Beinn Tharsuinn	25	NH 055433	______
862	2828	Sgurr na Feartaig	25	NH 055454	______
862	2827	Beinn a'Bha'ach Ard	26	NH 361435	______
849	2787	Bac an Eich	25	NH 222489	______
840	2756	Meallan nan Uan	25	NH 264545	______
814	2671	An Sidhean	25	NH 171454	______
797	2615	Beinn Dronaig	25	NH 037382	______
693	2272	Beinn na Muice	25	NH 219402	______
680	2230	Meall na Faochaig	25	NH 257525	______
673	2209	Carn na Coinnich	26	NH 324511	______
663	2175	Beinn Mheadhoin	25	NH 259478	______
612	2008	Creag Dhubh Mhor	25	NG 983405	______
580	1904	Sgurr Marcasaidh	26	NH 354593	______
537	1762	Creag Loch nan Dearcag	26	NH 333568	______

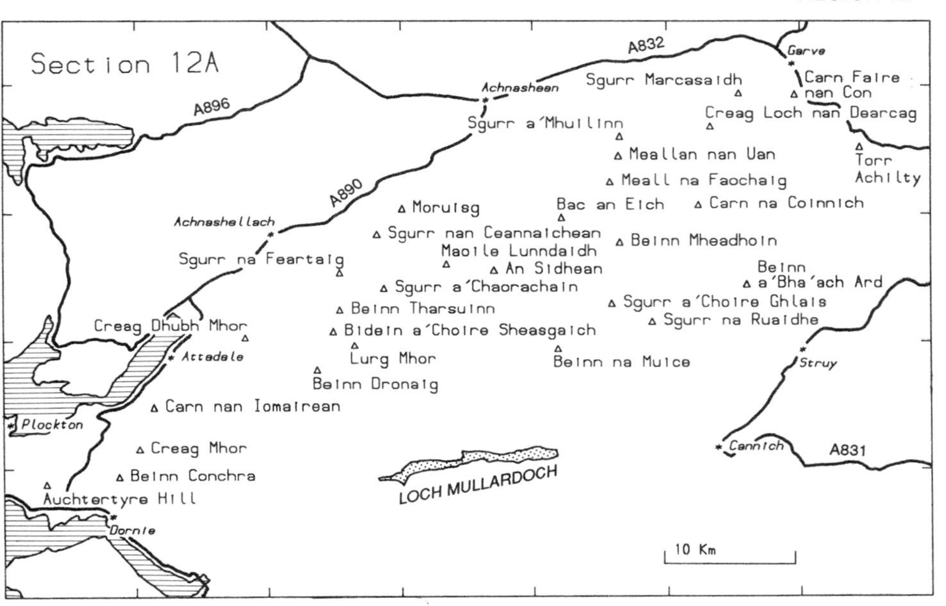

Metres	Feet	Name	Map	Grid Ref	Date
486	1594	Carn nan Iomairean	25	NG 914352	______
453	1487	Beinn Conchra	33	NG 887292	______
452	1483	Auchtertyre Hill	33	NG 832289	______
407	1335	Creag Mhor	25	NG 903316	______
370	1215	Carn Faire nan Con	26	NH 396592	______
256	840	Torr Achilty	26	NH 447551	______

Section 12B Killilan to Inverness

South of River Ling, Loch Cruoshie, Loch Monar, Glen Strathfarrar and River Beauly

Metres	Feet	Name	Map	Grid Ref	Date
1150	3774	Sgurr na Lapaich	25	NH 161351	______
1129	3704	An Riabhachan	25	NH 134345	______
1069	3508	An Socach *	25	NH 100332	______
992	3255	Carn nan Gobhar	25	NH 182344	______
899	2949	Aonach Buidhe	25	NH 058324	______
879	2883	Sguman Coinntich	25	NG 977304	______
868	2847	Faochaig	25	NH 022317	______

Metres	Feet	Name	Map	Grid Ref	Date
818	2684	Sgorr na Diollaid	25	NH 282362	______
706	2316	An Cruachan	25	NH 094359	______
678	2224	Carn na Breabaig	25	NH 067301	______
677	2221	Carn Gorm	26	NH 328355	______
601	1972	Meallan Odhar Doire nan Gillean	25	NH 156378	______
591	1939	Beinn Dubh an Iaruinn	25	NH 182392	______
501	1643	Carn a'Bhodaich	26	NH 570375	______
465	1526	Meall na h-Eilrig	26	NH 537326	______
457	1499	Carn nam Bad	26	NH 402339	______
390	1280	Meall Innis an Loichel	25	NH 204389	______

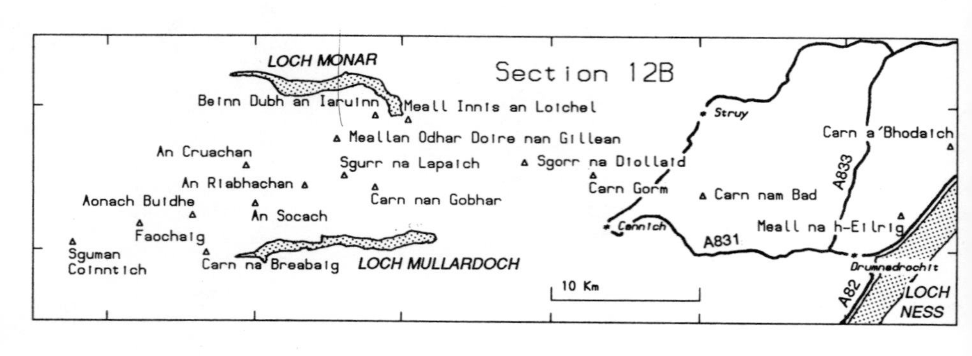

REGION 13
Loch Carron to Loch Maree

Poolewe; Loch Maree to Kinlochewe; A832 to Achnasheen; railway to Strathcarron; Loch Carron and coast to Poolewe.

Section 13A Loch Torridon to Loch Maree

North of Loch Torridon and A896 from Torridon to Kinlochewe

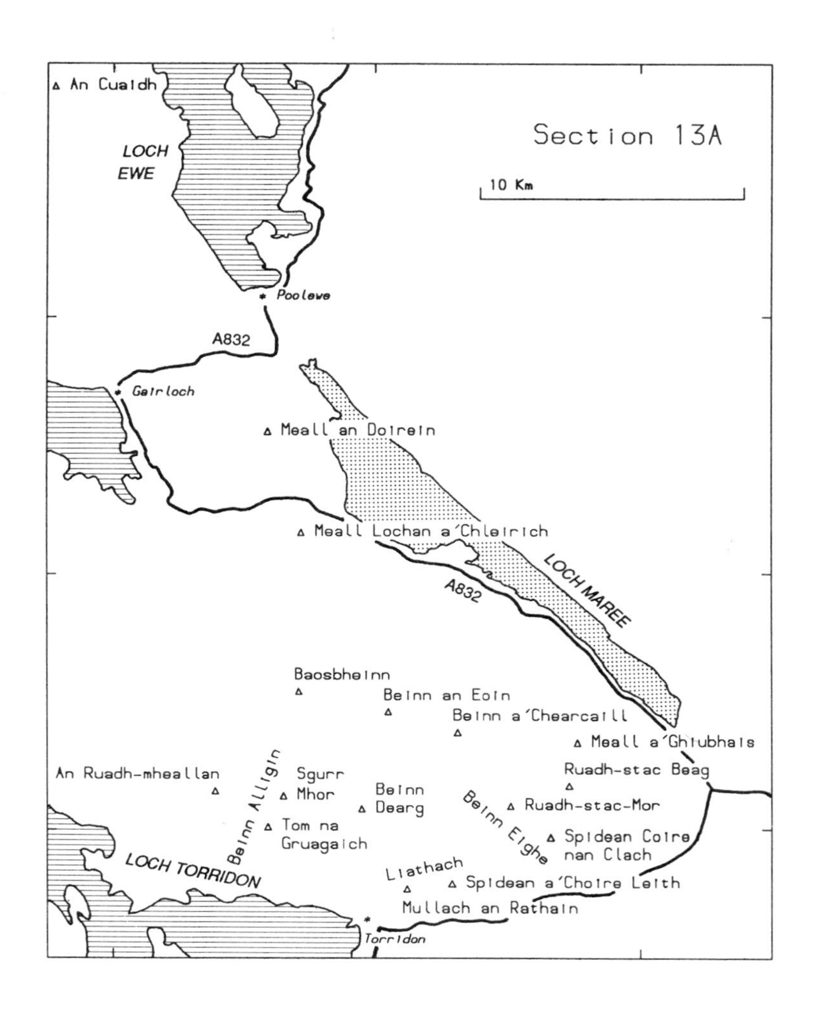

Metres	Feet	Name	Map	Grid Ref	Date
1055	3460	Liathach - Spidean a'Choire Leith	25	NG 929579	______
1023	3356	Liathach - Mullach an Rathain	25	NG 912577	______
1010	3313	Beinn Eighe - Ruadh-stac Mor	19	NG 951611	______
993	3258	Beinn Eighe - Spidean Coire nan Clach	25	NG 966597	______
986	3235	Beinn Alligin - Sgurr Mhor	19/24	NG 865613	______
922	3025	Beinn Alligin - Tom na Gruagaich	19/24	NG 859601	______
914	2998	Beinn Dearg	19/24	NG 895608	______
896	2940	Ruadh-stac Beag	19	NG 973614	______
887	2910	Meall a'Ghiubhais	19	NG 976634	______
875	2871	Baosbheinn	19/24	NG 871654	______
855	2805	Beinn an Eoin	19	NG 905646	______
725	2378	Beinn a'Chearcaill	19	NG 931638	______
672	2205	An Ruadh-mheallan	19/24	NG 836615	______
420	1378	Meall an Doirein	19	NG 859754	______
403	1322	Meall Lochan a'Chleirich	19	NG 872716	______
296	972	An Cuaidh	19	NG 765891	______

Section 13B Applecross to Achnasheen

South of Loch Torridon and A896 from Torridon to Kinlochewe

Metres	Feet	Name	Map	Grid Ref	Date
960	3150	Sgorr Ruadh	25	NG 959504	______
933	3060	Maol Chean-dearg	25	NG 924498	______
925	3036	Beinn Liath Mhor	25	NG 964519	______
907	2976	Fuar Tholl	25	NG 975489	______
902	2959	Beinn Damh	24	NG 893502	______
896	2938	Beinn Bhan	24	NG 804450	______
892	2926	An Ruadh-stac	25	NG 922481	______
873	2863	Sgorr nan Lochan Uaine	25	NG 969531	______
792	2598	Sgurr a'Chaorachain	24	NG 797417	______
782	2566	Sgurr Dubh	25	NG 979558	______
737	2418	Beinn na h-Eaglaise	25	NG 909523	______
732	2402	Sgurr a'Gharaidh	24	NG 884443	______
678	2223	Carn Breac	25	NH 045530	______
626	2053	Meall an Doireachain	24	NG 724491	______

Metres	Feet	Name	Map	Grid Ref	Date
625	2050	Beinn na Feusaige	25	NH 093543	______
530	1739	Ben Shieldaig	24	NG 833524	______
513	1682	An Staonach	24	NG 830481	______
466	1529	Bidein Clann Raonaild	25	NH 054592	______
437	1435	Seana Mheallan	25	NG 929551	______
395	1296	Bad a'Chreamha	24	NG 858367	______
392	1286	An Sgurr	24	NG 857387	______

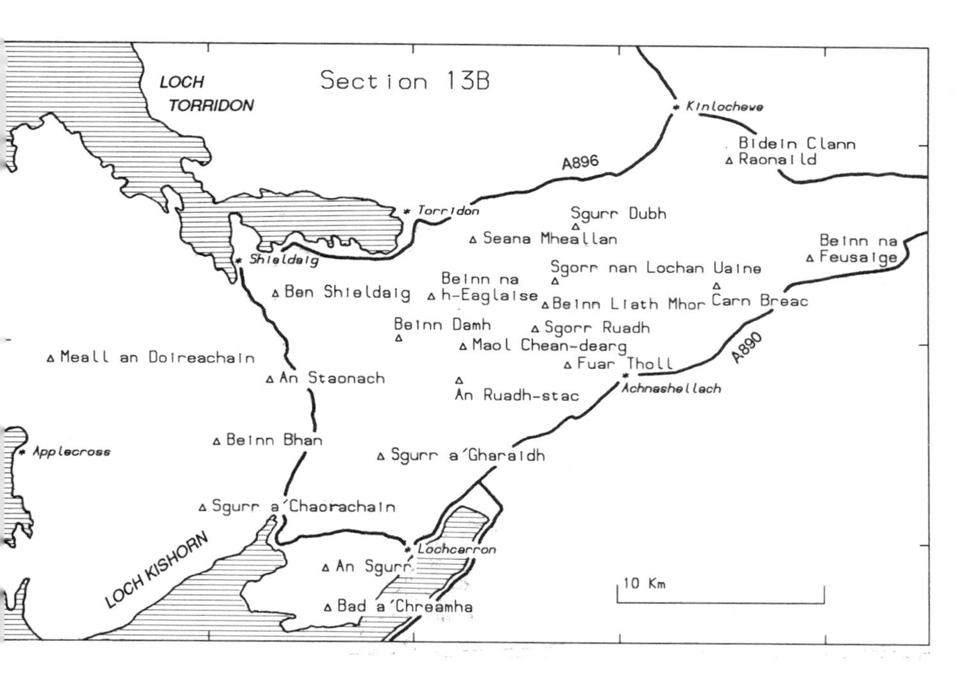

REGION 14

Loch Maree to Loch Broom and Garve

Ullapool; Loch Broom and A835 to Garve; railway to Achnasheen; A832 to Kinlochewe; Loch Maree and coast to Ullapool.

Section 14A Loch Maree to Loch Broom

North-west of Heights of Kinlochewe, Gleann Tanagaidh, Bealach na Croise and Loch a'Bhraoin

Metres	*Feet*	*Name*	*Map*	*Grid Ref*	*Date*
1062	3484	An Teallach - Bidein a'Ghlas Thuill	19	NH 069843	______
1019	3343	Mullach Coire Mhic Fhearchair	19	NH 052735	______
989	3245	Sgurr Ban	19	NH 055745	______
981	3217	Slioch	19	NH 004691	______
967	3173	A'Mhaighdean	19	NH 007748	______
937	3075	Beinn Tarsuinn	19	NH 039727	______
918	3012	Ruadh Stac Mor	19	NH 018756	______
916	3005	Beinn a'Chlaidheimh	19	NH 061775	______
910	2985	Beinn Dearg Mor	19	NH 032799	______
860	2821	Beinn Lair	19	NG 982732	______
857	2812	Beinn a'Chaisgein Mor	19	NG 983785	______
820	2690	Beinn Dearg Bheag	19	NH 020811	______
807	2647	Creag Rainich	19	NH 097751	______
791	2595	Beinn Airigh Charr	19	NG 930762	______
767	2516	Sail Mhor	19	NH 033887	______
722	2370	Meall Mheinnidh	19	NG 955748	______
692	2270	Beinn a'Mhuinidh	19	NH 032660	______
680	2230	Beinn a'Chaisgein Beag	19	NG 965821	______
635	2082	Beinn Ghobhlach	19	NH 056943	______
580	1903	Beinn nam Ban	19	NH 109908	______
545	1788	Cnoc a'Bhaid-rallaich	19	NH 066930	______
521	1709	Meall Glac Tigh-fail	20	NH 161828	______

Looking north-west from Tullich Hill (Section 1E) to The Cobbler, probably the most difficult mainland peak, and Beinn Ime, the southernmost 1000-metre peak in Scotland.

A rare clear day on the dramatic north-east face of Ben Nevis, Britain's highest mountain, seen from near the top of Carn Mor Dearg (Section 4A).

Contemplating the view from the top of Beinn Bhreac (Section 6A), possibly the most remote Marilyn of all. It is possible to cycle ten miles along a track up Glen Bruar to get within walking range of the mountain, but it is a very rough ride.

The summits of Lurg Mhor and Bidean a'Choire Sheasgaich (Section 12A), two very remote mountains in the sparsely-populated region on Monar.

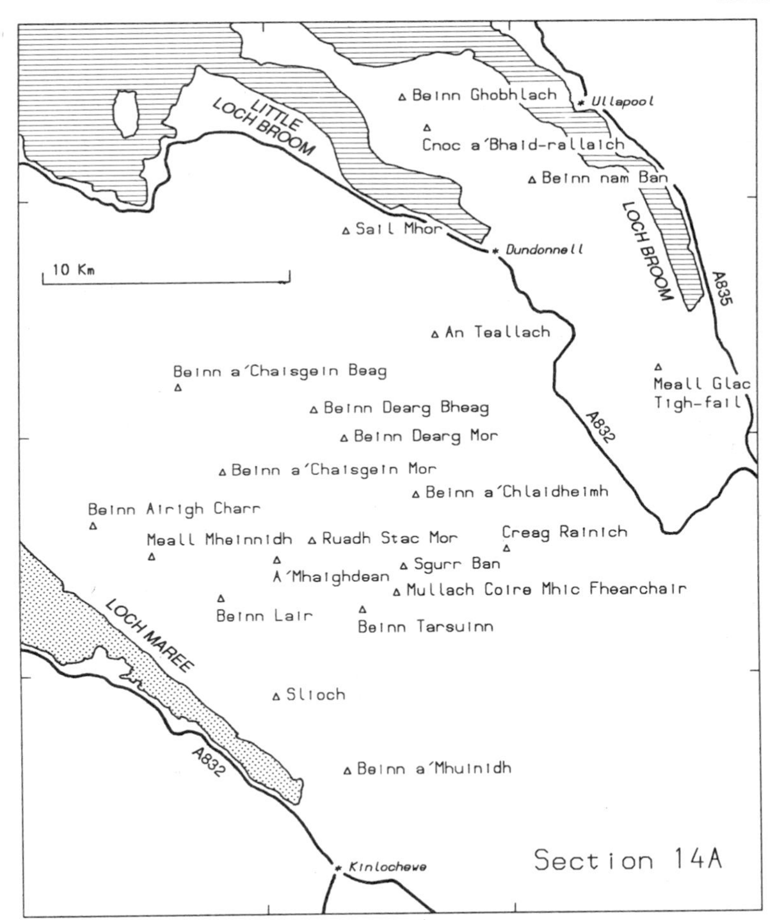

Section 14B The Fannaichs

South-east of Heights of Kinlochewe, Gleann Tanagaidh, Bealach na Croise and Loch a'Bhraoin

Metres	*Feet*	*Name*	*Map*	*Grid Ref*	*Date*
1110	3642	Sgurr Mor	20	NH 203718	______
1093	3586	Sgurr nan Clach Geala	20	NH 184715	______
1000	3281	Sgurr Breac	20	NH 158711	______
999	3276	A'Chailleach	19	NH 136714	______
933	3062	Fionn Bheinn	20	NH 147621	______

Metres	*Feet*	*Name*	*Map*	*Grid Ref*	*Date*
766	2513	Beinn Liath Mhor a'Ghiubhais Li	20	NH 281713	______
749	2457	Groban	19	NH 099709	______
711	2333	Beinn nan Ramh	19	NH 139662	______
705	2313	Meall a'Chaorainn	19	NH 136604	______
668	2192	Beinn Bheag	19	NH 084714	______
558	1832	An Cabar	20	NH 257641	______
479	1571	Carn na Dubh Choille	20	NH 387674	______

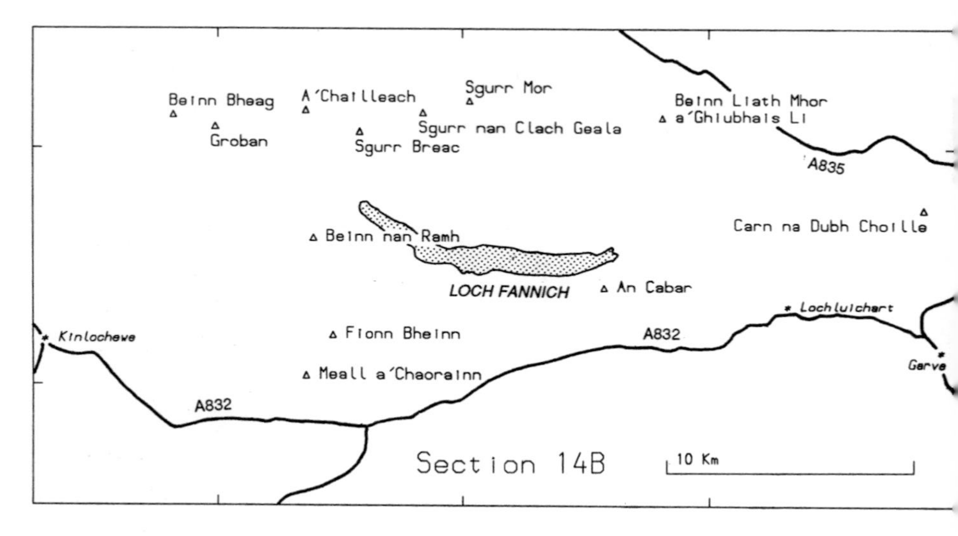

REGION 15
Ullapool to the Moray Firth

Ullapool; A835 to Ledmore; A837 and River Oykel to Bonar Bridge; Dornoch Firth and coast to Inverness; Beauly Firth to Beauly; A832 to Garve; A835 and Loch Broom to Ullapool.

Section 15A Loch Broom to Strath Oykel
North-west of Loch Vaich, Gleann Mor and River Carron

Metres	*Feet*	*Name*	*Map*	*Grid Ref*	*Date*
1084	3556	Beinn Dearg	20	NH 259812	______
980	3215	Cona' Mheall	20	NH 274816	______
954	3130	Am Faochagach	20	NH 303793	______
928	3045	Eididh nan Clach Geala	20	NH 257842	______
927	3040	Seana Bhraigh	20	NH 281878	______
889	2915	Beinn Enaiglair	20	NH 225805	______
845	2772	Carn Ban	20	NH 339876	______
730	2395	Meall Doire Faid	20	NH 221792	______

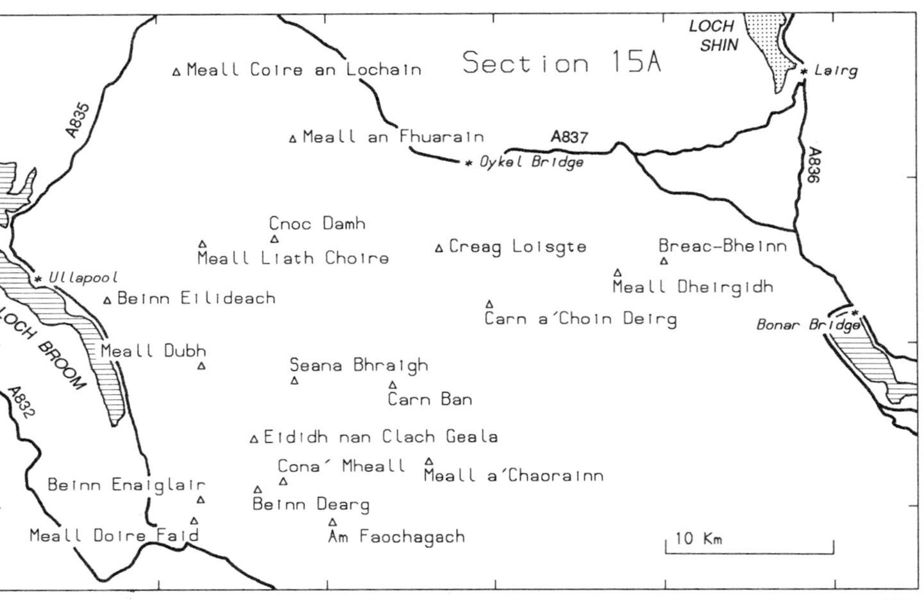

Metres	Feet	Name	Map	Grid Ref	Date
701	2301	Carn a'Choin Deirg	20	NH 397924	______
665	2183	Meall Dubh	20	NH 226887	______
632	2073	Meall a'Chaorainn	20	NH 360828	______
591	1939	Cnoc Damh	20	NH 270963	______
578	1895	Meall an Fhuarain	15	NC 281024	______
559	1835	Beinn Eilideach	20	NH 170927	______
548	1798	Meall Liath Choire	20	NH 227962	______
517	1696	Meall Coire an Lochain	15	NC 212065	______
507	1663	Meall Dheirgidh	20	NH 473943	______
462	1516	Breac-Bheinn	20	NH 500950	______
412	1353	Creag Loisgte	20	NH 367958	______

Section 15B Loch Vaich to the Moray Firth

South-east of Loch Vaich, Gleann Mor and River Carron

Metres	Feet	Name	Map	Grid Ref	Date
1046	3433	Ben Wyvis	20	NH 463684	______
838	2750	Carn Chuinneag	20	NH 484833	______
787	2582	Beinn a'Chaisteil	20	NH 370801	______
764	2507	Little Wyvis	20	NH 429645	______
743	2436	Beinn nan Eun	20	NH 448759	______
738	2421	Meall Mor	20	NH 515746	______
714	2342	Beinn Tharsuinn	20	NH 413829	______
698	2290	Carn Loch nan Amhaichean	20	NH 411757	______
692	2270	Beinn Tharsuinn	21	NH 607792	______
645	2116	Carn Salachaidh	20	NH 518875	______
523	1716	Cnoc Ceislein	21	NH 589706	______
397	1301	Cnoc Corr Guinie	21	NH 672754	______
380	1246	Cnoc an t-Sabhail	21	NH 694787	______
373	1225	Struie	21	NH 658850	______
321	1054	Cnoc an t-Sabhail	21	NH 722817	______
269	883	Cnoc Mor	26	NH 490569	______
256	841	Mount Eagle	26	NH 649590	______
203	665	Hill of Nigg *	21	NH 828713	______

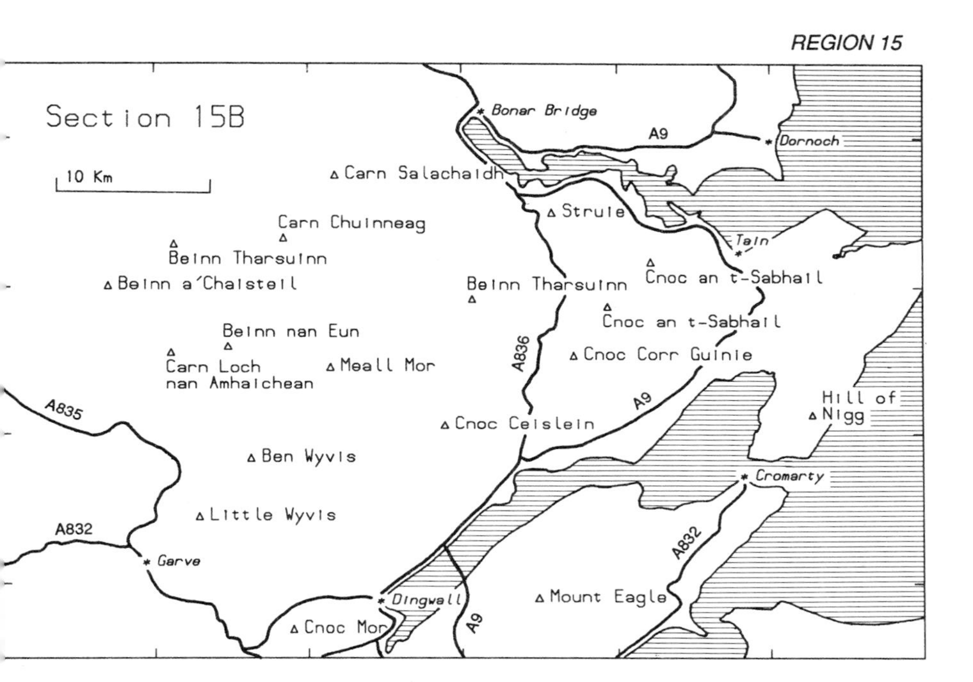
Section 15B
10 Km
Bonar Bridge
A9
Dornoch
Carn Salachaidh
Strule
Carn Chuinneag
Tain
Beinn Tharsuinn
Beinn a'Chaisteil
Beinn Tharsuinn
Cnoc an t-Sabhail
Cnoc an t-Sabhail
Beinn nan Eun
A836
Cnoc Corr Guinie
Carn Loch
nan Amhaichean
Meall Mor
A9
Hill of
Nigg
A835
Cnoc Ceislein
Ben Wyvis
Cromarty
Little Wyvis
A832
A832
Garve
Dingwall
Mount Eagle
A9
Cnoc Mor

REGION 16
The Far North

Ullapool; coast to Cape Wrath, Wick and Dornoch; Dornoch Firth, River Oykel and A837 to Ledmore; A835 to Ullapool.

Section 16A Cape Wrath Peninsula

North-west of A838 from Laxford Bridge to Durness

Metres	*Feet*	*Name*	*Map*	*Grid Ref*	*Date*
521	1709	Farrmheall	9	NC 308588	______
485	1592	Creag Riabhach	9	NC 279638	______
467	1532	An Grianan	9	NC 264627	______
460	1508	Fashven	9	NC 313674	______
371	1216	Sgribhis-bheinn	9	NC 319713	______

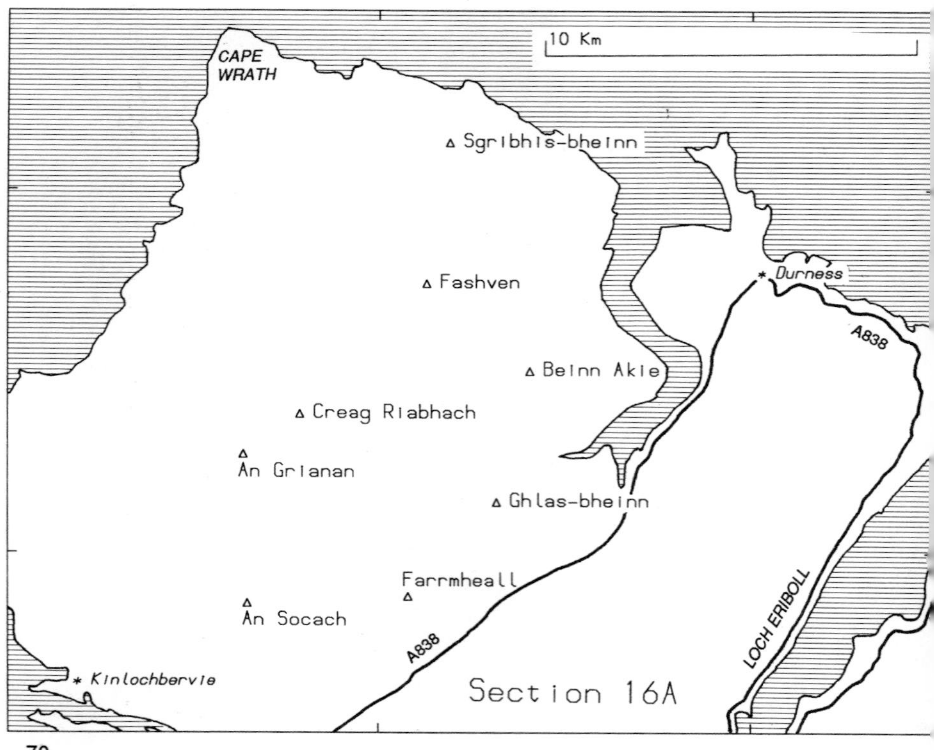

Metres	Feet	Name	Map	Grid Ref	Date
362	1187	An Socach	9	NC 265586	______
332	1089	Ghlas-bheinn	9	NC 332614	______
288	944	Beinn Akie	9	NC 341650	______

Section 16B Durness to Loch Shin
East of A838 and west of A836

Metres	Feet	Name	Map	Grid Ref	Date
927	3040	Ben Hope	9	NC 477501	______
914	2998	Foinaven - Ganu Mor	9	NC 315507	______

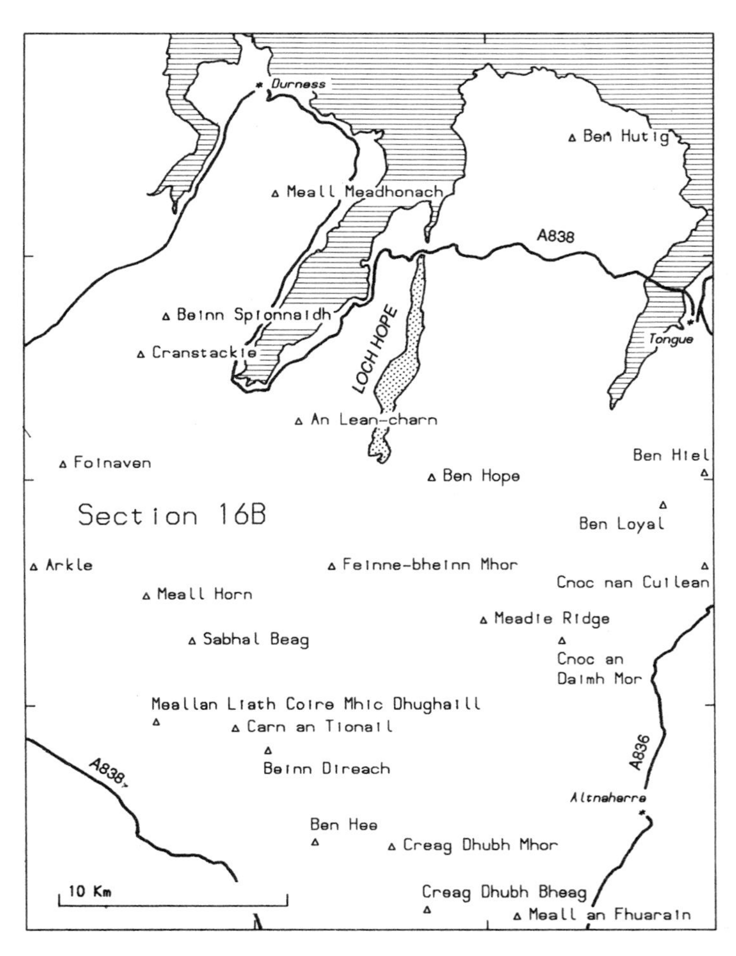

Metres	Feet	Name	Map	Grid Ref	Date
873	2863	Ben Hee	16	NC 426339	______
801	2627	Meallan Liath Coire Mhic Dhughaill	15	NC 357392	______
800	2625	Cranstackie	9	NC 351556	______
787	2582	Arkle	9	NC 303462	______
777	2548	Meall Horn	9	NC 353449	______
772	2534	Beinn Spionnaidh	9	NC 362573	______
764	2506	Ben Loyal - An Caisteal	10	NC 578489	______
759	2490	Carn an Tionail	16	NC 392390	______
732	2401	Sabhal Beag	9	NC 373429	______
688	2257	Beinn Direach	16	NC 406380	______
557	1828	Cnoc nan Cuilean	10	NC 597462	______
553	1814	Creag Dhubh Mhor	16	NC 459337	______
535	1754	Ben Hiel	10	NC 596501	______
521	1709	An Lean-charn	9	NC 420526	______
473	1552	Meall an Fhuarain	16	NC 513306	______
472	1549	Creag Dhubh Bheag	16	NC 474307	______
465	1526	Feinne-bheinn Mhor	9	NC 434462	______
422	1385	Meall Meadhonach	9	NC 410628	______
416	1364	Meadie Ridge	9	NC 499438	______
408	1338	Ben Hutig	10	NC 538653	______
356	1167	Cnoc an Daimh Mor	10	NC 533429	______

Section 16C Tongue to Wick and Helmsdale

North of B873, B871 and River Helmsdale from Altnaharra to Helmsdale

Metres	Feet	Name	Map	Grid Ref	Date
706	2315	Morven	17	ND 004286	______
626	2055	Scaraben	17	ND 066268	______
590	1936	Ben Griam Mor	17	NC 806389	______
580	1902	Ben Griam Beg	10	NC 832412	______
555	1820	Creag Scalabsdale	17	NC 970241	______
527	1728	Beinn Stumanadh	10	NC 641499	______
509	1670	Smean	17	ND 032277	______
484	1587	Maiden Pap	11/17	ND 048293	______
422	1385	Braigh na h-Eaglaise	17	ND 065221	______

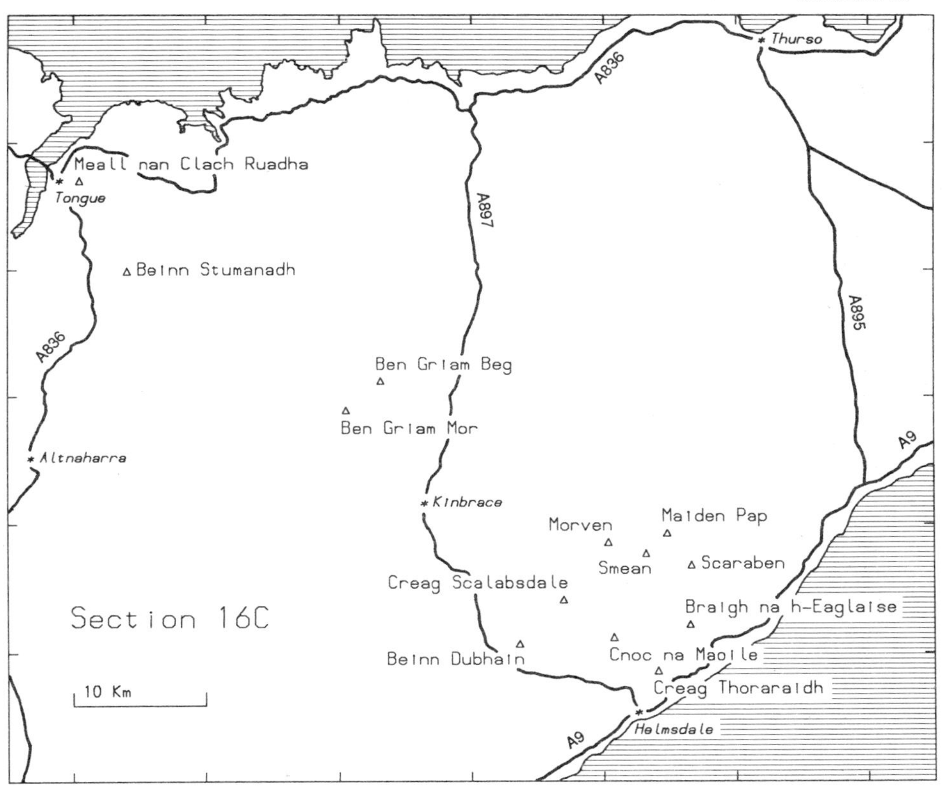

Metres	Feet	Name	Map	Grid Ref	Date
417	1368	Beinn Dubhain	17	NC 937207	______
405	1329	Creag Thoraraidh	17	ND 041187	______
402	1319	Cnoc na Maoile	17	ND 008212	______
336	1102	Meall nan Clach Ruadha	10	NC 605570	______

Section 16D Altnaharra to Dornoch

South of B873, B871 and River Helmsdale from Altnaharra to Helmsdale

Metres	Feet	Name	Map	Grid Ref	Date
961	3154	Ben Klibreck - Meall nan Con	16	NC 585299	______
713	2338	Creag Mhor	16	NC 698240	______
705	2312	Ben Armine - Creag a'Choire Ghlais	16	NC 695273	______
628	2060	Beinn Dhorain	17	NC 925157	______

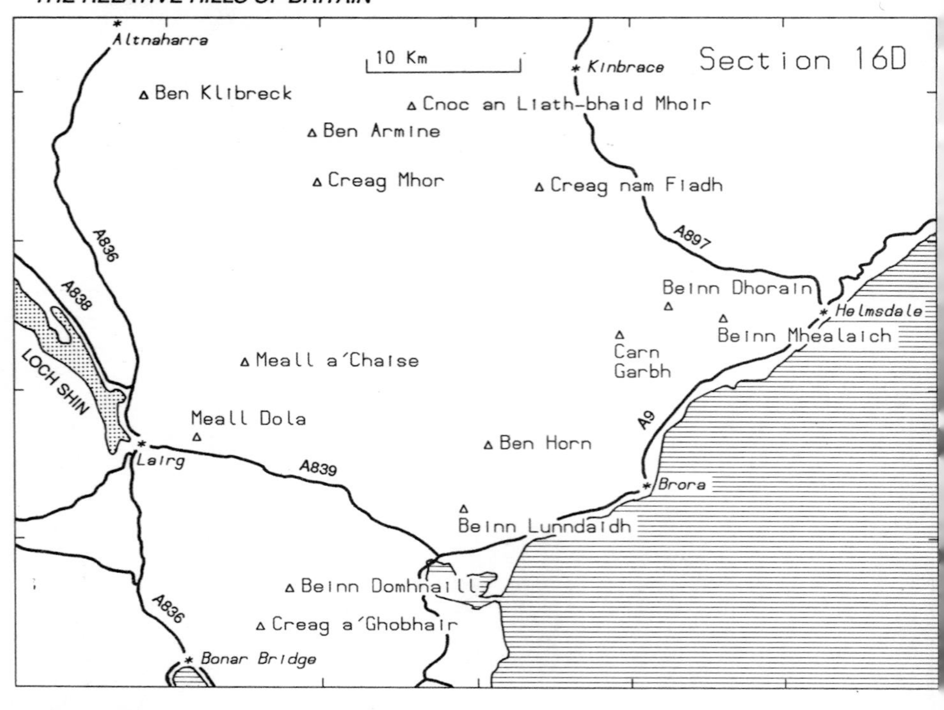

Metres	Feet	Name	Map	Grid Ref	Date
592	1942	Beinn Mhealaich	17	NC 961149	______
545	1788	Carn Garbh	17	NC 893138	______
521	1710	Ben Horn	17	NC 807064	______
446	1463	Beinn Lunndaidh	17	NC 791020	______
434	1423	Cnoc an Liath-bhaid Mhoir	16	NC 759291	______
387	1271	Creag nam Fiadh	17	NC 841237	______
370	1214	Meall a'Chaise	16	NC 651119	______
349	1144	Beinn Domhnaill	21	NH 679967	______
346	1135	Creag a'Ghobhair	21	NH 655939	______
323	1059	Meall Dola	16	NC 619069	______

Section 16E Scourie to Lairg

North of A837 and River Oykel from Lochinver to Invershin

Metres	Feet	Name	Map	Grid Ref	Date
998	3273	Ben More Assynt	15	NC 318201	______
814	2670	Breabag	15	NC 287158	______

Metres	Feet	Name	Map	Grid Ref	Date
808	2651	Quinag - Sail Gharbh	15	NC 209292	______
792	2599	Beinn Leoid	15	NC 320295	______
776	2546	Glas Bheinn	15	NC 255265	______
776	2546	Quinag - Sail Gorm	15	NC 198304	______
764	2507	Quinag - Spidean Coinich	15	NC 205278	______
750	2461	Meallan a'Chuail	15	NC 345293	______
721	2364	Ben Stack	9	NC 269423	______
613	2010	Meall an Fheur Loch	16	NC 362310	______
544	1786	Beinn an Eoin	16	NC 389083	______
512	1680	Maovally	16	NC 378212	______
510	1674	Ben Dreavie	15	NC 261398	______
476	1561	Beinn Sgeireach	16	NC 453118	______

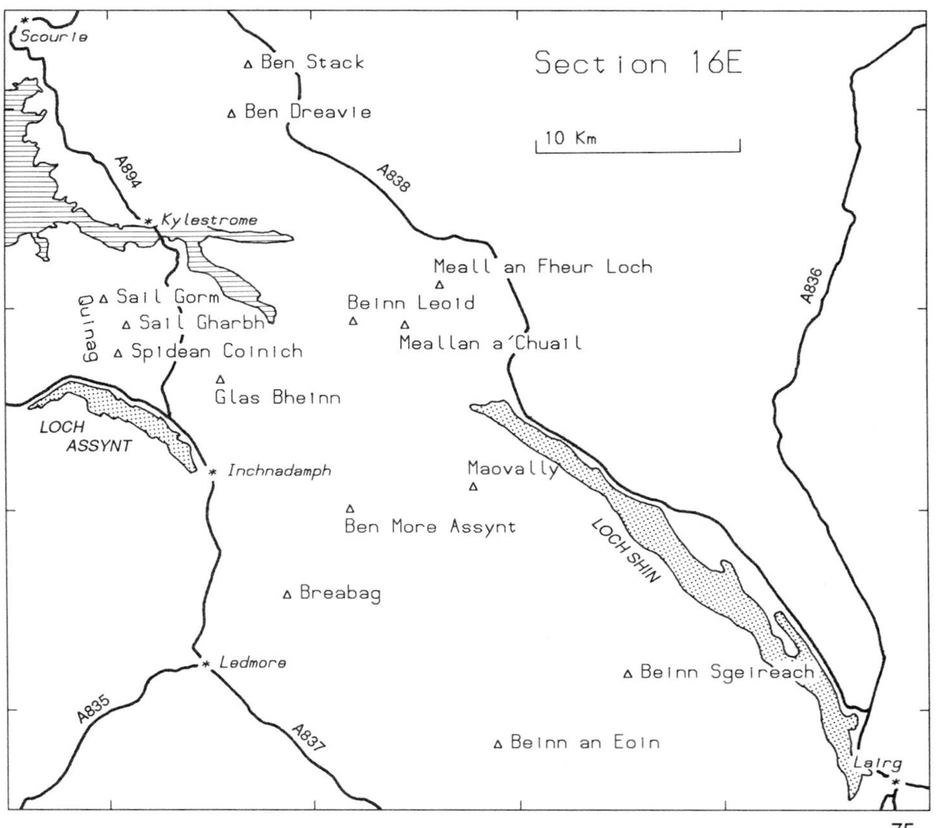

Section 16F Lochinver to Ullapool

West of A837 and A835 from Loch Assynt to Ullapool

Metres	Feet	Name	Map	Grid Ref	Date
849	2787	Cul Mor	15	NC 162119	______
846	2775	Canisp	15	NC 203187	______
769	2523	Cul Beag	15	NC 140088	______
743	2438	Ben Mor Coigach	15	NC 094042	______
731	2399	Suilven - Caisteal Liath	15	NC 153183	______
703	2306	Sgurr an Fhidhleir	15	NC 094054	______
618	2028	Beinn an Eoin	15	NC 105064	______
613	2010	Stac Pollaidh	15	NC 107106	______
588	1928	Sgorr Tuath	15	NC 110075	______
567	1860	Beinn Reidh	15	NC 212213	______
203	667	Meall an Fheadain	15	NB 999109	______

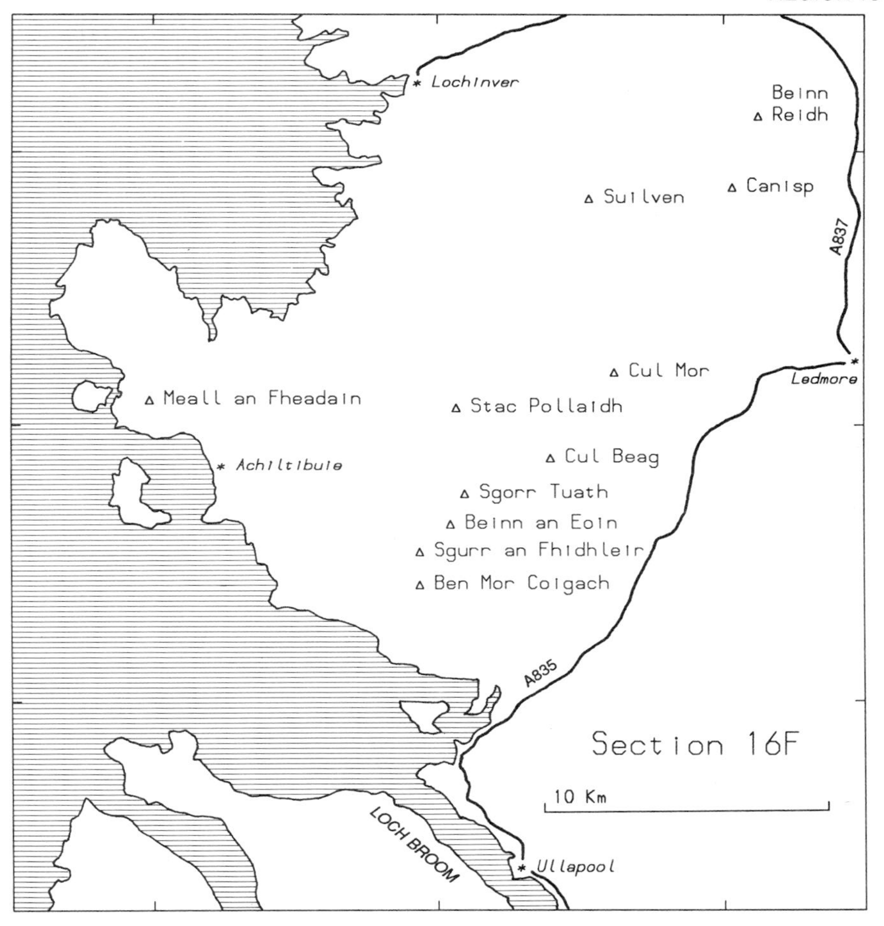
Lochinver
Beinn Reidh
Canisp
Suilven
A837
Cul Mor
Ledmore
Meall an Fheadain
Stac Pollaidh
Achiltibuie
Cul Beag
Sgorr Tuath
Beinn an Eoin
Sgurr an Fhidhleir
Ben Mor Coigach
A835
Section 16F
10 Km
LOCH BROOM
Ullapool

REGION 17
Skye, Rhum, Mull and Nearby Islands

All the islands in the Inner Hebrides, from the Inner Sound to the Firth of Lorn.

Section 17A North Skye and Raasay

North of A863 from Loch Harport to Loch Sligachan, plus the island of Raasay

719	2358	The Storr	23	NG 495540	1.1.95
669	2195	Hartaval	23	NG 480551	______
552	1812	Ben Dearg	23	NG 477504	______
543	1781	Meall na Suiramach	23	NG 446695	______
489	1604	Healabhal Bheag	23	NG 225422	______
471	1544	Healabhal Mhor	23	NG 219445	______
466	1530	Bioda Buidhe	23	NG 439664	______

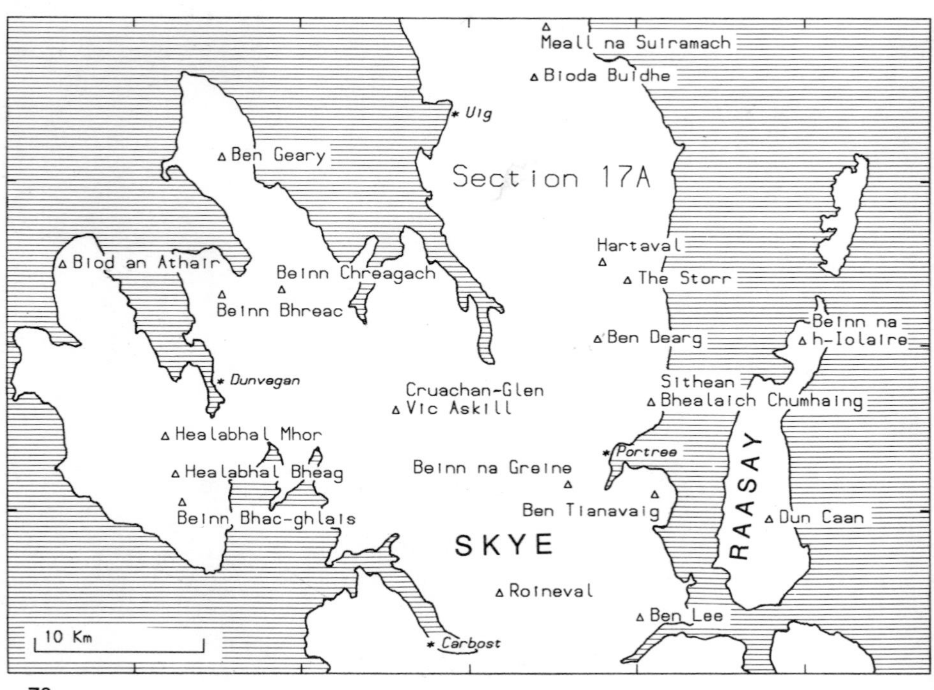

Metres	Feet	Name	Map	Grid Ref	Date
445	1460	Ben Lee	24/32	NG 502335	______
444	1457	Dun Caan	24/32	NG 579395	______
439	1440	Roineval	32	NG 418350	______
417	1367	Beinn na Greine	23	NG 459416	______
413	1355	Ben Tianavaig	23/24	NG 511410	______
409	1341	Beinn Bhac-ghlais	23	NG 229405	______
392	1287	Sithean Bhealaich Chumhaing	23/24	NG 509466	______
328	1075	Beinn Chreagach	23	NG 289534	______
327	1074	Beinn Bhreac	23	NG 253531	______
313	1028	Biod an Athair	23	NG 158549	______
295	969	Cruachan-Glen Vic Askill	23	NG 357461	______
284	931	Ben Geary	23	NG 253615	______
254	833	Beinn na h-Iolaire	24	NG 599503	______

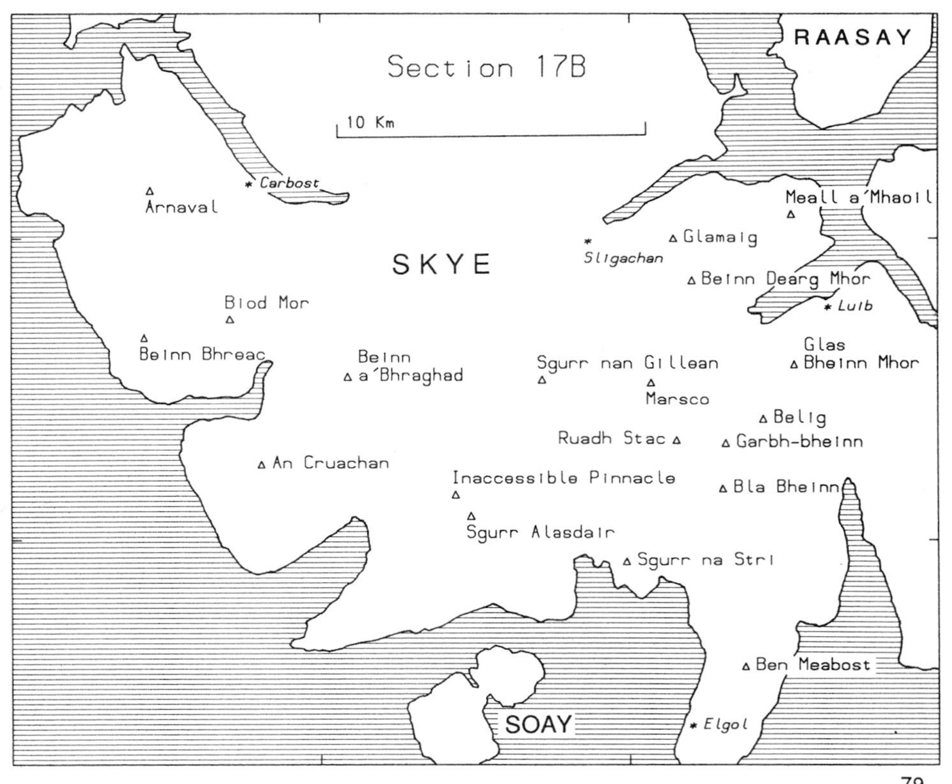

Section 17B Minginish and the Cuillin Hills

West of Strath Mor, from Luib to Loch Slapin

Metres	Feet	Name	Map	Grid Ref	Date
993	3257	Sgurr Alasdair	32	NG 449208	______
986	3234	Sgurr Dearg - Inaccessible Pinnacle	32	NG 444215	______
965	3167	Sgurr nan Gillean	32	NG 472253	______
928	3046	Bla Bheinn (Blaven)	32	NG 530217	______
808	2650	Garbh-bheinn	32	NG 531232	______
775	2542	Glamaig - Sgurr Mhairi	32	NG 514300	______
736	2414	Marsco	32	NG 507252	______
731	2398	Beinn Dearg Mhor	32	NG 520285	______
702	2303	Belig	32	NG 543240	______
570	1870	Glas Bheinn Mhor	32	NG 553258	______
497	1631	Sgurr na Stri	32	NG 499193	______
493	1619	Ruadh Stac	32	NG 515233	______
461	1512	Beinn a'Bhraghad	32	NG 409254	______
445	1460	Beinn Bhreac	32	NG 343267	______
435	1428	An Cruachan	32	NG 381225	______
383	1257	Biod Mor	32	NG 371273	______
369	1210	Arnaval	32	NG 345316	______
346	1135	Ben Meabost	32	NG 537158	______
284	932	Meall a'Mhaoil	24/32	NG 553308	______

Section 17C South-East Skye and Scalpay

East of Strath Mor, from Luib to Loch Slapin, plus the island of Scalpay

Metres	Feet	Name	Map	Grid Ref	Date
739	2424	Sgurr na Coinnich	33	NG 762222	______
733	2405	Beinn na Caillich	33	NG 771229	______
732	2403	Beinn na Caillich	32	NG 601233	______
709	2326	Beinn Dearg Mhor	32	NG 587228	______
610	2000	Ben Aslak	33	NG 751191	______
572	1878	Ben na Cro	32	NG 569242	______
561	1841	Beinn na Seamraig	33	NG 729178	______
396	1298	Mullach na Carn	32	NG 606292	______
301	988	Beinn nan Carn	32	NG 636180	______
299	981	Sgorach Breac	32	NG 651132	______

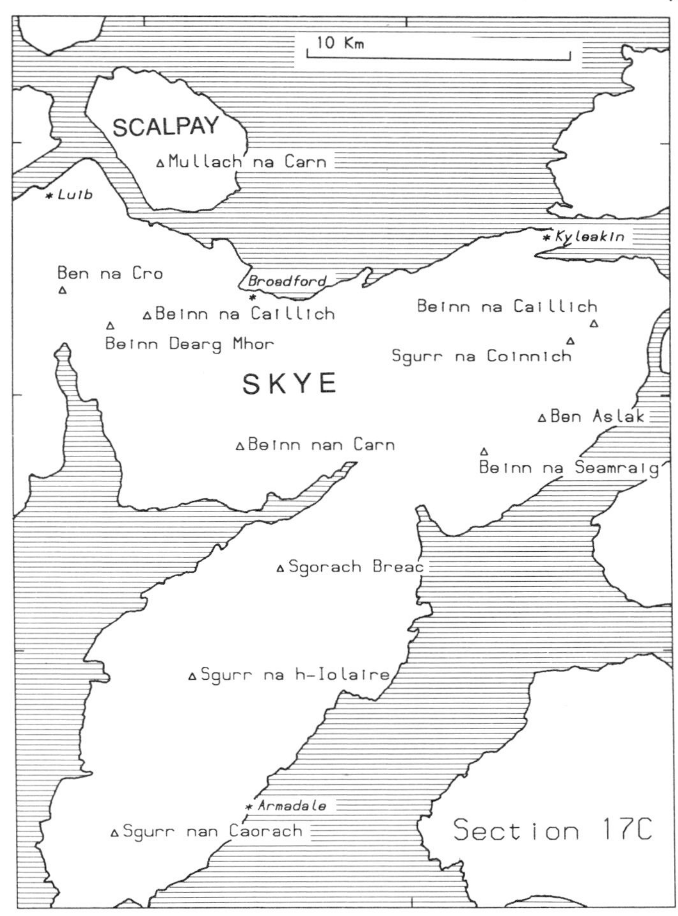

Metres	Feet	Name	Map	Grid Ref	Date
292	959	Sgurr na h-Iolaire	32	NG 617090	______
280	920	Sgurr nan Caorach	32/39	NG 587029	______

Section 17D Canna, Rhum and Eigg
Three islands between Skye and Mull

Metres	Feet	Name	Map	Grid Ref	Date
812	2663	Askival	39	NM 393952	______
781	2562	Ainshval	39	NM 379944	______
702	2303	Trallval	39	NM 377952	______

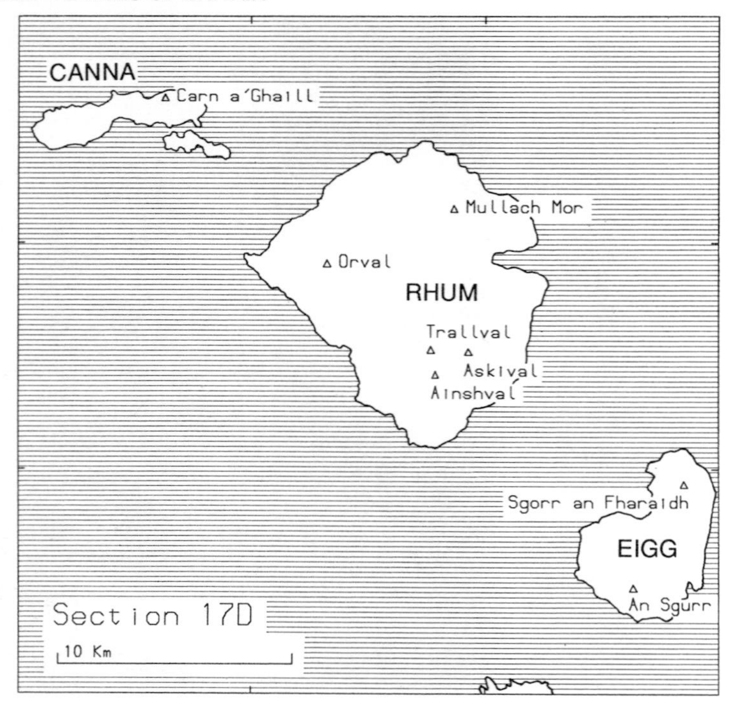

Metres	*Feet*	*Name*	*Map*	*Grid Ref*	*Date*
571	1874	Orval	39	NM 333991	______
393	1290	An Sgurr	39	NM 463847	______
340	1115	Sgorr an Fharaidh	39	NM 485893	______
304	997	Mullach Mor	32/39	NG 387015	______
210	690	Carn a'Ghaill	39	NG 263064	______

Section 17E Mull and Nearby Islands

The island of Mull plus the islands of Ulva and Gometra

966	3170	Ben More	47/48	NM 526331	______
766	2512	Dun da Ghaoithe	49	NM 672362	______
763	2502	Beinn Talaidh	49	NM 625347	______
741	2430	Sgurr Dearg	49	NM 665340	______
717	2353	Ben Buie	49	NM 604271	______
704	2311	Corra-bheinn	48	NM 573322	______

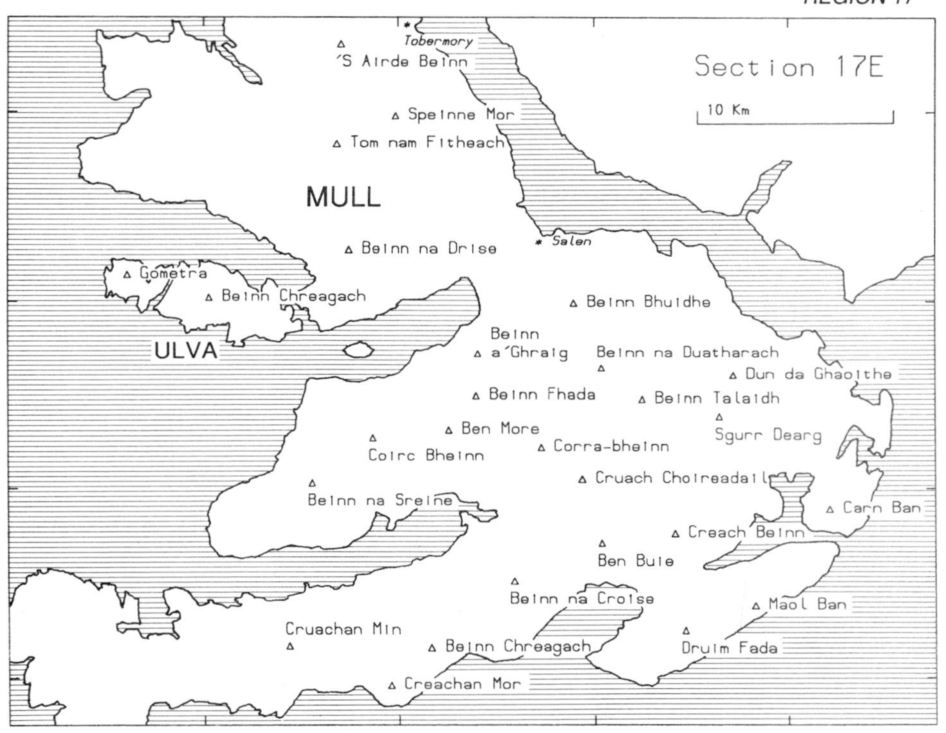

Metres	Feet	Name	Map	Grid Ref	Date
702	2303	Beinn Fhada	47/48	NM 540349	______
698	2290	Creach Beinn	49	NM 642276	______
618	2028	Cruach Choireadail	48	NM 594305	______
591	1939	Beinn a'Ghraig	47/48	NM 541372	______
561	1841	Coirc Bheinn	48	NM 487327	______
521	1710	Beinn na Sreine	48	NM 456303	______
503	1649	Beinn na Croise	48	NM 559251	______
456	1495	Beinn na Duatharach	49	NM 604363	______
444	1458	Speinne Mor	47/48	NM 499498	______
424	1392	Beinn na Drise	47/48	NM 475427	______
413	1355	Beinn Bhuidhe	47/48	NM 590399	______
405	1329	Druim Fada	49	NM 647225	______
377	1236	Beinn Chreagach	48	NM 517216	______

Metres	Feet	Name	Map	Grid Ref	Date
376	1232	Cruachan Min	48	NM 445217	______
338	1109	Maol Ban	49	NM 683238	______
331	1086	Creachan Mor	48	NM 496196	______
313	1026	Beinn Chreagach	47/48	NM 403402	______
295	968	'S Airde Beinn	47	NM 471537	______
275	901	Tom nam Fitheach	47/48	NM 469483	______
248	812	Carn Ban	49	NM 721289	______
155	509	Gometra	47/48	NM 361414	______

REGION 18
Ardnamurchan to Loch Linnhe

Fort William; Loch Linnhe and coast to Ardnamurchan Point and Lochailort; A830 and Loch Eil to Fort William.

Section 18A Moidart and Ardnamurchan

North and west of A861 and Loch Shiel from Salen to Glenfinnan, including Eilean Shona

Metres	*Feet*	*Name*	*Map*	*Grid Ref*	*Date*
882	2895	Beinn Odhar Bheag	40	NM 846778	______
882	2895	Rois-Bheinn	40	NM 756778	______
874	2867	Sgurr na Ba Glaise	40	NM 770777	______
814	2671	An Stac	40	NM 763793	______
783	2569	Beinn Mhic Cedidh	40	NM 829788	______
666	2185	Beinn Gaire	40	NM 781749	______
663	2175	Croit Bheinn	40	NM 810773	______
528	1731	Ben Hiant	47	NM 537632	______
512	1679	Ben Laga	40	NM 645621	______
490	1607	Meall nan Each	40	NM 632643	______
437	1433	Meall nan Con	47	NM 503681	______
344	1130	Beinn na Seilg	47	NM 458642	______
265	869	Beinn a'Bhaillidh	40	NM 649741	______
240	787	Beinn Bhreac	40	NM 681715	______

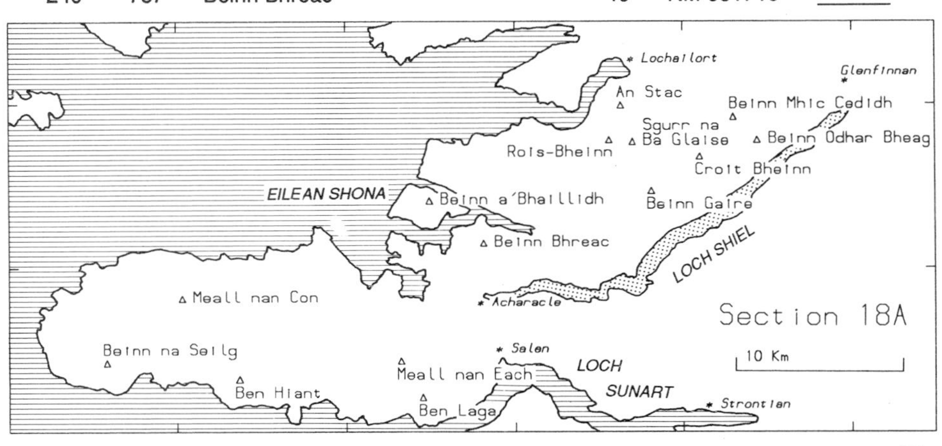

Section 18B Sunart and Ardgour

North of Loch Sunart and Glen Tarbert

Metres	*Feet*	*Name*	*Map*	*Grid Ref*	*Date*
888	2914	Sgurr Dhomhnuill	40	NM 889679	_______
885	2903	Garbh Bheinn	40	NM 904622	_______
849	2784	Sgurr Ghiubhsachain	40	NM 876751	_______
845	2772	Beinn Resipol	40	NM 766655	_______
786	2579	Carn na Nathrach	40	NM 887699	_______
775	2543	Sgorr Craobh a'Chaorainn	40	NM 895758	_______
771	2528	Stob Coire a'Chearcaill	41	NN 017727	_______
770	2525	Druim Tarsuinn	40	NM 875727	_______
762	2500	Beinn na h-Uamha	40	NM 918665	_______
761	2497	Sgurr a'Chaorainn	40	NM 895662	_______
736	2415	Beinn Bheag	40	NM 914635	_______
734	2407	Druim na Sgriodain *	40	NM 978656	_______
723	2371	Meall nan Damh	40	NM 919745	_______
721	2365	Stob Mhic Bheathain	40	NM 914713	_______
701	2300	Sgurr nan Cnamh	40	NM 887643	_______
650	2133	Sgorr Mhic Eacharna	40	NM 928630	_______
636	2086	Glas Bheinn	40	NM 939758	_______

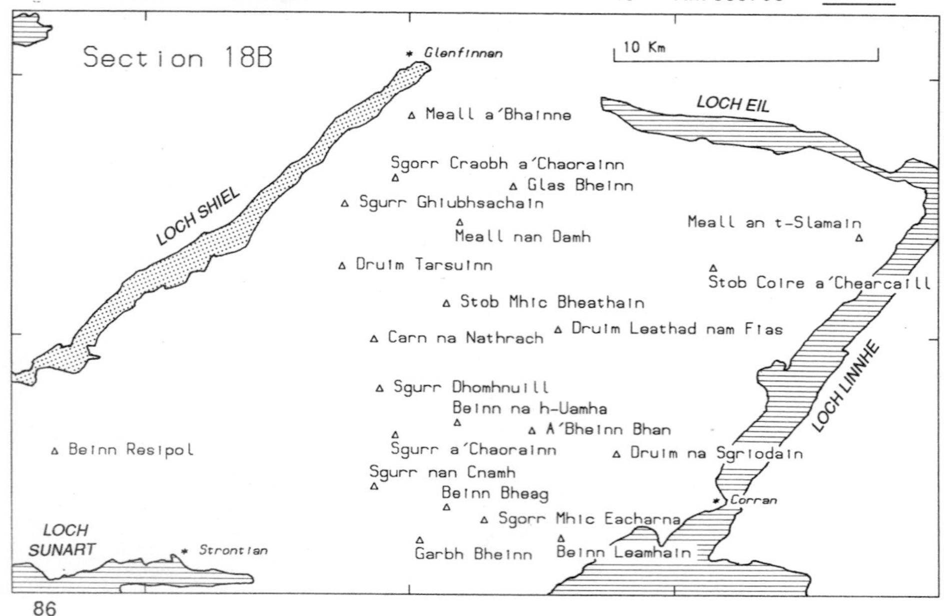

Metres	Feet	Name	Map	Grid Ref	Date
576	1890	Druim Leathad nam Fias	40	NM 956703	______
559	1835	Meall a'Bhainne	40	NM 901785	______
508	1666	Beinn Leamhain	40	NM 957623	______
477	1565	A'Bheinn Bhan	40	NM 946665	______
467	1531	Meall an t- Slamain	41	NN 070739	______

Section 18C Morvern and Kingairloch

South of Loch Sunart and Glen Tarbert, including the island of Carna

Metres	Feet	Name	Map	Grid Ref	Date
853	2798	Creach Bheinn	49	NM 871577	______
766	2512	Fuar Bheinn	49	NM 853564	______
739	2423	Beinn Mheadhoin	49	NM 799514	______
652	2140	Beinn na Cille	49	NM 854542	______
582	1911	Beinn nam Beathrach	49	NM 752572	______
551	1807	Sidhean na Raplaich	49	NM 635517	______
513	1684	An Sleaghach	49	NM 764434	______
479	1572	Beinn Chlaonleud	49	NM 748543	______
465	1525	Beinn na h-Uamha	49	NM 682534	______
437	1435	Beinn a'Chaisil	49	NM 780477	______
170	558	Cruachan Charna	49	NM 618590	______

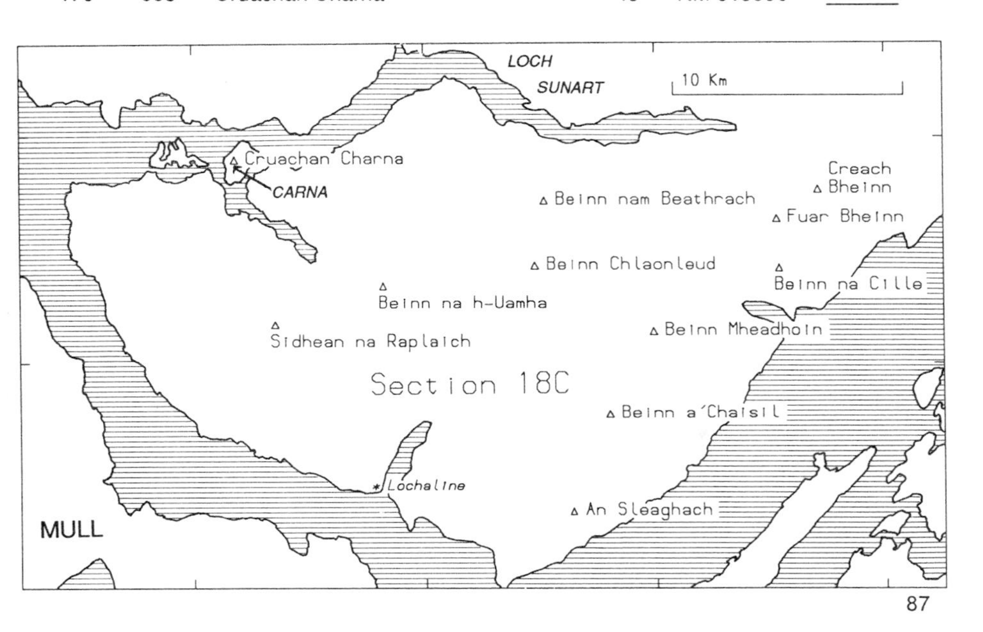

REGION 19

Oban to Dunoon and the Mull of Kintyre

Oban; coast to Taynuilt; A85 and A819 to Inveraray; A83 to Arrochar; Loch Long and coast to Oban, plus the islands of Kerrera and Bute.

Section 19A Oban to Loch Fyne

North of the Crinan Canal, including the island of Kerrera

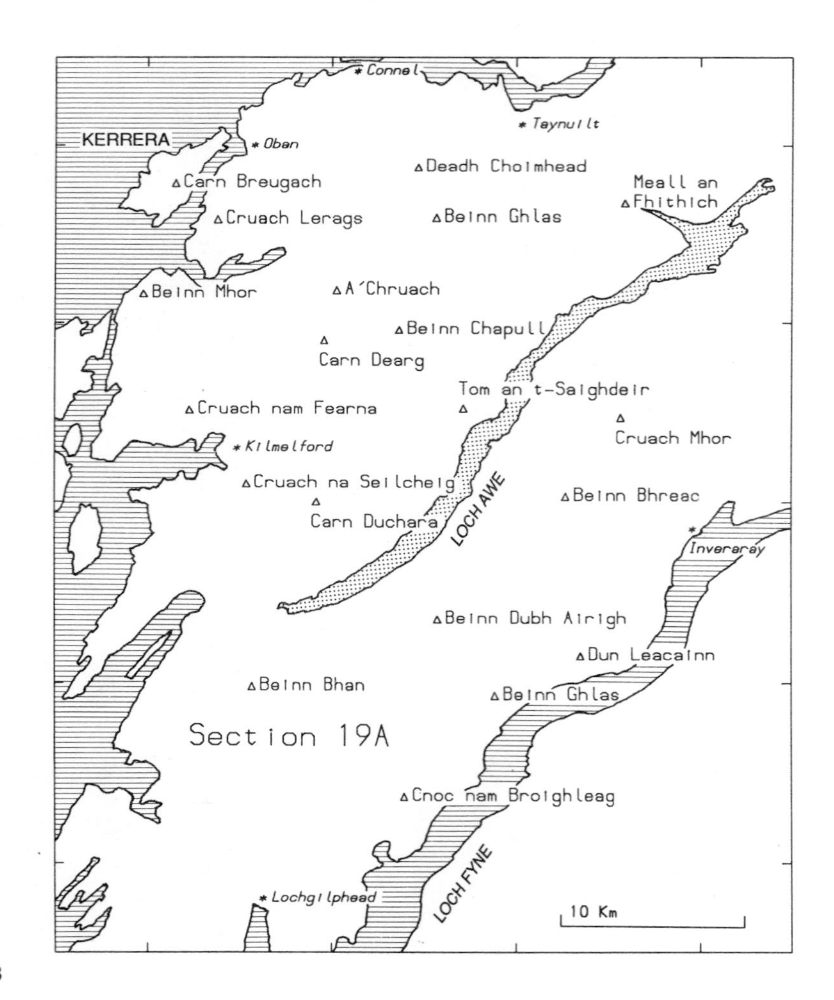

Metres	Feet	Name	Map	Grid Ref	Date
589	1932	Cruach Mhor	50/56	NN 057147	______
526	1726	Beinn Bhreac	50/55	NN 027103	______
515	1691	Beinn Ghlas	49	NM 957259	______
515	1690	Beinn Chapull	55	NM 937196	______
491	1610	Carn Duchara	55	NM 892102	______
459	1506	Beinn Dubh Airigh	55	NM 958035	______
438	1436	Carn Dearg	55	NM 896190	______
420	1378	Beinn Ghlas	55	NR 989993	______
383	1257	Deadh Choimhead	49	NM 947287	______
380	1247	Cruach na Seilcheig	55	NM 854110	______
368	1208	A'Chruach	49	NM 903218	______
359	1179	Dun Leacainn	55	NN 035015	______
332	1089	Cruach nam Fearna	55	NM 823151	______
319	1048	Beinn Bhan	55	NR 857998	______
314	1031	Cnoc nam Broighleag	55	NR 940937	______
303	993	Tom an t-Saighdeir	55	NM 972152	______
294	965	Meall an Fhithich *	50	NN 059267	______
252	827	Cruach Lerags	49	NM 838258	______
194	637	Beinn Mhor	49	NM 798216	______
189	620	Carn Breugach	49	NM 815278	______

Section 19B Knapdale and Kintyre
South of the Crinan Canal

Metres	Feet	Name	Map	Grid Ref	Date
562	1843	Stob Odhar	62	NR 818742	______
466	1530	Cruach Lusach	55	NR 786832	______
454	1490	Beinn an Tuirc	68/69	NR 752362	______
446	1464	Cnoc Moy	68	NR 611152	______
428	1404	Beinn na Lice	68	NR 602085	______
422	1383	Cnoc a'Bhaile-shios	62	NR 863629	______
397	1302	Sgreadan Hill	68	NR 741295	______
385	1263	The Slate	68	NR 633164	______
354	1160	Beinn Ghuilean	68	NR 729171	______
265	870	Cnoc Reamhar	55	NR 766912	______

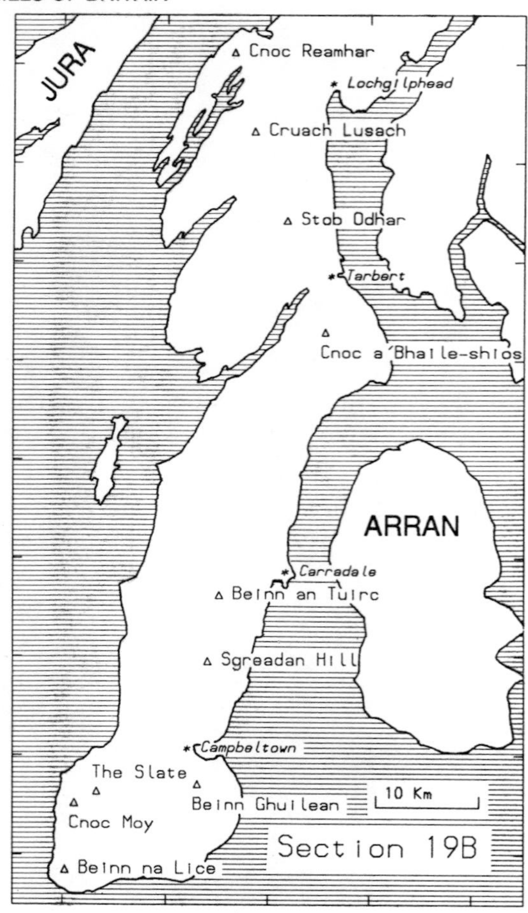

Section 19C Loch Fyne to Bute and the Firth of Clyde

South-west of the A83 from Inveraray to Arrochar, plus the island of Bute

Metres	*Feet*	*Name*	*Map*	*Grid Ref*	*Date*
901	2956	Beinn an Lochain	56	NN 218079	______
847	2778	Ben Donich	56	NN 218043	______
787	2582	The Brack	56	NN 246031	______
779	2556	Beinn Bheula	56	NS 154983	______
761	2497	Cnoc Coinnich	56	NN 233008	______
741	2430	Beinn Mhor	56	NS 108908	______

Metres	Feet	Name	Map	Grid Ref	Date
732	2401	Stob an Eas	56	NN 185074	______
703	2306	Beinn Lochain	56	NN 160007	______
664	2178	Beinn Ruadh	56	NS 155883	______
658	2159	Stob na Boine Druim-fhinn	56	NN 169025	______
643	2110	Creag Tharsuinn	56	NS 088913	______
618	2029	Beinn Bheag	56	NS 125932	______
611	2005	Cruach nam Mult	56	NN 169056	______
611	2005	Cruach nan Capull	63	NS 095795	______
607	1991	Cruach Neuran	56	NS 083820	______

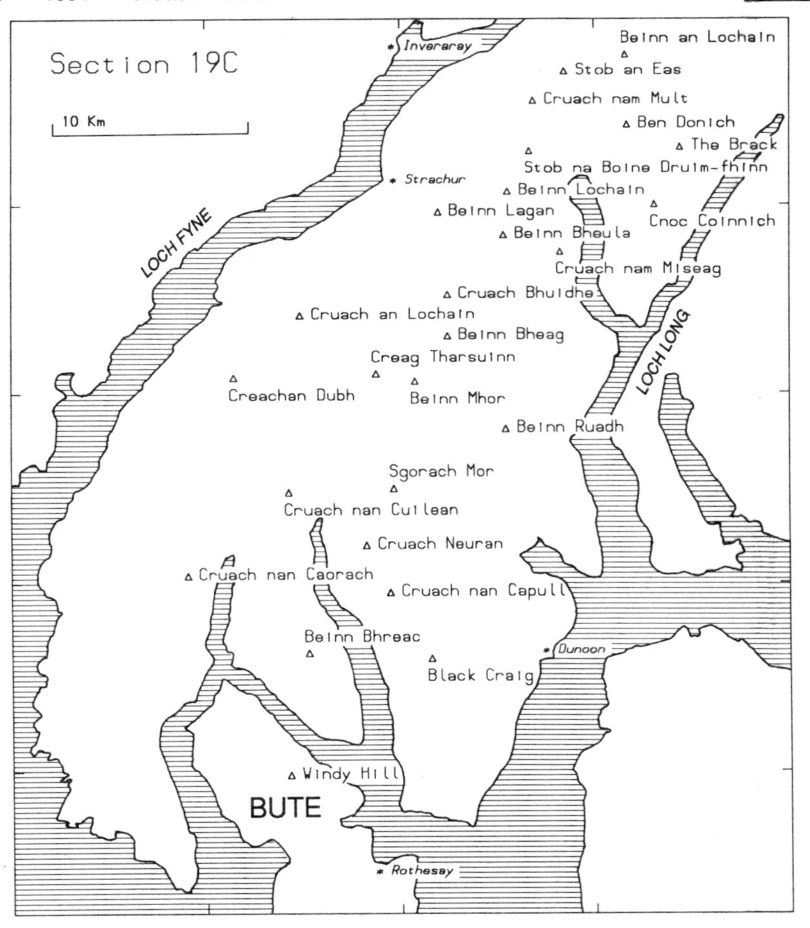

Metres	Feet	Name	Map	Grid Ref	Date
606	1988	Cruach nam Miseag	56	NS 183981	______
601	1972	Sgorach Mor	56	NS 097850	______
568	1863	Cruach Bhuidhe	56	NS 125947	______
522	1713	Black Craig	63	NS 116760	______
508	1666	Cruach an Lochain	56	NS 049938	______
507	1662	Beinn Bhreac	63	NS 053763	______
470	1542	Creachan Dubh	55	NS 015910	______
465	1526	Beinn Lagan	56	NS 120996	______
458	1503	Cruach nan Caorach	55	NR 991804	______
432	1416	Cruach nan Cuilean	56	NS 043848	______
278	913	Windy Hill	63	NS 043698	______

REGION 20
Jura, Islay, Arran and Nearby Islands

All the islands from the Firth of Lorn to the Firth of Clyde, except Kerrera and Bute.

Section 20A Jura and Scarba

Two islands west of Knapdale and north of Islay

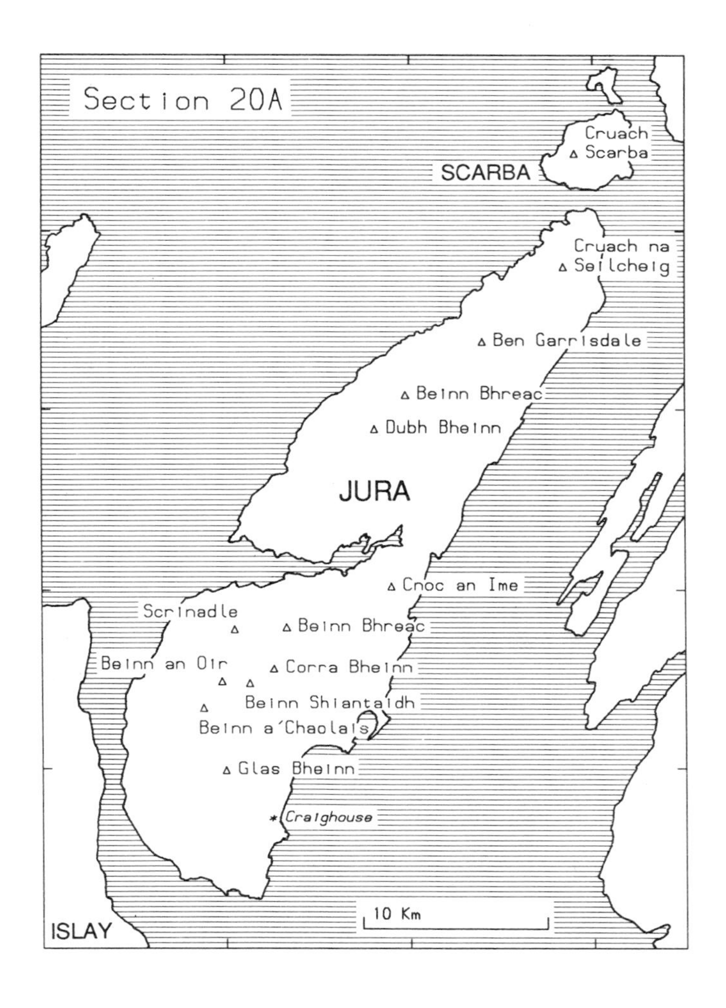

Metres	Feet	Name	Map	Grid Ref	Date
785	2576	Beinn an Oir	60/61	NR 498749	______
757	2485	Beinn Shiantaidh	61	NR 513748	______
734	2408	Beinn a'Chaolais	60/61	NR 488734	______
575	1886	Corra Bheinn	61	NR 526755	______
562	1845	Glas Bheinn	61	NR 500699	______
508	1667	Scrinadle	61	NR 505778	______
485	1590	Dubh Bheinn	61	NR 581889	______
467	1532	Beinn Bhreac	61	NR 598908	______
449	1474	Cruach Scarba	55	NM 690044	______

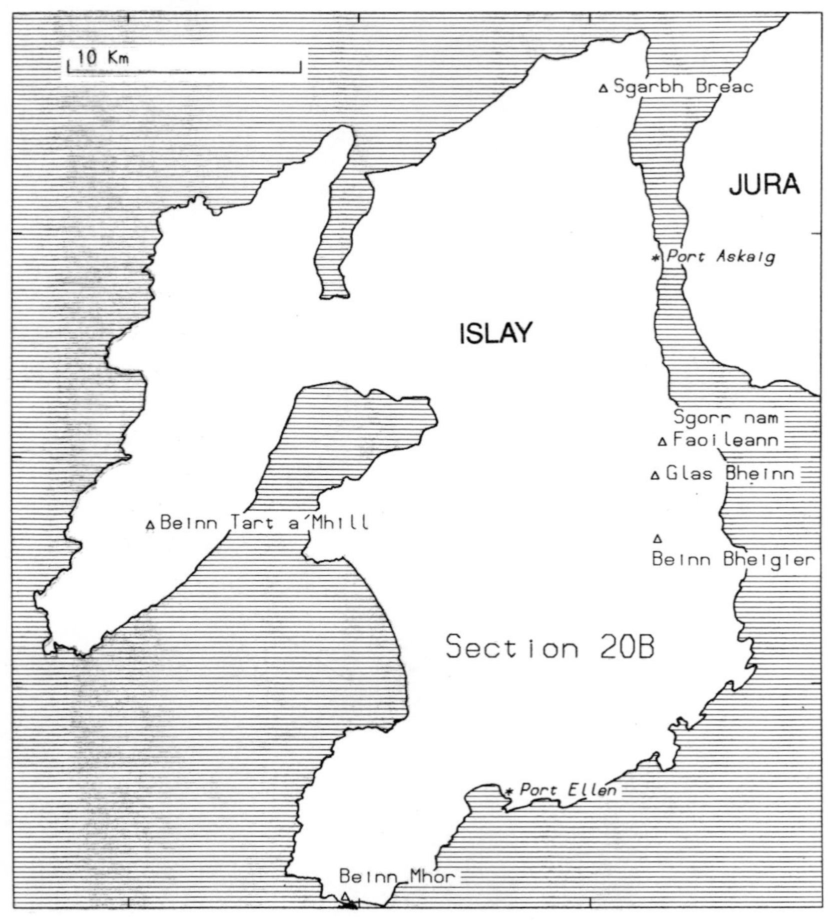

Metres	Feet	Name	Map	Grid Ref	Date
441	1446	Beinn Bhreac	61	NR 533779	______
371	1217	Ben Garrisdale	55/61	NR 640938	______
303	994	Cnoc an Ime	61	NR 590802	______
296	971	Cruach na Seilcheig	55/61	NR 684980	______

Section 20B Islay
Large island south-west of Jura

Metres	Feet	Name	Map	Grid Ref	Date
491	1612	Beinn Bheigier	60	NR 430564	______
472	1548	Glas Bheinn	60	NR 429592	______
429	1407	Sgorr nam Faoileann	60	NR 432607	______
364	1195	Sgarbh Breac	60	NR 406766	______
232	760	Beinn Tart a'Mhill	60	NR 210570	______
202	662	Beinn Mhor	60	NR 294404	______

Section 20C Arran and Holy Island
Two islands between Kintyre and the Firth of Clyde

Metres	Feet	Name	Map	Grid Ref	Date
874	2868	Goat Fell	62/69	NR 991415	______
859	2817	Caisteal Abhail	62/69	NR 969444	______
826	2710	Beinn Tarsuinn	62/69	NR 959412	______
799	2620	Cir Mhor	62/69	NR 973432	______
721	2366	Beinn Bharrain - Mullach Buidhe	62/69	NR 902428	______
575	1885	Beinn Bhreac	62/69	NR 943456	______
570	1870	Meall nan Damh	62/69	NR 911469	______
514	1685	A'Chruach	68/69	NR 969335	______
458	1503	Tighvein	69	NR 997274	______
444	1456	Creag Ghlas Laggan	62/69	NR 977497	______
314	1030	Mullach Mor	69	NS 063297	______

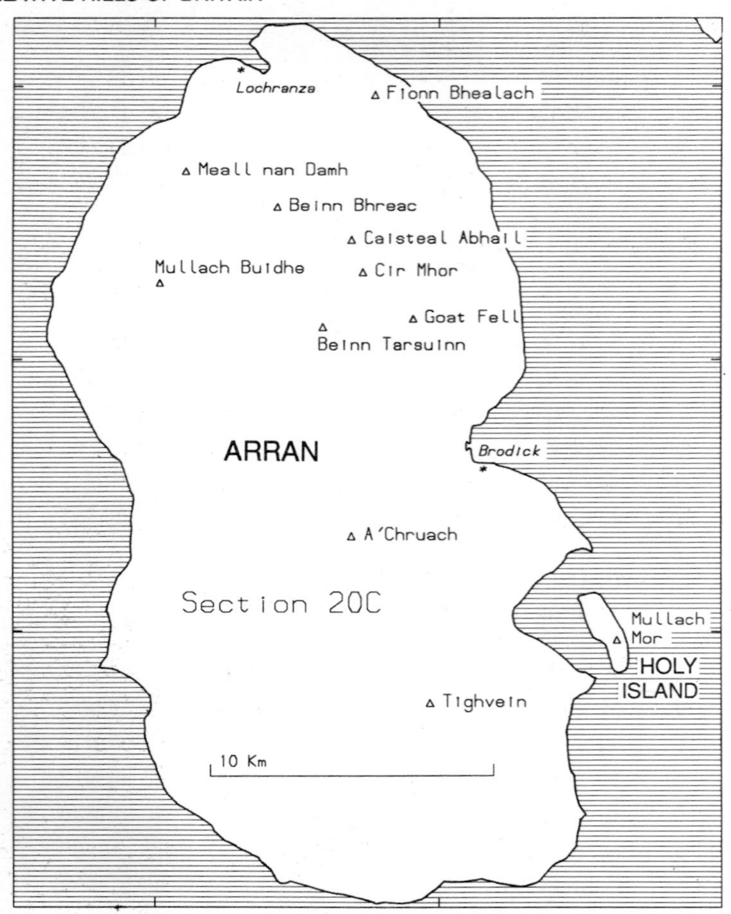
Lochranza
Fionn Bhealach
Meall nan Damh
Beinn Bhreac
Caisteal Abhail
Mullach Buidhe
Cir Mhor
Goat Fell
Beinn Tarsuinn
ARRAN
Brodick
A'Chruach
Section 20C
Mullach
Mor
HOLY
ISLAND
Tighvein
10 Km

›ove:

.e massive southern
›pes of Beinn Eighe
:ction 13A), one of
ly three Munros that
asts two Marilyns.
e highest point is
t of sight on the
rthern side.

ght:

e spectacular gash
it eats into the
nmit ridge of Beinn
igin (Section 13A),
iich like Beinn Eighe
s two Marilyns but
ly one Munro.

The rocky summit of Sgurr Alasdair (Section 17B), the highest point in Britain outwith th mainland. It is difficult to reach the top from this side; the most common route of ascent follows a steep scree slope on the far (west) side.

The contrasting peaks of Sgurr nan Gillean and Marsco seen from Bla Bheinn (Section 17I one of the finest viewpoints in Britain. The mountains of Harris in the Outer Hebrides ar just discernible on the horizon.

REGION 21
Strathspey to Aberdeen

Fraserburgh; coast to Aberdeen; River Dee to Ballater; A939 to Grantown-on-Spey; River Spey to Spey Bey; coast to Fraserburgh.

Section 21A Tomintoul to Banff
West of A97 from Banff to the River Dee

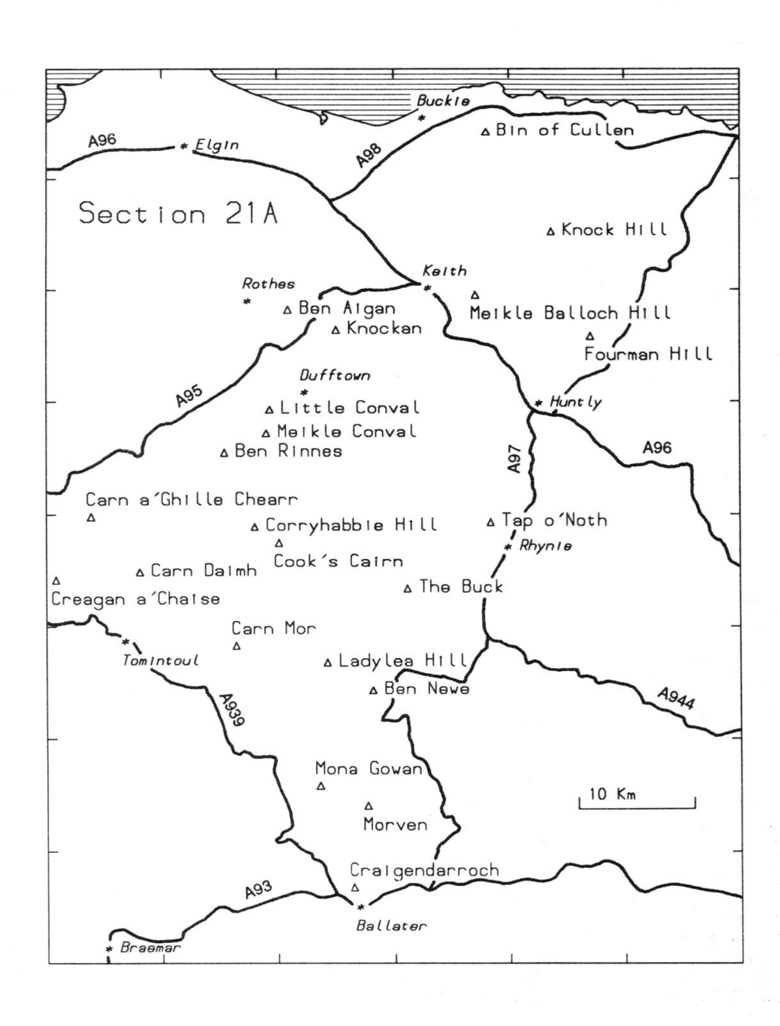

Metres	Feet	Name	Map	Grid Ref	Date
872	2861	Morven	37	NJ 377040	______
840	2756	Ben Rinnes	28	NJ 255355	______
804	2639	Carn Mor	37	NJ 265183	______
781	2561	Corryhabbie Hill	37	NJ 281289	______
756	2479	Cook's Cairn	37	NJ 302278	______
749	2456	Mona Gowan	37	NJ 336058	______
722	2369	Creagan a'Chaise	36	NJ 104242	______
721	2366	The Buck	37	NJ 412234	______
710	2330	Carn a'Ghille Chearr	36	NJ 139298	______
609	1998	Ladylea Hill	37	NJ 343168	______
571	1873	Meikle Conval	28	NJ 291372	______
570	1870	Carn Daimh	36	NJ 181249	______
565	1854	Ben Newe	37	NJ 382143	______
563	1848	Tap o'Noth	37	NJ 484293	______
552	1811	Little Conval	28	NJ 294393	______
471	1546	Ben Aigan	28	NJ 310482	______
430	1412	Knock Hill	29	NJ 537552	______
402	1319	Craigendarroch	37/44	NO 365965	______
372	1220	Knockan	28	NJ 351464	______
366	1200	Meikle Balloch Hill	28/29	NJ 471495	______
344	1128	Fourman Hill	29	NJ 571458	______
320	1051	Bin of Cullen	28/29	NJ 480643	______

Section 21B Fraserburgh to the Dee Valley

East of A97 from Banff to the River Dee

Metres	Feet	Name	Map	Grid Ref	Date
619	2031	Pressendye	37	NJ 490089	______
533	1748	Coiliochbhar Hill	37	NJ 503163	______
529	1735	Bennachie - Oxen Craig	38	NJ 662227	______
518	1699	Lord Arthur's Hill	37	NJ 513198	______
494	1621	Benaquhallie	37	NJ 606087	______
476	1562	Craiglich	37	NJ 533054	______
471	1545	Hill of Fare	38	NJ 672028	______
467	1531	Hill of Foudland	29	NJ 603332	______

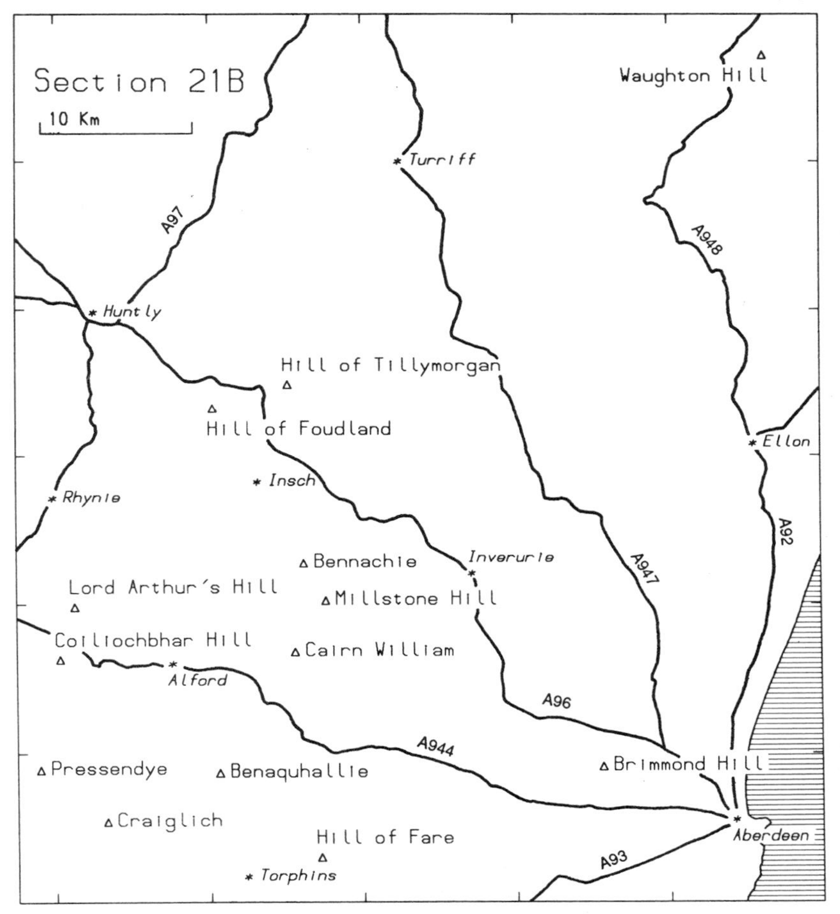

Metres	Feet	Name	Map	Grid Ref	Date
448	1469	Cairn William	38	NJ 656168	______
409	1342	Millstone Hill	38	NJ 676202	______
381	1249	Hill of Tillymorgan	29	NJ 652348	______
266	874	Brimmond Hill	38	NJ 856091	______
234	768	Waughton Hill	30	NJ 963572	______

REGION 22
Shetland Islands

All the islands north of the Orkneys, including Unst, Yell, Fetlar, Mainland, Bressay, Isle of Noss, Foula and Fair Isle.

Metres	*Feet*	*Name*	*Map*	*Grid Ref*	*Date*
450	1475	Ronas Hill	3	HU 305835	______
418	1373	The Sneug	4	HT 948395	______
293	962	Royl Field	4	HU 396285	______
285	935	Saxa Vord	1	HP 631167	______
283	930	Fitful Head	4	HU 346135	______
281	922	Scalla Field	2/3	HU 389572	______
263	863	Ward of Scousburgh	4	HU 388188	______
252	827	Dalescord Hill	2/3	HU 393684	______
249	817	Sandness Hill	3	HU 192557	______
248	814	The Noup	4	HT 954375	______
226	740	Ward of Bressay	4	HU 502387	______
217	712	Ward Hill	4	HZ 208734	______
216	709	Scrae Field	4	HU 418361	______
216	708	Valla Field	1	HP 584079	______
210	690	Hill of Arisdale	1/2	HU 495842	______
181	594	Noss Head	4	HU 554399	______
176	577	Cunnigill Hill	2/3	HU 432675	______
173	567	White Grunafirth	3	HU 276808	______
172	565	Mid Ward	3	HU 320652	______
159	522	Vord Hill	1/2	HU 622935	______

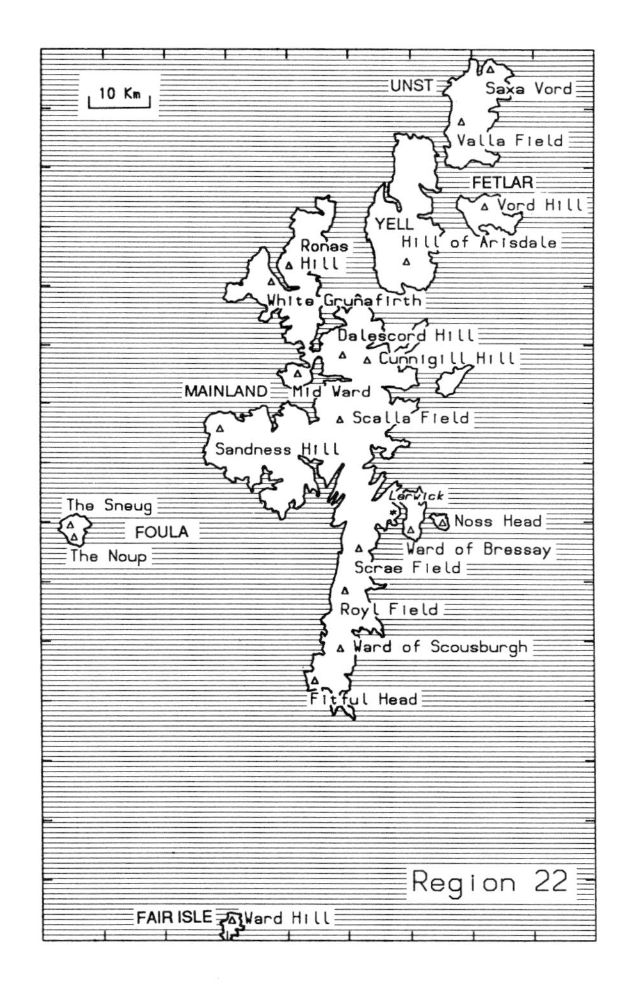
10 Km
UNST
Saxa Vord
Valla Field
FETLAR
Vord Hill
YELL
Hill of Arisdale
Ronas
Hill
White
Gruñafirth
Dalescord Hill
Cunnigill Hill
MAINLAND
Mid Ward
Scalla Field
Sandness Hill
Lerwick
Noss Head
The Sneug
FOULA
The Noup
Ward of Bressay
Scrae Field
Royl Field
Ward of Scousburgh
Fitful Head
Region 22
FAIR ISLE
Ward Hill

REGION 23
Orkney Islands

All the islands between Fair Isle and the Scottish mainland, including Westray, Rousay, Mainland and Hoy.

Metres	*Feet*	*Name*	*Map*	*Grid Ref*	*Date*
481	1577	Ward Hill	6/7	HY 229022	______
435	1427	Cuilags	7	HY 210033	______
399	1310	Knap of Trowieglen	7	ND 240985	______
275	901	Mid Hill	6/7	HY 335087	______
250	821	Blotchnie Fiold	5/6	HY 418289	______
225	738	Wideford Hill	6	HY 411116	______
224	735	Milldoe - Mid Tooin	6	HY 358207	______
221	724	Keelylang Hill	6	HY 378103	______
169	555	Fitty Hill	5	HY 429448	______

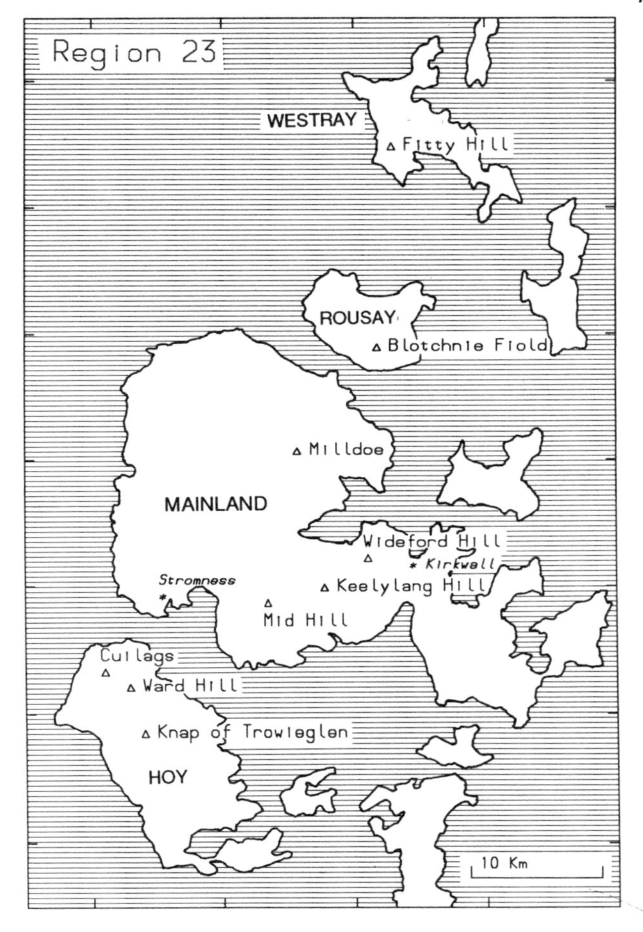
Region 23
WESTRAY
Fitty Hill
ROUSAY
Blotchnie Fiold
Milldoe
MAINLAND
Wideford Hill
Kirkwall
Stromness
Keelylang Hill
Mid Hill
Cuilags
Ward Hill
Knap of Trowieglen
HOY
10 Km

REGION 24

Western Isles

All the islands in the Outer Hebrides, from the Butt of Lewis to Barra Head.

Section 24A Lewis and Nearby Islands

Northern part of the Isle of Lewis and Harris, plus Seaforth Island and the Shiant Islands

Metres	*Feet*	*Name*	*Map*	*Grid Ref*	*Date*
574	1883	Mealisval	13	NB 022270	______
572	1877	Beinn Mhor	13/14	NB 254096	______
515	1690	Tahaval	13	NB 042264	______
514	1686	Cracaval	13	NB 030253	______
497	1631	Griomaval	13	NB 012220	______
492	1615	Liuthaid	13/14	NB 175136	______
470	1542	Gormol	13/14	NB 302069	______
449	1473	Caiteshal	13/14	NB 242044	______
429	1407	Suainaval	13	NB 078309	______
424	1391	Muaithabhal	13/14	NB 258114	______
406	1332	Guainemol	13/14	NB 262135	______
397	1303	Beinn Mheadhonach	13/14	NB 090236	______
378	1240	Kearnaval	13/14	NB 186157	______
374	1227	Uisenis	13/14	NB 337056	______
336	1102	Cipeagil Bheag	13/14	NB 247065	______
327	1073	Feirihisval	13/14	NB 301146	______
292	958	Beinn Mholach	8	NB 356387	______
281	922	Roineval	13/14	NB 233212	______
256	840	Conostom	13	NB 166300	______
248	814	Sleiteachal Mhor	13/14	NB 213188	______
248	813	Muirneag	8	NB 479489	______
228	748	Caultrashal Mor	13/14	NB 158228	______
217	713	Seaforth Island	13/14	NB 207111	______
205	673	Forsnaval	13	NB 061359	______
191	627	Beinn Bhreac	14	NB 407121	______
160	525	Mullach Buidhe *	14	NG 415987	______

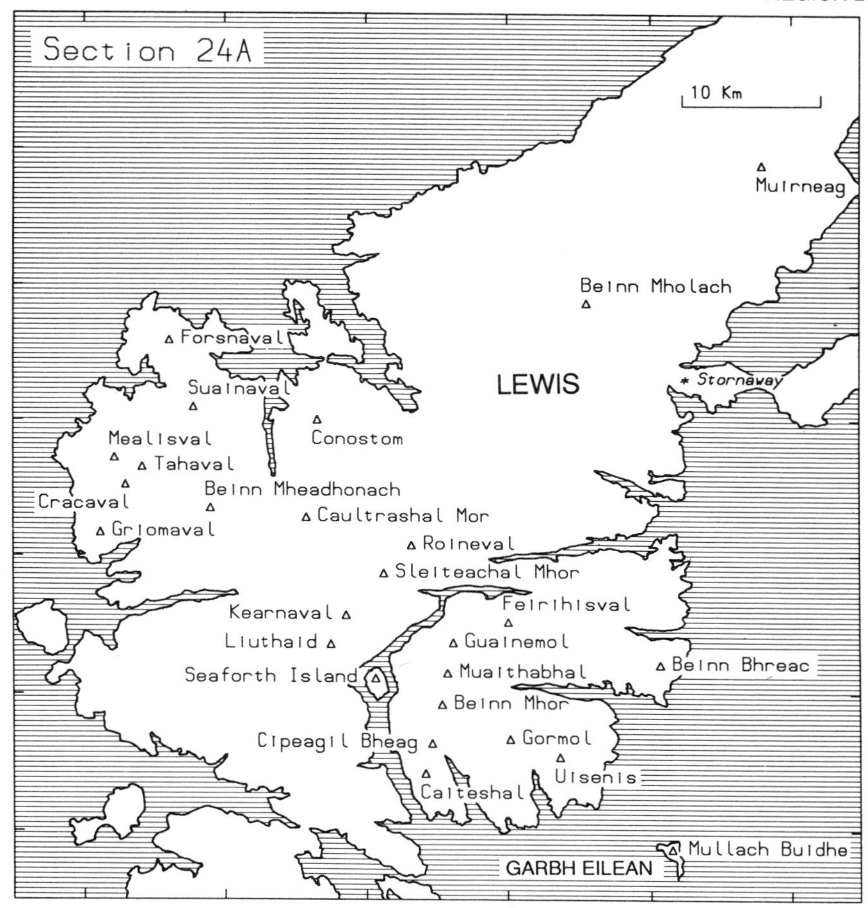

Section 24B Harris and Nearby Islands

Southern part of the Isle of Lewis and Harris, plus the islands of Scarp and Taransay

Metres	Feet	Name	Map	Grid Ref	Date
799	2622	Clisham	13/14	NB 155073	______
729	2392	Uisgnaval Mor	13/14	NB 120086	______
679	2227	Tirga Mor	13/14	NB 056115	______
662	2172	Oreval	13/14	NB 084099	______
579	1901	Stulaval	13/14	NB 133122	______

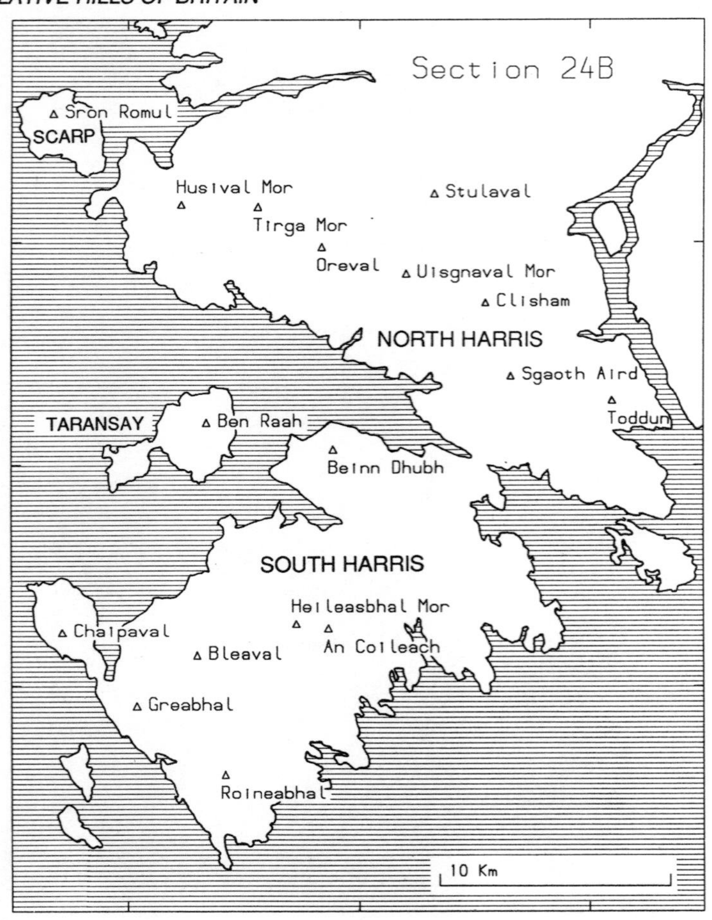

Metres	Feet	Name	Map	Grid Ref	Date
559	1834	Sgaoth Aird	13/14	NB 166040	______
528	1733	Toddun	14	NB 210029	______
506	1661	Beinn Dhubh	14/18	NB 089007	______
489	1603	Husival Mor	13	NB 023116	______
460	1508	Roineabhal	18	NG 042861	______
398	1305	Bleaval	18	NG 030914	______
389	1276	An Coileach	14/18	NG 087927	______
384	1260	Heileasbhal Mor	14/18	NG 073928	______

Metres	Feet	Name	Map	Grid Ref	Date
368	1207	Chaipaval	18	NF 972924	______
308	1012	Sron Romul	13	NA 968158	______
280	920	Greabhal	18	NG 004891	______
267	877	Ben Raah	18	NB 034019	______

Section 24C North Uist, South Uist and Nearby Islands

The islands of North Uist, South Uist, Pabbay (North) and Eriskay

Metres	Feet	Name	Map	Grid Ref	Date
620	2033	Beinn Mhor	22	NF 808311	______
606	1988	Hecla	22	NF 825345	______
527	1729	Ben Corodale	22	NF 819329	______
374	1228	Stulaval	22	NF 807241	______
357	1170	Triuirebheinn	31	NF 812212	______
347	1139	Eaval	22	NF 899605	______
281	922	South Lee	18	NF 919653	______
280	920	Beinn Ruigh Choinnich	31	NF 807197	______
262	860	North Lee	18	NF 927660	______
256	840	Arnaval	22	NF 785256	______
243	797	Easaval	31	NF 774158	______
230	756	Marrival	18	NF 808700	______
201	661	Roneval	31	NF 816140	______
196	642	Beinn a'Charnain	18	NF 894884	______
190	624	Beinn Mhor	18	NF 898762	______
185	607	Ben Scrien	31	NF 795112	______
180	590	Crogary Mor	18	NF 867731	______
154	504	Crogary na Hoe	18	NF 975724	______

Section 24D Barra to Barra Head

The islands of Barra, Vatersay, Muldoanich, Sandray, Pabbay (South), Mingulay and Berneray

Metres	Feet	Name	Map	Grid Ref	Date
383	1255	Heaval	31	NL 678994	______
333	1093	Ben Tangaval	31	NL 639990	______
273	896	Carnan	31	NL 553828	______
207	678	Cairn Galtar	31	NL 640915	______

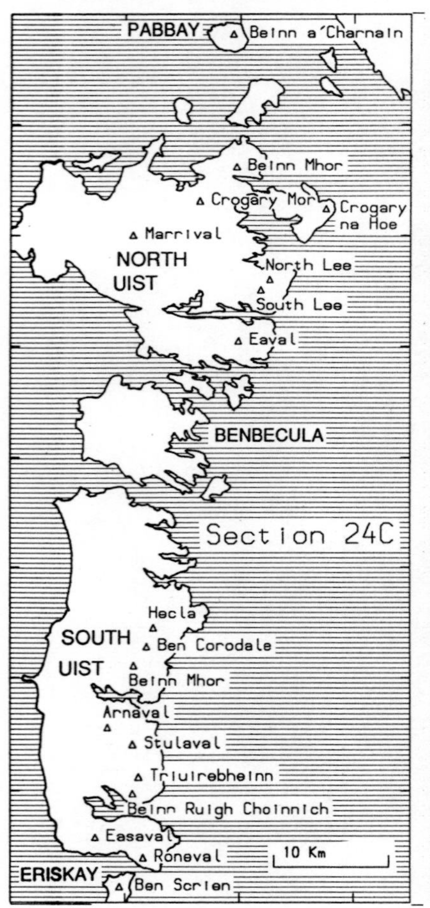

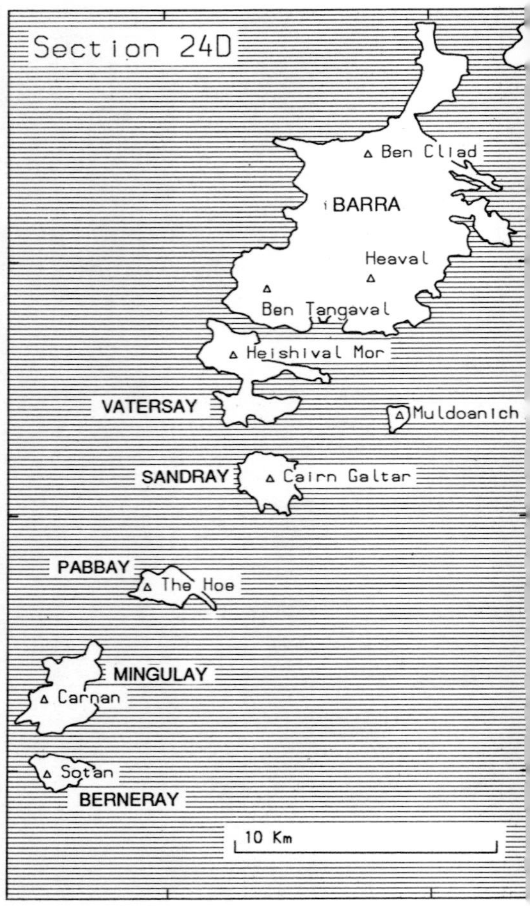

Metres	Feet	Name	Map	Grid Ref	Date
206	676	Ben Cliad	31	NF 677043	______
193	633	Sotan *	31	NL 553799	______
190	624	Heishival Mor	31	NL 626964	______
171	561	The Hoe	31	NL 593872	______
153	503	Muldoanich	31	NL 689940	______

REGION 25
St Kilda

Small group of islands several miles west of the Outer Hebrides, comprising the islands of Hirta, Soay, Dun and Boreray, plus two sea stacks; Stac Lee and Stac an Armin.

Metres	*Feet*	*Name*	*Map*	*Grid Ref*	*Date*
430	1411	Conachair	18	NA 100002	_____
384	1259	Mullach an Eilein *	18	NA 153053	_____
378	1239	Cnoc Glas	18	NA 062016	_____
196	644	Stac an Armin	18	NA 151064	_____
178	583	Bioda Mor *	18	NF 104973	_____
172	564	Stac Lee	18	NA 142049	_____

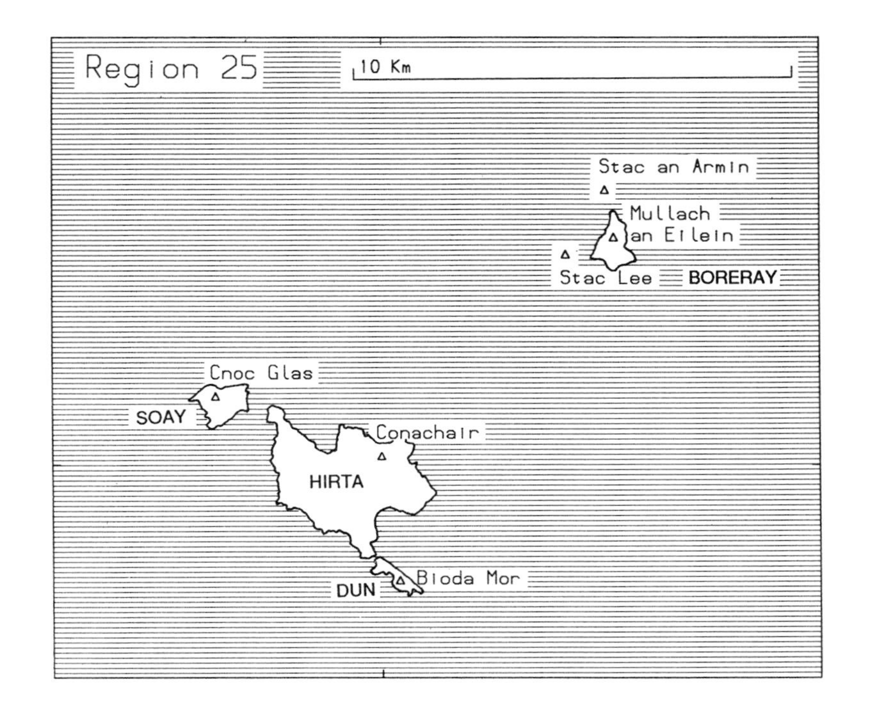

REGION 26
Central Scotland from Dumbarton to Montrose

Dumbarton; River Leven, Loch Lomond and Endrick Water to Drymen; A811 to Stirling; A9 to Perth; River Tay, Strathmore and River South Esk to Montrose; coast to Firth of Forth; Forth & Clyde Canal to Glasgow; River Clyde to Dumbarton.

Metres	*Feet*	*Name*	*Map*	*Grid Ref*	*Date*
721	2364	Ben Cleuch	58	NN 903006	______
578	1897	Earl's Seat	57/64	NS 569838	______
570	1870	Meikle Bin	57/64	NS 667822	______
522	1713	West Lomond	58	NO 197066	______
511	1678	Stronend	57	NS 629895	______
497	1630	Innerdouny Hill	58	NO 032073	______
485	1592	Carleatheran	57	NS 687918	______

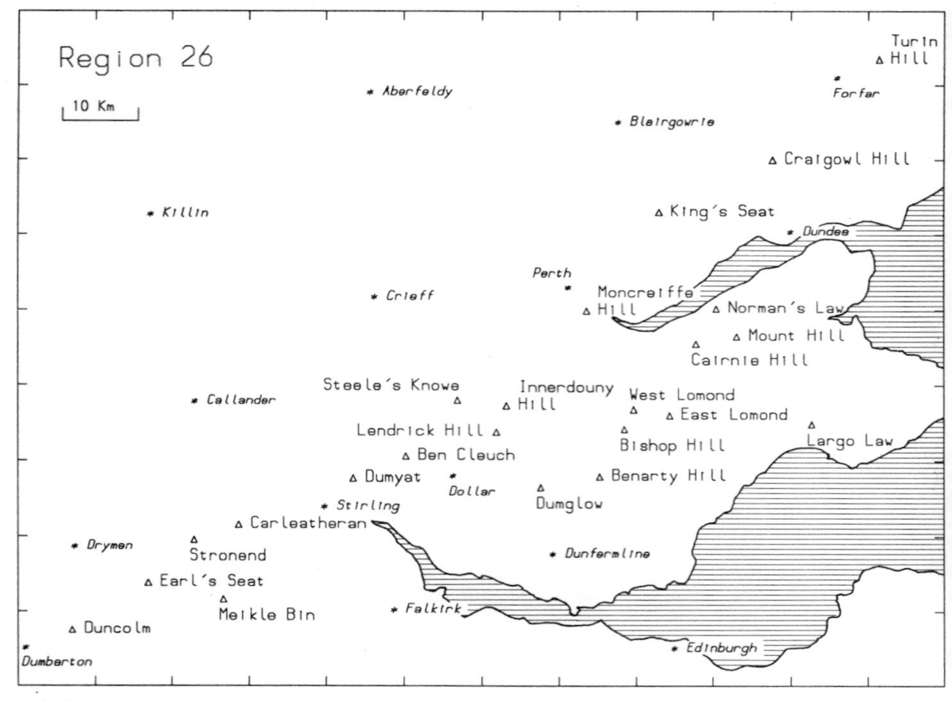

Metres	Feet	Name	Map	Grid Ref	Date
485	1592	Steele's Knowe	58	NN 969080	______
461	1512	Bishop Hill	58	NO 185043	______
456	1496	Lendrick Hill	58	NO 019036	______
455	1492	Craigowl Hill	54	NO 377400	______
448	1471	East Lomond	59	NO 244062	______
418	1373	Dumyat	57	NS 835977	______
401	1316	Duncolm	64	NS 470775	______
379	1243	Dumglow	58	NT 076965	______
377	1236	King's Seat	53	NO 230330	______
356	1168	Benarty Hill	58	NT 153979	______
290	952	Largo Law	59	NO 427049	______
285	936	Norman's Law	53/59	NO 305202	______
252	826	Turin Hill	54	NO 514535	______
228	749	Cairnie Hill *	59	NO 279155	______
223	732	Moncreiffe Hill	58	NO 136199	______
221	726	Mount Hill	59	NO 331165	______

REGION 27
South-West Scotland

Glasgow; River Clyde to Abington; A74 to Gretna; Solway Firth and coast to Firth of Clyde and Glasgow.

Section 27A Ayr to the River Clyde

North of A77, B742, A70 and A74 from Turnberry to Abington

Metres	*Feet*	*Name*	*Map*	*Grid Ref*	*Date*
711	2334	Tinto	72	NS 953344	______
522	1712	Hill of Stake	63	NS 273630	______
522	1712	Nutberry Hill	71	NS 743338	______
510	1673	Dungavel Hill	71/72	NS 942305	______
488	1600	Common Hill	71	NS 792308	______
466	1530	Middlefield Law	71	NS 681307	______

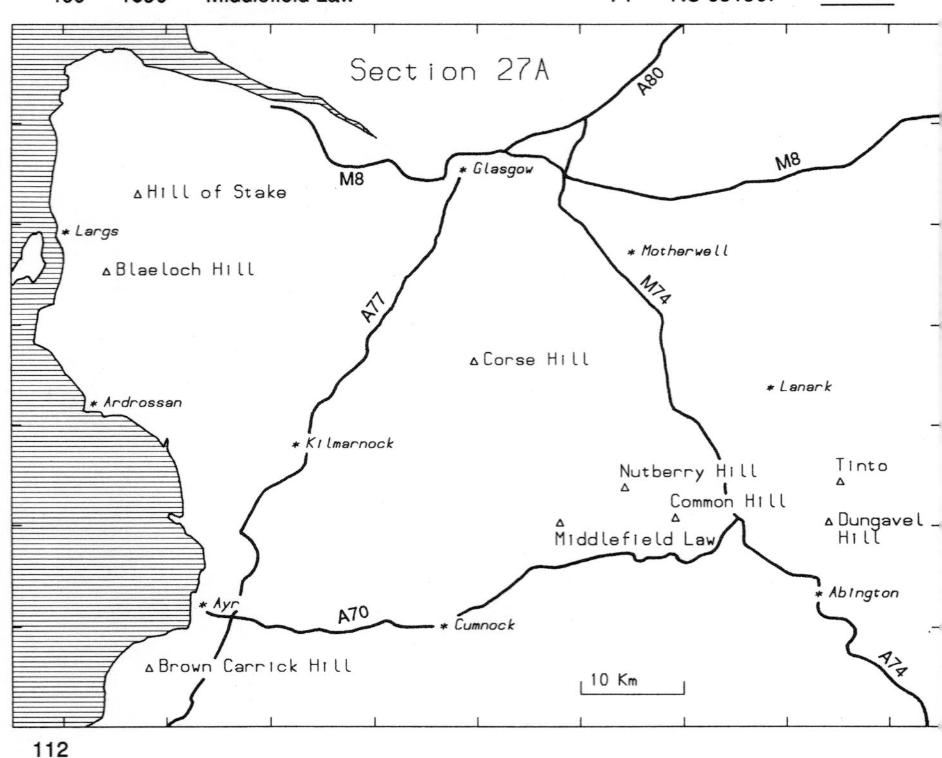

Metres	Feet	Name	Map	Grid Ref	Date
407	1335	Blaeloch Hill	63	NS 243553	______
376	1232	Corse Hill	64	NS 598464	______
287	943	Brown Carrick Hill	70	NS 283159	______

Section 27B Carrick and Galloway

West of A713, Loch Ken and River Dee from Dalmellington to Kirkcudbright, plus the island of Ailsa Craig

Metres	Feet	Name	Map	Grid Ref	Date
843	2766	Merrick	77	NX 428855	______
814	2669	Corserine	77	NX 497871	______
775	2543	Shalloch on Minnoch	77	NX 407906	______
717	2351	Lamachan Hill	77	NX 435769	______
711	2332	Cairnsmore of Fleet	83	NX 502671	______
692	2270	Mullwharchar	77	NX 454867	______
656	2152	Millfore	77	NX 478755	______
645	2116	Craignaw	77	NX 459833	______

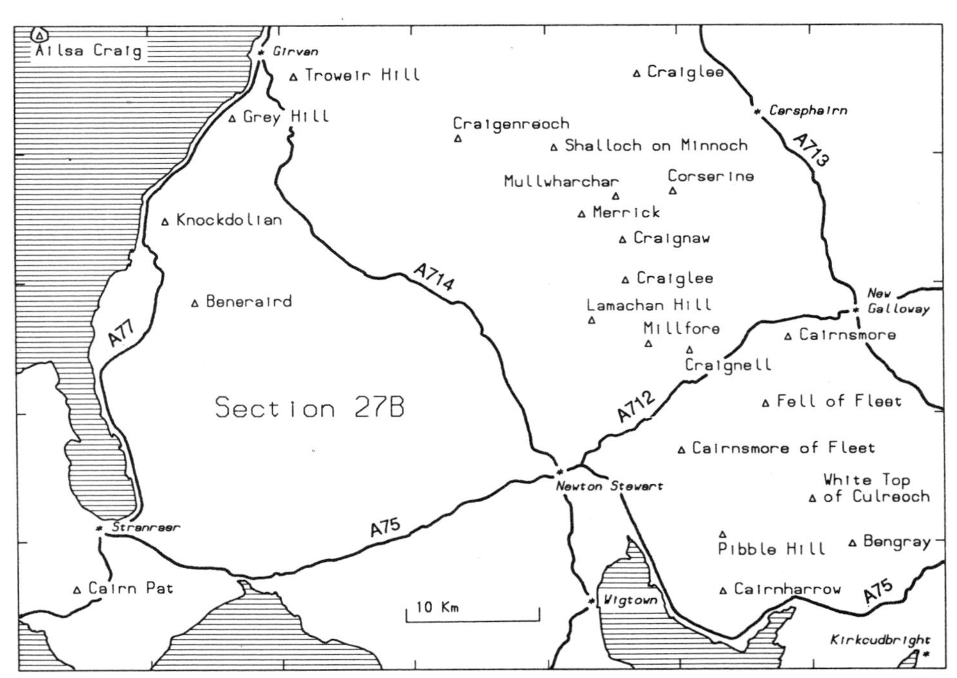

Metres	Feet	Name	Map	Grid Ref	Date
565	1854	Craigenreoch	76	NX 335910	_____
531	1742	Craiglee	77	NX 461801	_____
523	1716	Craiglee	77	NX 470962	_____
493	1617	Cairnsmore (Black Craig of Dee)	77	NX 583758	_____
477	1565	Craignell	77	NX 509751	_____
470	1542	Fell of Fleet	77	NX 566707	_____
456	1496	Cairnharrow	83	NX 533561	_____
439	1439	Beneraird	76	NX 135785	_____
383	1257	Pibble Hill	83	NX 533605	_____
366	1202	Bengray	83	NX 630598	_____
344	1130	White Top of Culreoch	83	NX 600633	_____
338	1109	Ailsa Craig	76	NX 019998	_____
297	975	Grey Hill	76	NX 164928	_____
296	971	Troweir Hill	76	NX 211960	_____
265	871	Knockdolian	76	NX 113848	_____
182	596	Cairn Pat	82	NX 044563	_____

Section 27C The Glenkens to Annandale

East of A713, Loch Ken and River Dee from Ayr to Kirkcudbright

Metres	Feet	Name	Map	Grid Ref	Date
797	2614	Cairnsmore of Carsphairn	77	NX 594980	_____
732	2403	Green Lowther	71/78	NS 900120	_____
700	2298	Blackcraig Hill	71/77	NS 648065	_____
698	2290	Windy Standard	77	NS 620015	_____
697	2286	Queensberry	78	NX 989998	_____
691	2268	Ballencleuch Law	78	NS 935049	_____
606	1987	Well Hill	71/78	NS 913064	_____
598	1963	Colt Hill	77	NX 698990	_____
593	1945	Cairn Table	71	NS 724242	_____
588	1930	Green Hill *	71/78	NS 862125	_____
569	1868	Criffel	84	NX 957618	_____
569	1866	Hods Hill	78	NT 001097	_____
554	1817	Cairnkinna Hill	78	NS 791018	_____
535	1755	Wether Hill	77	NX 696942	_____
511	1675	Kirkland Hill	71	NS 731163	_____

Metres	Feet	Name	Map	Grid Ref	Date
464	1522	Benbeoch	70/77	NS 495083	______
451	1480	Cairn Hill	71/78	NS 852070	______
432	1417	Bogrie Hill	78	NX 789859	______
417	1368	Fell Hill	77	NX 722844	______
398	1306	Bennan	84	NX 821769	______
392	1285	Bishop Forest Hill	84	NX 849796	______
391	1283	Bengairn	84	NX 770545	______
357	1172	Wauk Hill	78	NX 841909	______

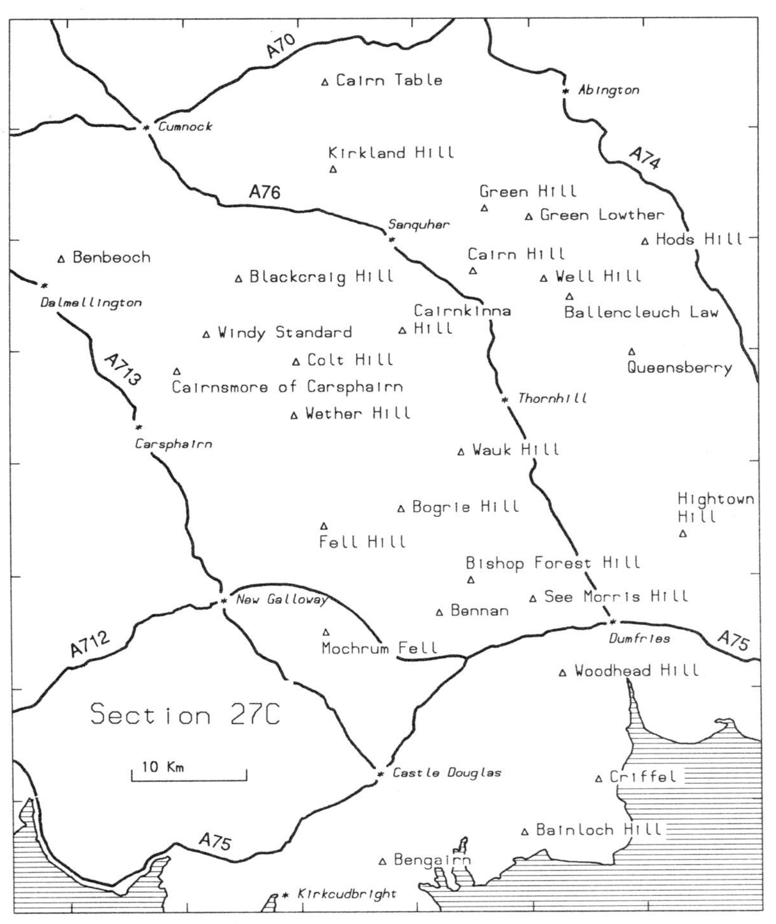

Metres	Feet	Name	Map	Grid Ref	Date
317	1040	Mochrum Fell	77/84	NX 723750	______
287	942	Bainloch Hill	84	NX 893571	______
258	846	Woodhead Hill	84	NX 927713	______
250	820	Hightown Hill	78	NY 036836	______
240	787	See Morris Hill	84	NX 902779	______

REGION 28
Firth of Forth to the English Border

Edinburgh; coast to Berwick; English border to Gretna; A74 to Abington; River Clyde to Glasgow; Forth & Clyde Canal to Firth of Forth and Edinburgh.

Section 28A Firth of Forth to the River Tweed
North-east of River Clyde from Glasgow to Biggar, and north of Biggar Water and River Tweed

Metres	*Feet*	*Name*	*Map*	*Grid Ref*	*Date*
659	2163	Windlestraw Law	73	NT 372431	______
651	2137	Blackhope Scar	73	NT 315483	______
579	1898	Scald Law	65/66	NT 192611	______
571	1874	Broughton Heights	72	NT 122411	______
562	1844	West Cairn Hill	65/72	NT 107584	______
549	1800	Trahenna Hill	72	NT 136374	______
538	1765	Penvalla	72	NT 151395	______
535	1755	Meikle Says Law	67	NT 581617	______
516	1692	Black Mount	72	NT 080459	______
501	1645	Black Hill	65/66	NT 188632	______
493	1618	Allermuir Hill	66	NT 227662	______
479	1570	Wether Law	72	NT 194483	______
468	1535	Spartleton	67	NT 653655	______
451	1481	Mendick Hill	65/72	NT 121505	______
427	1402	White Meldon	73	NT 219428	______
426	1399	Broomy Law	72	NT 085428	______
423	1389	Meigle Hill	73	NT 466360	______
398	1307	Dirrington Great Law	67/74	NT 698549	______
314	1030	Black Hill	73/74	NT 585370	______
312	1023	Cairnpapple Hill	65	NS 987711	______
251	822	Arthur's Seat	66	NT 275729	______
187	613	North Berwick Law	66	NT 556842	______

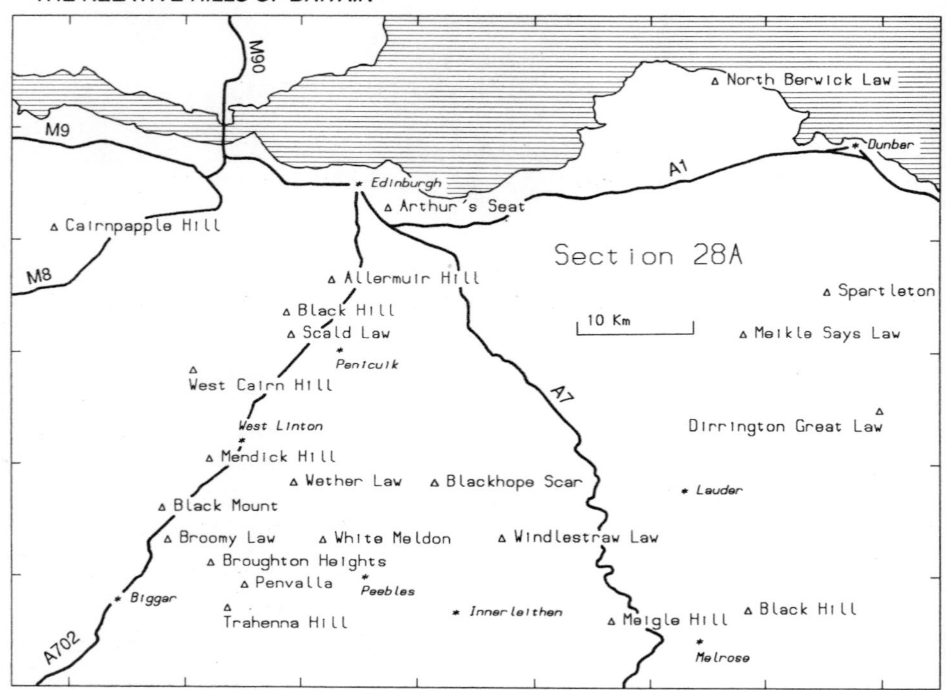

Section 28B The River Tweed to the English Border

South of Biggar Water and River Tweed

Metres	Feet	Name	Map	Grid Ref	Date
840	2756	Broad Law	72	NT 146235	______
822	2696	White Coomb	79	NT 163151	______
808	2651	Hart Fell	78	NT 114136	______
748	2455	Culter Fell	72	NT 053291	______
743	2438	Dun Rig	73	NT 253316	______
692	2270	Ettrick Pen	79	NT 199077	______
688	2257	Gathersnow Hill	72	NT 059257	______
678	2223	Capel Fell	79	NT 164069	______
677	2222	Andrewhinney Hill	79	NT 198139	______
637	2090	Croft Head	79	NT 153057	______
619	2030	Cauldcleuch Head	79	NT 458008	______
599	1966	Greatmoor Hill	79	NT 489007	______

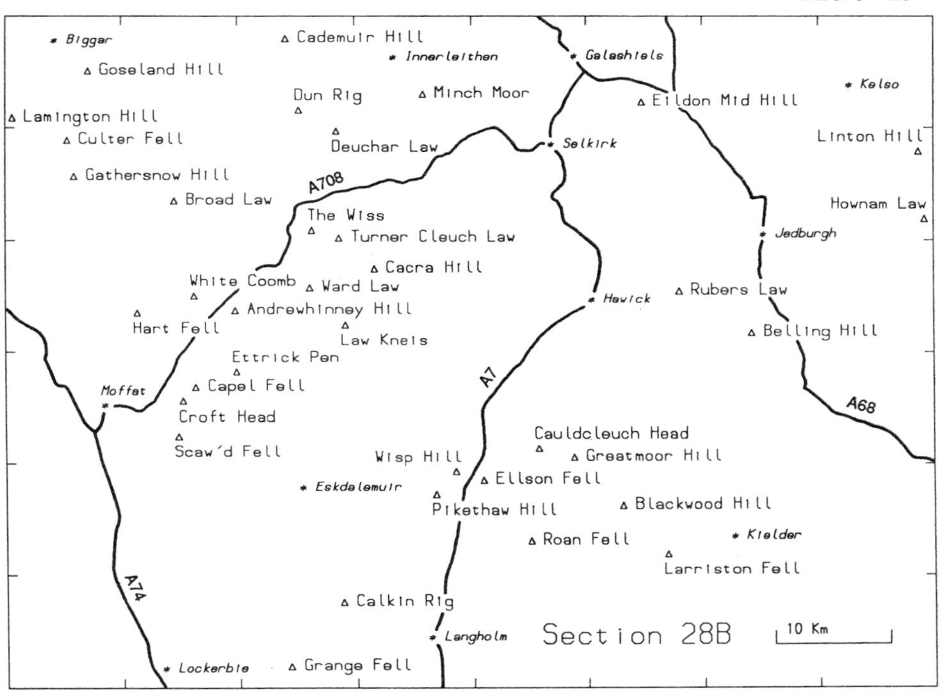

Metres	Feet	Name	Map	Grid Ref	Date
595	1953	Wisp Hill	79	NY 386993	______
594	1950	Ward Law	79	NT 262159	______
589	1933	The Wiss	73	NT 264206	______
568	1862	Roan Fell	79	NY 451931	______
567	1859	Minch Moor	73	NT 359330	______
564	1850	Pikethaw Hill	79	NY 369978	______
551	1808	Turner Cleuch Law	73	NT 287205	______
550	1805	Scaw'd Fell	78	NT 149028	______
543	1780	Deuchar Law	73	NT 285297	______
537	1762	Ellson Fell	79	NY 410985	______
512	1680	Larriston Fell	80	NY 569921	______
498	1634	Law Kneis	79	NT 292131	______
492	1615	Lamington Hill	72	NT 001305	______
471	1546	Cacra Hill	79	NT 317173	______

Metres	Feet	Name	Map	Grid Ref	Date
451	1480	Calkin Rig	79	NY 289876	______
449	1472	Hownam Law	74	NT 796219	_____
447	1467	Blackwood Hill	79	NY 531962	______
435	1427	Goseland Hill	72	NT 071351	______
424	1391	Rubers Law	80	NT 580155	______
422	1385	Eildon Mid Hill *	73	NT 548323	______
415	1362	Cademuir Hill	73	NT 242377	______
354	1161	Belling Hill	80	NT 642118	______
319	1047	Grange Fell	79	NY 244819	______
282	926	Linton Hill	74	NT 787279	_____

REGION 29
Isle of Man

Large island in the Irish Sea.

Metres	*Feet*	*Name*	*Map*	*Grid Ref*	*Date*
621	2036	Snaefell	95	SC 397881	______
488	1601	Slieau Freoaghane	95	SC 340883	______
483	1586	South Barrule	95	SC 257759	______
230	756	Bradda Hill	95	SC 193711	______
169	554	Mull Hill	95	SC 189676	______

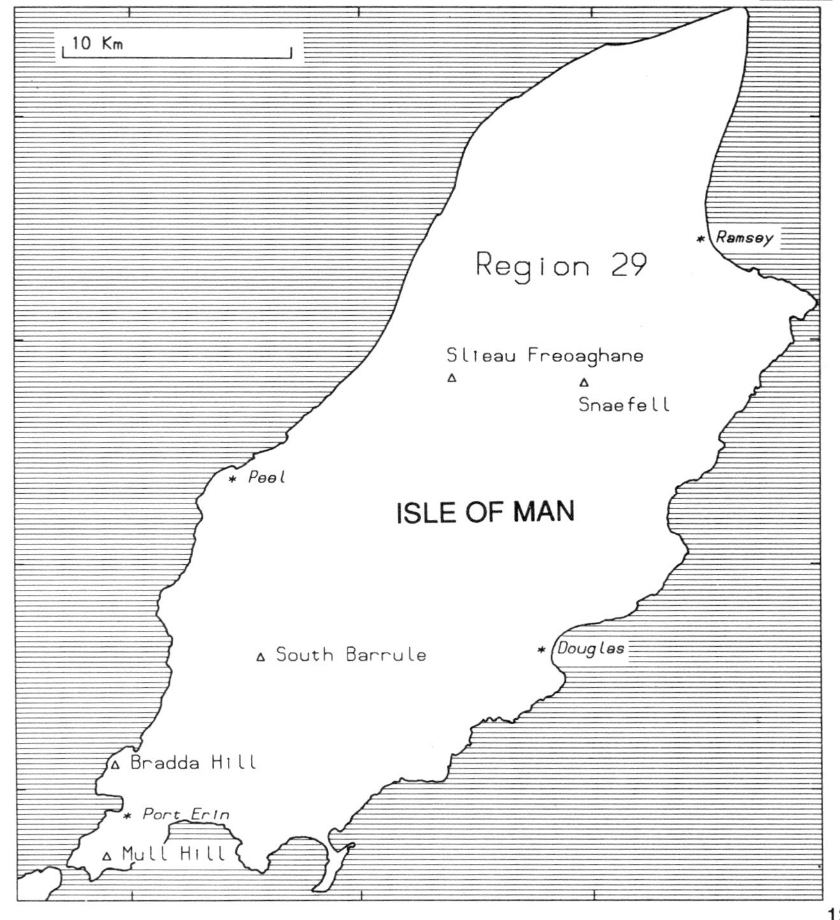

REGION 30
North Wales

Caernarfon; coast to River Dee; English border and River Severn to Welshpool; A458 to Mallwyd; River Dyfi to Aberdyfi; coast to Caernarfon, plus the islands of Anglesey, Holy Island and Bardsey Island.

Section 30A Anglesey and the Lleyn Peninsula
West of A487 from Caernarfon to Porthmadog, plus Bardsey Island, Anglesey and Holy Island

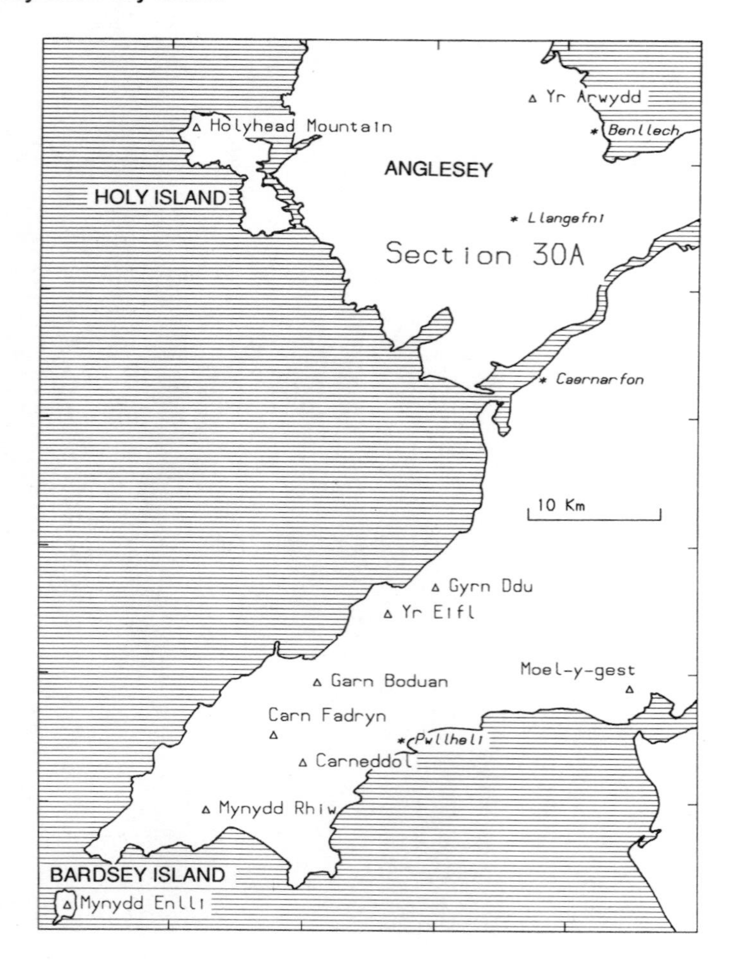

Metres	Feet	Name	Map	Grid Ref	Date
564	1850	Yr Eifl	123	SH 365447	______
522	1712	Gyrn Ddu	115/123	SH 401468	______
371	1218	Carn Fadryn	123	SH 279352	______
304	999	Mynydd Rhiw	123	SH 228294	______
279	915	Garn Boduan	123	SH 312393	______
262	858	Moel-y-gest	124	SH 549389	______
235	770	Carneddol	123	SH 301331	______
220	722	Holyhead Mountain	114	SH 218829	______
178	584	Yr Arwydd *	114	SH 472854	______
167	548	Mynydd Enlli	123	SH 122219	______

Section 30B Snowdonia

West of River Conwy, A470 and A496 from Conwy to Maentwrog

Metres	Feet	Name	Map	Grid Ref	Date
1085	3560	Snowdon - Yr Wyddfa	115	SH 609544	______
1064	3490	Carnedd Llewelyn	115	SH 684644	______
999	3279	Glyder Fawr	115	SH 642579	______
947	3107	Y Garn	115	SH 631596	______
923	3029	Elidir Fawr	115	SH 612613	______
915	3002	Tryfan	115	SH 664594	______
898	2946	Y Lliwedd	115	SH 622533	______
872	2861	Moel Siabod	115	SH 705546	______
799	2622	Pen Llithrig y Wrach	115	SH 716623	______
782	2566	Moel Hebog	115	SH 565469	______
770	2527	Moelwyn Mawr	124	SH 658449	______
747	2451	Yr Aran	115	SH 604515	______
734	2408	Craig Cwm Silyn	115	SH 525503	______
726	2382	Moel Eilio	115	SH 556577	______
709	2326	Trum y Ddysgl	115	SH 545516	______
698	2290	Allt Fawr	115	SH 682475	______
698	2290	Mynydd Mawr	115	SH 539547	______
678	2224	Creigiau Gleision	115	SH 729615	______
674	2210	Moel Cynghorion	115	SH 586564	______
610	2000	Tal y Fan	115	SH 729727	______
553	1814	Moel-ddu	124	SH 579442	______
382	1254	Moel y Dyniewyd	115	SH 613477	______

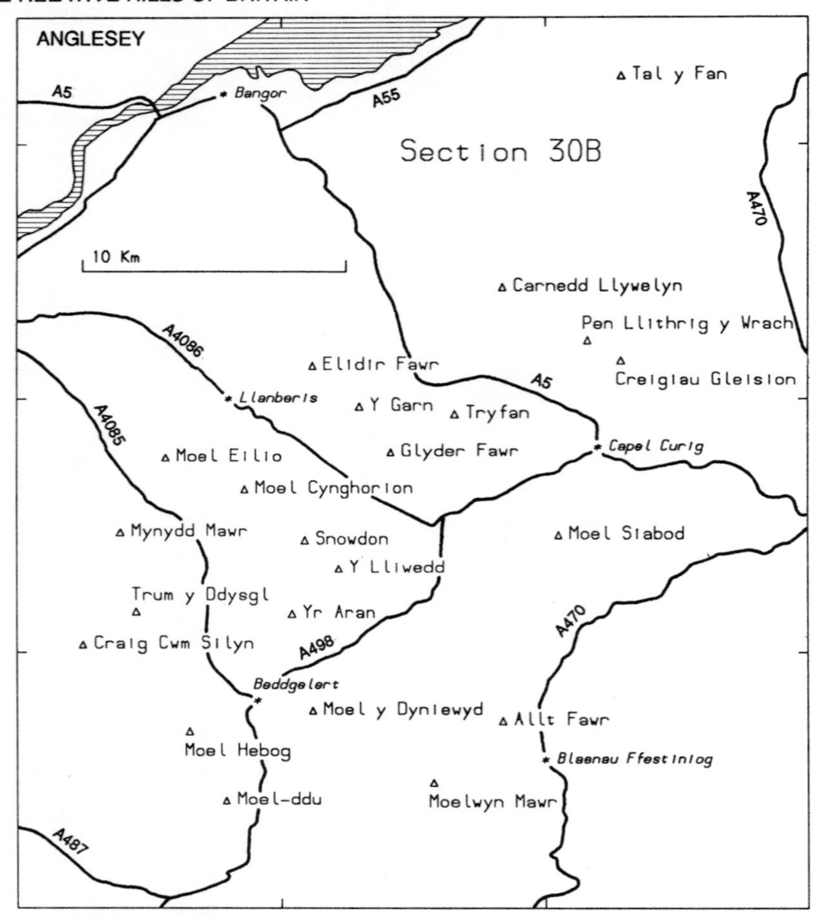

Section 30C Llandudno to Wrexham

North of A5 from Betws-y-Coed to the English border

Metres	Feet	Name	Map	Grid Ref	Date
578	1896	Moel y Gamelin	116	SJ 176465	______
565	1853	Cyrn-y-Brain	117	SJ 208488	______
554	1818	Moel Famau	116	SJ 161627	______
532	1744	Mwdwl-eithin	116	SH 917540	______
511	1676	Foel Fenlli	116	SJ 164600	______
467	1531	Moel Gyw	116	SJ 171575	______

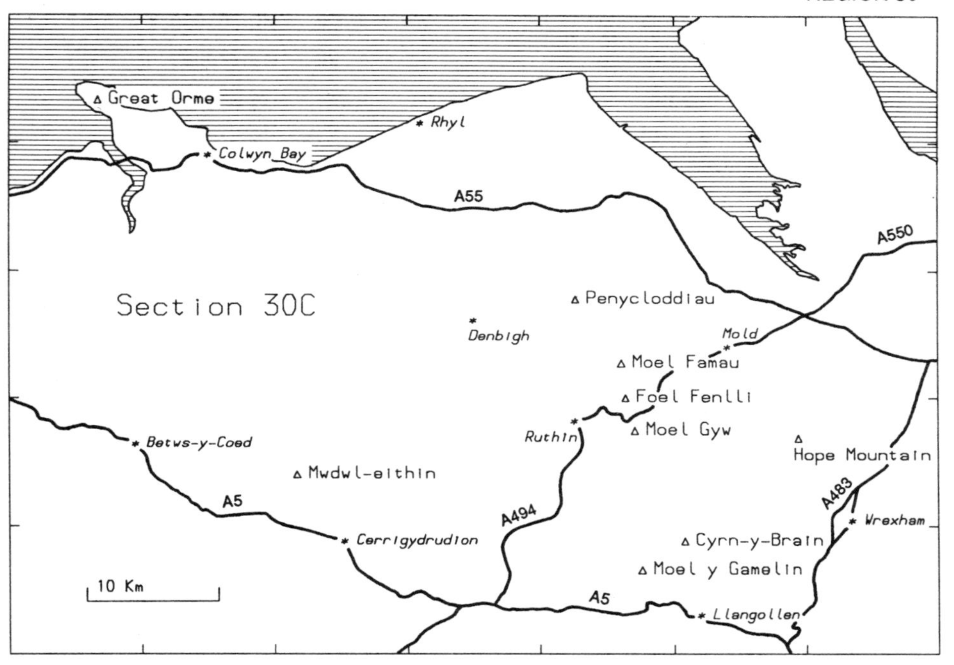

Metres	Feet	Name	Map	Grid Ref	Date
440	1443	Penycloddiau	116	SJ 127678	______
330	1083	Hope Mountain	117	SJ 294569	______
207	679	Great Orme	115	SH 767833	______

Section 30D Barmouth to Betws-y-Coed and Bala

North-west of A494 from Dolgellau to the A5

Metres	Feet	Name	Map	Grid Ref	Date
854	2801	Arenig Fawr	124/125	SH 827369	______
756	2480	Y Llethr	124	SH 661258	______
751	2464	Moel Llyfnant	124/125	SH 808352	______
734	2408	Rhobell Fawr	124	SH 787257	______
720	2362	Rhinog Fawr	124	SH 657290	______
689	2259	Arenig Fach	124/125	SH 821416	______
669	2196	Carnedd y Filiast	124/125	SH 871446	______
661	2168	Manod Mawr	124	SH 724447	______

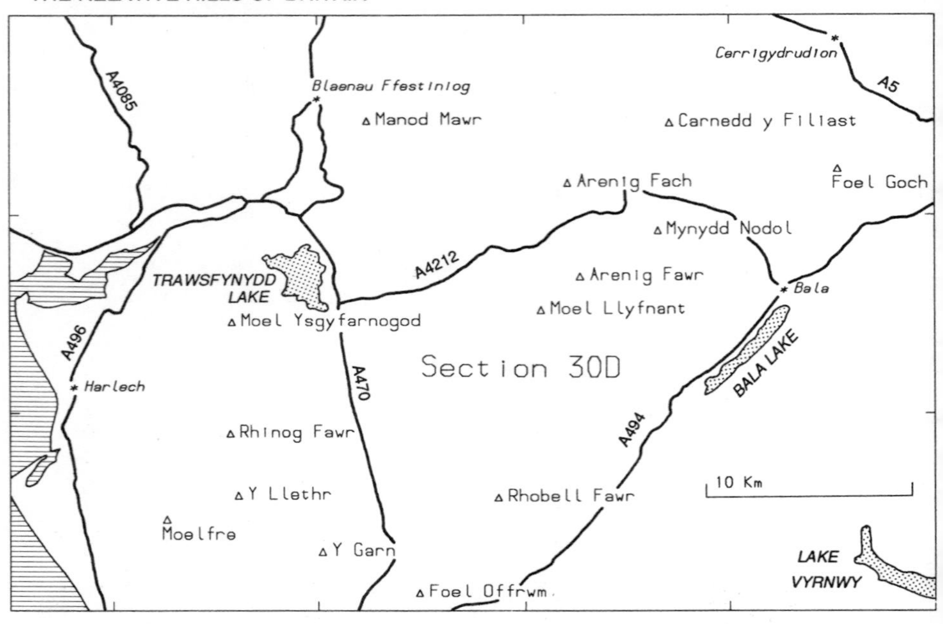

Metres	Feet	Name	Map	Grid Ref	Date
629	2063	Y Garn	124	SH 702230	______
623	2044	Moel Ysgyfarnogod	124	SH 658346	______
611	2004	Foel Goch	125	SH 953423	______
589	1932	Moelfre	124	SH 626246	______
530	1740	Mynydd Nodol	124/125	SH 865392	______
405	1329	Foel Offrwm	124	SH 749209	______

Section 30E Bala to Welshpool

South of A494 and A5 from Dolgellau to the English border

Metres	Feet	Name	Map	Grid Ref	Date
905	2970	Aran Fawddwy	124/125	SH 863224	______
830	2723	Cadair Berwyn	125	SJ 071323	______
779	2557	Glasgwm	124/125	SH 837194	______
671	2201	Foel Rhudd	124/125	SH 889236	______
667	2188	Cyrniau Nod	125	SH 988279	______
540	1772	Rhialgwm	125	SJ 054212	______
523	1715	Gyrn Moelfre	125	SJ 184294	______

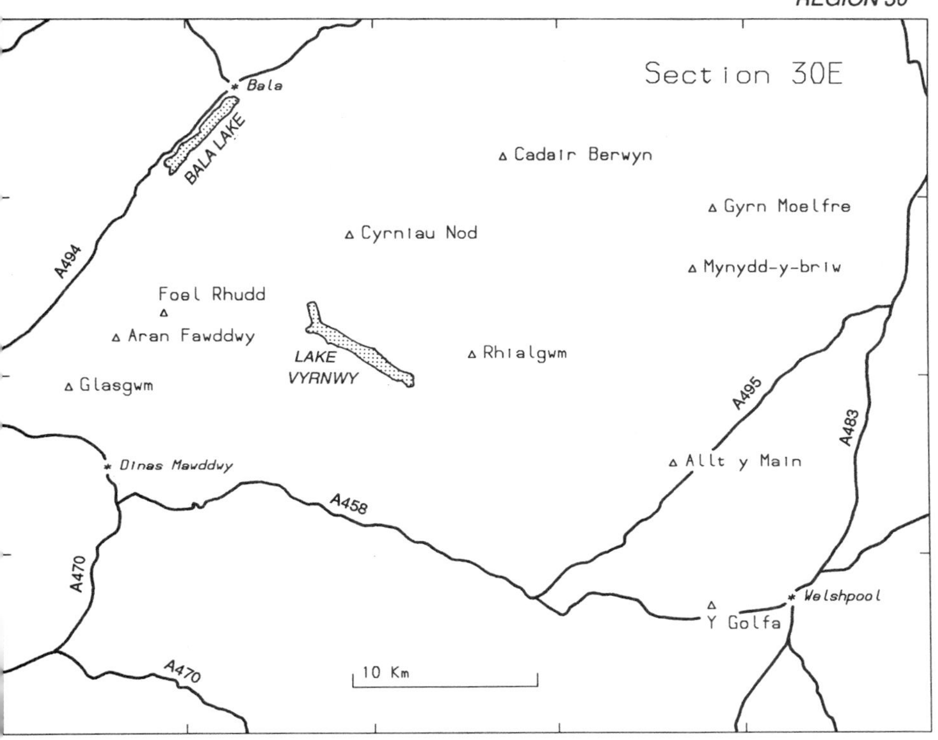

Metres	Feet	Name	Map	Grid Ref	Date
356	1169	Allt y Main	125	SJ 162151	______
341	1119	Mynydd-y-briw	125	SJ 173260	______
341	1119	Y Golfa	125	SJ 182071	______

Section 30F Dolgellau to Machynlleth

West of A470 and River Dyfi from Dolgellau to Machynlleth

Metres	Feet	Name	Map	Grid Ref	Date
893	2929	Cadair Idris - Penygadair	124	SH 711130	______
675	2213	Maesglase - Maen Du	124/125	SH 823152	______
667	2189	Tarren y Gesail	124	SH 711059	______
634	2080	Tarrenhendre	135	SH 683041	______
469	1538	Mynydd Cwmcelli	124	SH 804099	______
380	1246	Foel Cae'rberllan	124	SH 676082	______

Metres	Feet	Name	Map	Grid Ref	Date
313	1027	Ffridd Cocyn	135	SH 623042	______
294	965	Gamallt	124	SH 665068	______

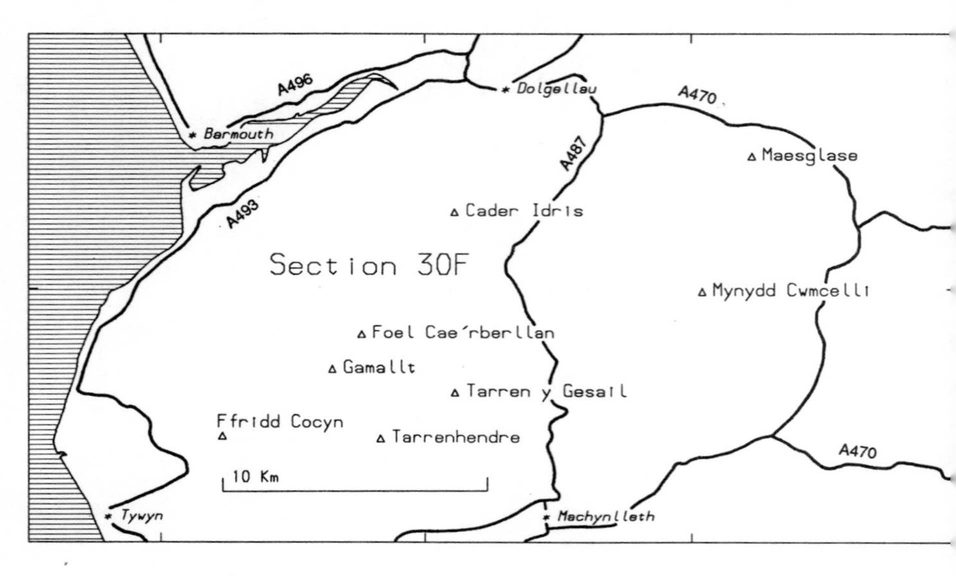

REGION 31
Mid Wales and Pembrokeshire

Aberdyfi; River Dyfi to Mallwyd; A458 to Welshpool; River Severn and English border to Hay-on-Wye; River Wye to Builth Wells; A483 to Llandovery; River Tywi to Carmarthen Bay; coast to Aberdyfi.

Section 31A Aberystwyth to Welshpool

North of River Rheidol, A44, A470 and River Severn from Aberystwyth to Welshpool

Metres	*Feet*	*Name*	*Map*	*Grid Ref*	*Date*
752	2467	Plynlimon - Pen Pumlumon Fawr	135	SN 789869	______
560	1837	Banc Llechwedd-mawr	135	SN 775899	______
550	1806	Drosgol	135	SN 759878	______
523	1715	Carnedd Wen	125	SH 923099	______
488	1602	Bryn Amlwg	136	SN 921974	______
485	1590	Garreg-hir	136	SN 998977	______
482	1582	Bryn y Fan	136	SN 931885	______

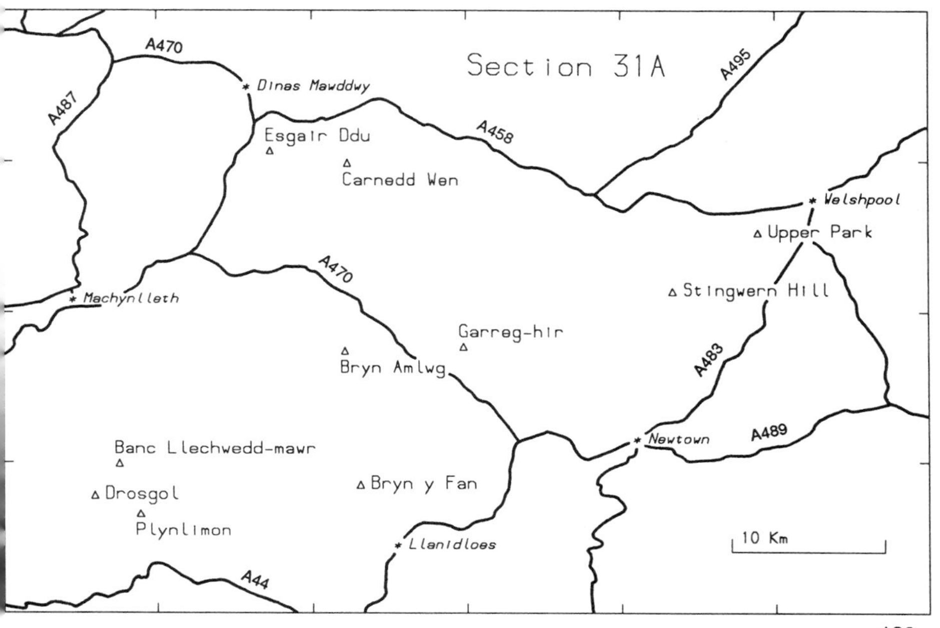

Metres	Feet	Name	Map	Grid Ref	Date
464	1523	Esgair Ddu	125	SH 873107	______
358	1175	Stingwern Hill	136	SJ 133014	______
352	1155	Upper Park *	125	SJ 189053	______

Section 31B Welshpool to Hay-on-Wye
East of River Severn, A470 and River Wye from Welshpool to Hay-on-Wye

Metres	Feet	Name	Map	Grid Ref	Date
660	2166	Great Rhos	148	SO 182639	______
586	1921	Pegwn Mawr	136	SO 023812	______

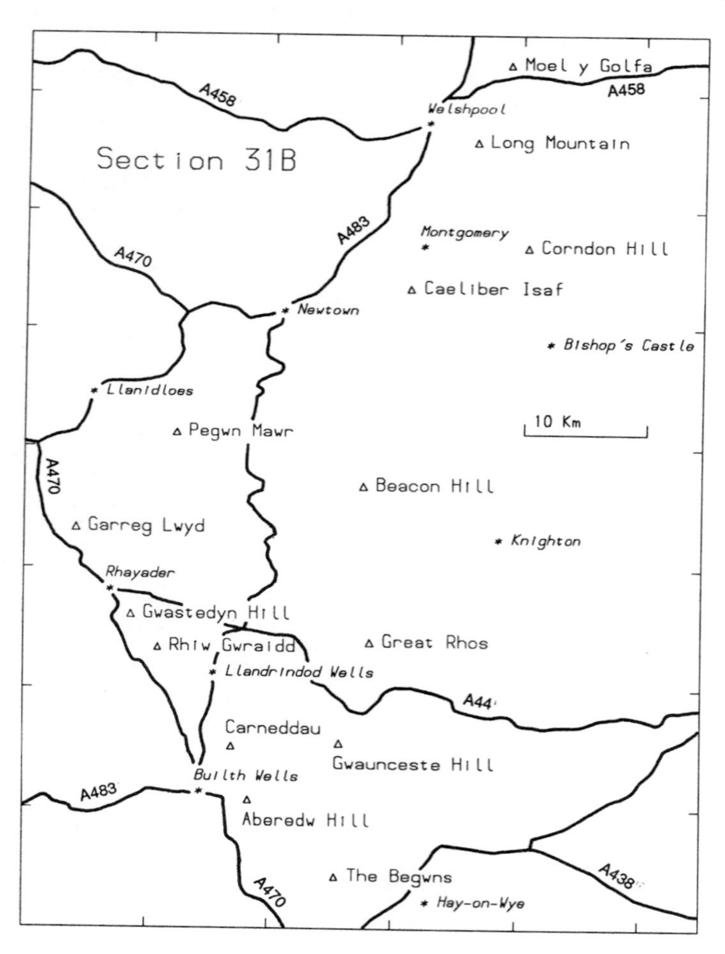

Metres	Feet	Name	Map	Grid Ref	Date
547	1796	Beacon Hill	136/148	SO 176768	______
542	1777	Gwaunceste Hill	148	SO 158555	______
513	1683	Corndon Hill	137	SO 306969	______
499	1636	Garreg Lwyd	136/147	SN 942733	______
477	1566	Gwastedyn Hill	136/147	SN 987661	______
451	1480	Aberedw Hill	147	SO 084507	______
445	1460	Carneddau	147	SO 070552	______
442	1450	Rhiw Gwraidd	147	SO 009634	______
415	1363	The Begwns	148/161	SO 155443	______
408	1338	Long Mountain - Beacon Ring	126	SJ 264058	______
404	1324	Moel y Golfa	126	SJ 290125	______
355	1164	Caeliber Isaf	137	SO 212934	______

Section 31C South-West Wales
South and west of River Rheidol, A44 and A470 from Aberystwyth to Builth Wells

Metres	Feet	Name	Map	Grid Ref	Date
645	2115	Drygarn Fawr	147	SN 862584	______
610	2002	Pen y Garn	135	SN 798771	______
594	1950	Waun Claerddu	135/147	SN 790704	______
536	1759	Foel Cwmcerwyn	145	SN 094311	______
487	1599	Pen y Garn-goch	147	SN 884502	______
462	1515	Crugiau Merched	146/147	SN 722455	______
395	1295	Frenni Fawr	145	SN 203348	______
361	1183	Hafod Ithel	135	SN 610678	______
347	1138	Mynydd Carningli	145	SN 062372	______
329	1079	Mynydd Cynros	146	SN 620327	______
327	1073	Rhos Ymryson	146	SN 459500	______
326	1070	Pen-crug-melyn *	146	SN 502285	______
205	673	Brandy Hill	158	SN 213133	______

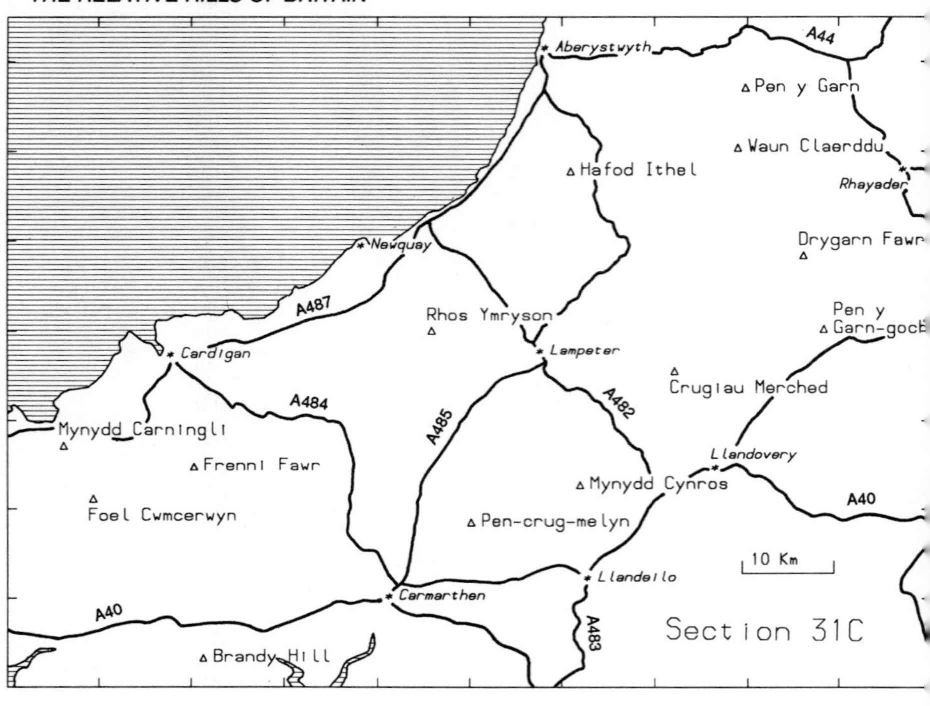
Aberystwyth
A44
Pen y Garn
Waun Claerddu
Rhayader
Hafod Ithel
Drygarn Fawr
Newquay
A487
Rhos Ymryson
Pen y
Garn-goch
Cardigan
Lampeter
Crugiau Merched
A484
A485
A482
Mynydd Carningli
Llandovery
Frenni Fawr
Mynydd Cynros
A40
Foel Cwmcerwyn
Pen-crug-melyn
10 Km
Llandeilo
Carmarthen
A40
A483
Section 31C
Brandy Hill

REGION 32
South Wales

Carmarthen; River Tywi to Llandovery; A483 to Builth Wells; River Wye to Hay-on-Wye; English border to the Severn estuary; coast to Carmarthen.

Section 32A Llandovery to Monmouth

East of A4069 and north of county boundary, A465 and A40 from Llandovery to Monmouth

Metres	*Feet*	*Name*	*Map*	*Grid Ref*	*Date*
886	2906	Pen y Fan	160	SO 012216	______
811	2660	Waun Fach	161	SO 215300	______
802	2630	Fan Brycheiniog	160	SN 825218	______
769	2523	Waun Rydd	160	SO 062206	______
734	2409	Fan Fawr	160	SN 970193	______
725	2379	Fan Gyhirych	160	SN 881191	______
663	2175	Fan Nedd	160	SN 913184	______
617	2024	Cefn yr Ystrad	160	SO 087137	______
609	1997	Mynydd Troed	161	SO 166293	______
596	1955	Sugar Loaf	161	SO 272188	______

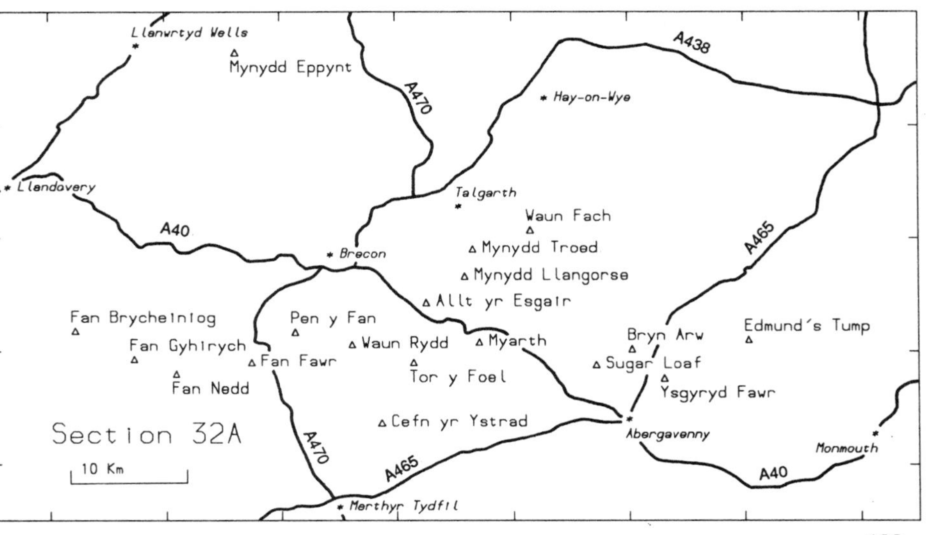

Metres	Feet	Name	Map	Grid Ref	Date
551	1807	Tor y Foel	161	SO 115195	______
515	1690	Mynydd Llangorse	161	SO 159267	______
486	1595	Ysgyryd Fawr	161	SO 331182	______
478	1568	Mynydd Eppynt	147	SN 961464	______
423	1389	Edmund's Tump *	161	SO 404210	______
393	1290	Allt yr Esgair	161	SO 126243	______
381	1250	Bryn Arw	161	SO 303197	______
292	959	Myarth	161	SO 171208	______

Section 32B Carmarthen to the Vale of Neath

West of A4069, county boundary and River Neath from Llangadog to Neath

Metres	Feet	Name	Map	Grid Ref	Date
481	1578	Hirfynydd	160	SN 839076	______
418	1370	Mynydd Marchywel	170	SN 768038	______
415	1360	Trichrug	160	SN 699229	______
374	1226	Mynydd y Betws	159	SN 664094	______
358	1173	Mynydd Uchaf	160	SN 716103	______

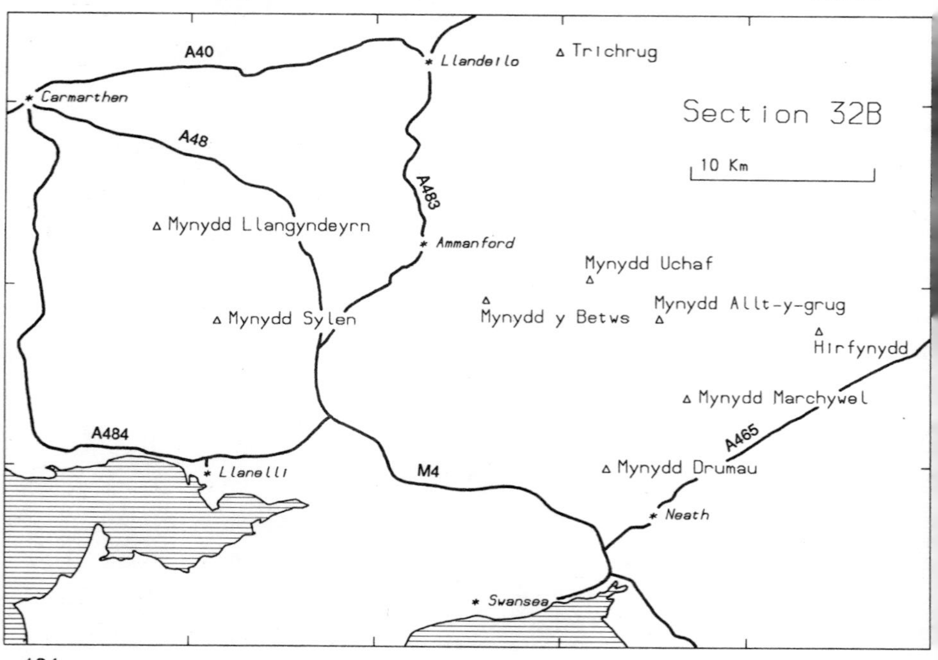

Metres	Feet	Name	Map	Grid Ref	Date
339	1113	Mynydd Allt-y-grug	160	SN 751079	______
284	933	Mynydd Sylen	159	SN 515080	______
272	893	Mynydd Drumau	170	SN 725002	______
262	861	Mynydd Llangyndeyrn	159	SN 482132	______

Section 32C Neath to Chepstow

South of River Neath, A465 and A40 from Neath to Monmouth

Metres	Feet	Name	Map	Grid Ref	Date
600	1969	Craig y Llyn	170	SN 907032	______
581	1905	Coity Mountain	161	SO 231080	______
550	1804	Mynydd Carn-y-cefn	161	SO 187085	______
472	1550	Mynydd Twyn-glas	171	ST 259978	______
385	1264	Mynydd y Lan	171	ST 208923	______
382	1253	Cefn Eglwysilan	171	ST 097905	______
381	1250	Mynydd y Glyn	170	ST 032896	______
370	1214	Foel Fynyddau	170	SS 782936	______
362	1188	Mynydd Machen	171	ST 223900	______
309	1013	Wentwood	171/172	ST 411943	______
307	1007	Garth Hill	171	ST 103835	______
274	899	Craig yr Allt	171	ST 133850	______

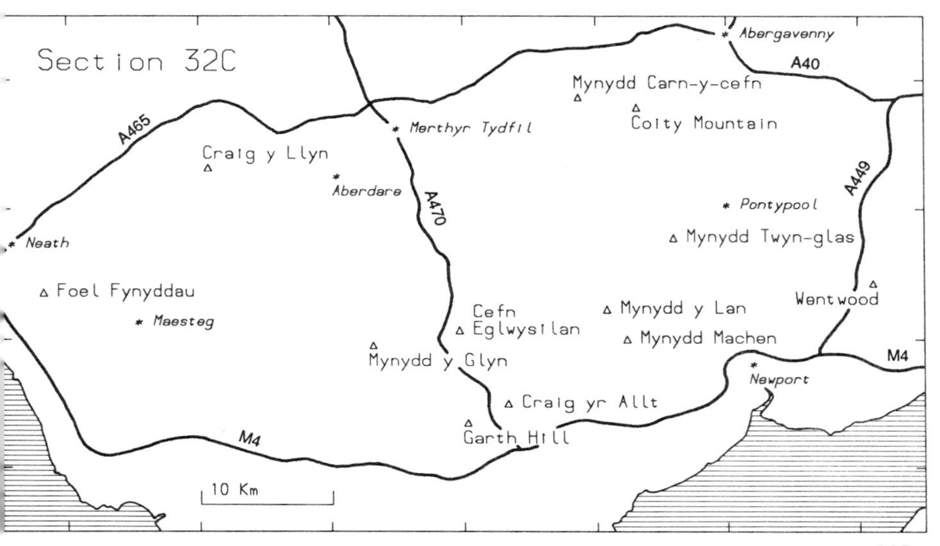

REGION 33
The Scottish Border to the River Tyne

Berwick; coast to Tynemouth; River Tyne and South Tyne to Haltwhistle; A69 and River Eden to the Solway Firth; Scottish border to Berwick.

Metres	Feet	Name	Map	Grid Ref	Date
815	2674	The Cheviot	74/75	NT 909205	______
714	2342	Hedgehope Hill	80	NT 943197	______
616	2020	Cushat Law	80	NT 928137	______

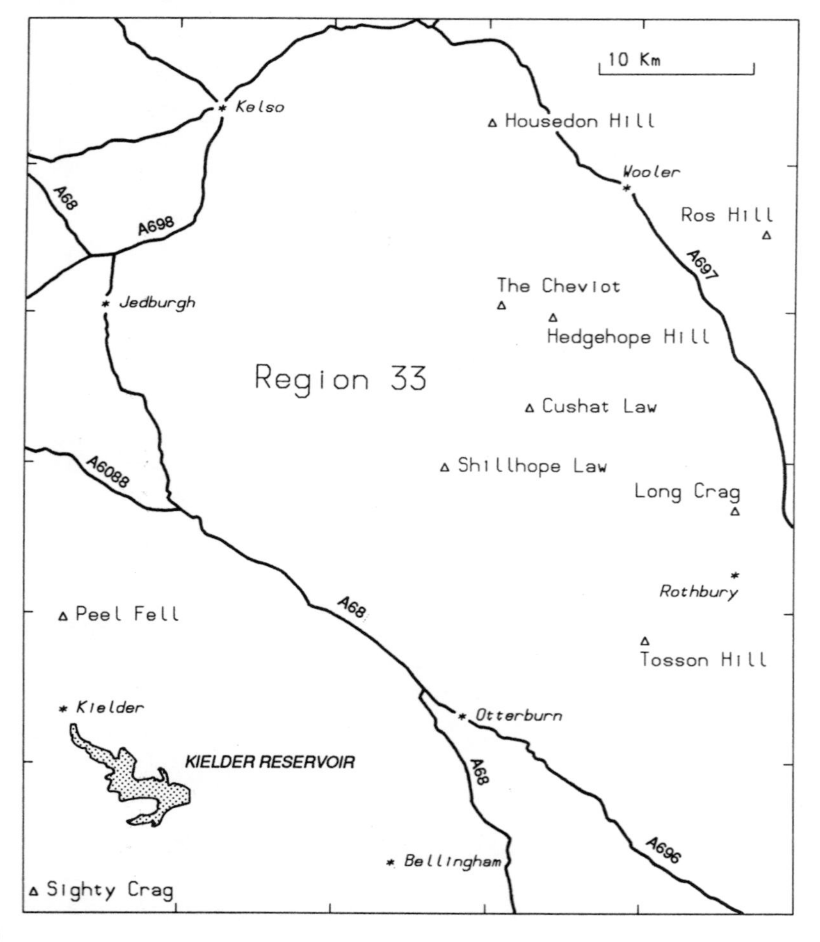

Metres	*Feet*	*Name*	*Map*	*Grid Ref*	*Date*
602	1975	Peel Fell	80	NY 626997	______
518	1701	Sighty Crag	80	NY 601809	______
501	1644	Shillhope Law	80	NT 873097	______
440	1444	Tosson Hill	81	NZ 004982	______
319	1047	Long Crag	81	NU 062069	______
315	1034	Ros Hill	75	NU 081253	______
267	877	Housedon Hill	74/75	NT 902329	______

REGION 34
The Lake District

Carlisle; M6 to Tebay; River Lune to Kirkby Lonsdale; Lancashire border to the coast, coast to the Solway Firth; River Eden to Carlisle.

Section 34A
Northern Fells

North of River Derwent, B5292 and A66 from Workington to Penrith

Metres	*Feet*	*Name*	*Map*	*Grid Ref*	*Date*
931	3054	Skiddaw	89/90	NY 260290	______
868	2847	Blencathra	90	NY 323277	______
710	2329	Knott	89/90	NY 296329	______
552	1811	Lord's Seat	89/90	NY 204265	______
447	1467	Binsey	89/90	NY 225355	______
254	833	Watch Hill	89	NY 158318	______

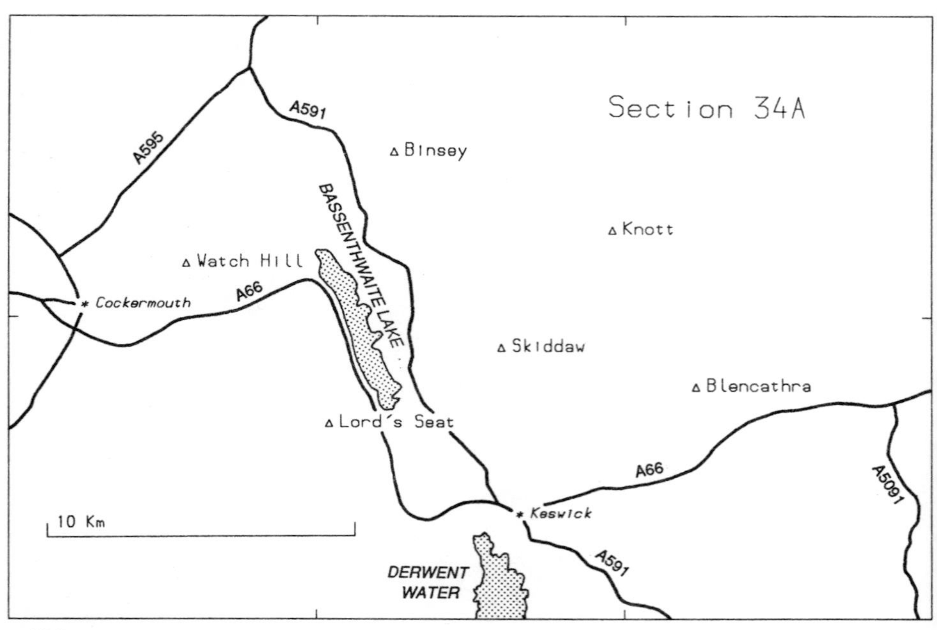

Section 34B Central and Western Fells

West of A591 from Keswick to Ambleside and north of the Eskdale railway and Hardknott Pass

Metres	*Feet*	*Name*	*Map*	*Grid Ref*	*Date*
978	3210	Scafell Pike	89/90	NY 215072	______
964	3162	Scafell	89/90	NY 206064	______
899	2949	Great Gable	89/90	NY 211103	______
892	2927	Pillar	89/90	NY 171120	______
852	2795	Grasmoor	89/90	NY 174203	______
807	2648	High Stile	89	NY 170148	______
802	2631	Kirk Fell	89/90	NY 194104	______
791	2595	Grisedale Pike	89/90	NY 198225	______
762	2500	High Raise	89/90	NY 280095	______
753	2470	Dale Head	89/90	NY 223153	______
737	2417	Robinson	89/90	NY 201168	______
705	2313	Pike of Blisco	89/90	NY 271042	______
692	2270	Seatallan	89	NY 139083	______
609	1998	Illgill Head	89	NY 169049	______

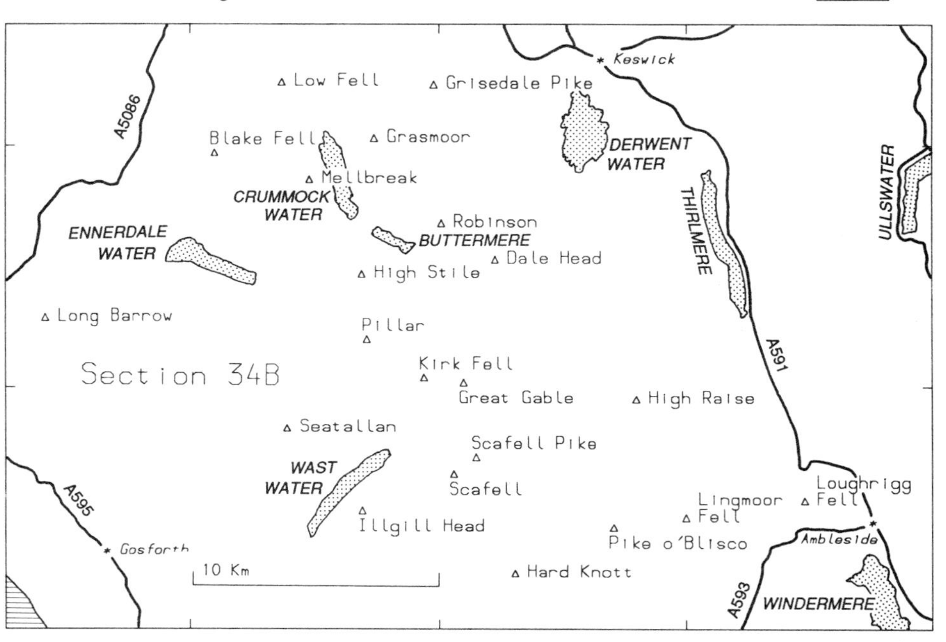

Metres	Feet	Name	Map	Grid Ref	Date
573	1879	Blake Fell	89	NY 110197	______
549	1801	Hard Knott	89/90	NY 231023	______
512	1680	Mellbreak	89	NY 148186	______
469	1540	Lingmoor Fell	90	NY 302046	______
423	1388	Low Fell	89	NY 137226	______
352	1155	Long Barrow	89	NY 041129	______
335	1100	Loughrigg Fell	90	NY 347051	______

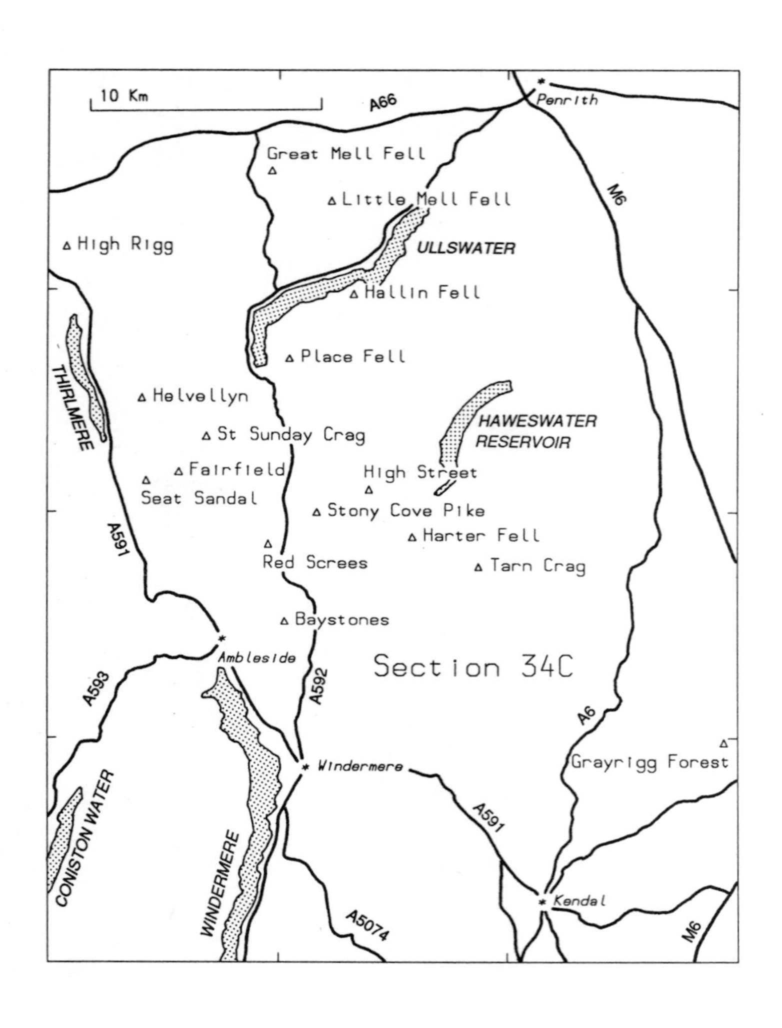

Section 34C Eastern Fells

East of A591 and north of A685 from Keswick to the M6

Metres	Feet	Name	Map	Grid Ref	Date
950	3116	Helvellyn	90	NY 341151	_____
873	2863	Fairfield	90	NY 358117	_____
841	2760	St Sunday Crag	90	NY 369134	_____
828	2718	High Street	90	NY 440110	_____
778	2552	Harter Fell	90	NY 459092	_____
776	2547	Red Screes	90	NY 396087	_____
763	2502	Stony Cove Pike	90	NY 417100	_____
736	2415	Seat Sandal	90	NY 343115	_____
664	2178	Tarn Crag	90	NY 488078	_____
657	2154	Place Fell	90	NY 405169	_____
537	1761	Great Mell Fell	90	NY 397254	_____
505	1657	Little Mell Fell	90	NY 423240	_____
494	1620	Grayrigg Forest	97	SD 598998	_____
487	1597	Baystones	90	NY 403052	_____
388	1273	Hallin Fell	90	NY 433198	_____
357	1170	High Rigg	90	NY 308220	_____

Section 34D Southern Cumbria

South of Eskdale railway, Hardknott Pass, A591 and A685 from Ravenglass to the M6

Metres	Feet	Name	Map	Grid Ref	Date
803	2635	The Old Man of Coniston	96/97	SD 272978	_____
653	2143	Harter Fell	96	SD 218997	_____
600	1970	Black Combe	96	SD 135854	_____
573	1881	Whitfell	96	SD 159930	_____
338	1109	Lambrigg Fell	97	SD 586943	_____
335	1100	Top o'Selside	96	SD 309919	_____
333	1092	Lowick High Common	96	SD 260840	_____
321	1054	Gummer's How	96	SD 390885	_____
317	1040	Holm Fell	90	NY 315006	_____
274	899	Hutton Roof Crags	97	SD 556775	_____
270	885	Claife Heights	96	SD 382973	_____

Metres	Feet	Name	Map	Grid Ref	Date
231	758	Muncaster Fell	96	SD 112983	______
215	706	Whitbarrow	97	SD 441870	______

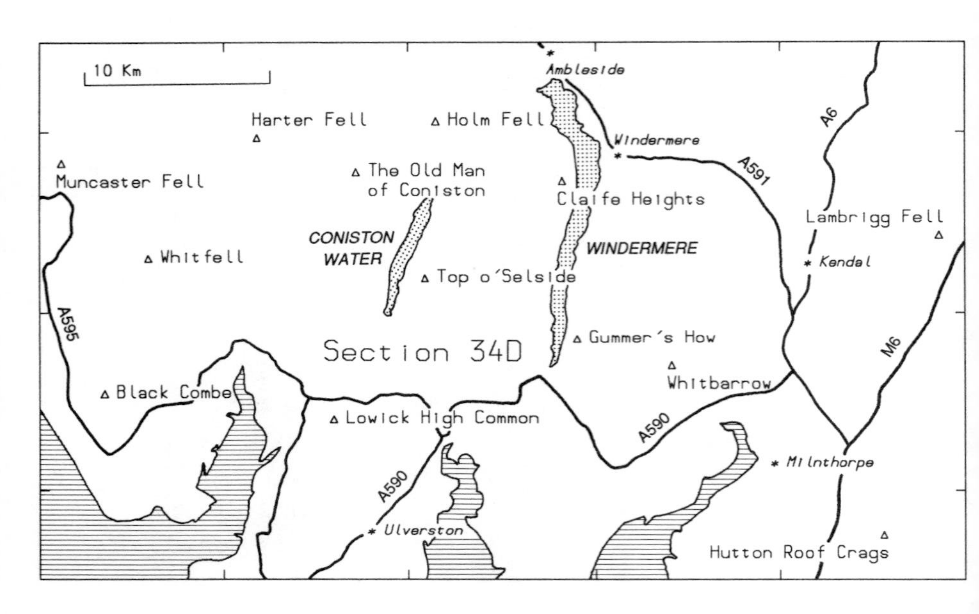

REGION 35
The Northern and Central Pennines

South Shields; coast to Middlesbrough; River Tees to Darlington; A1 to Knottingley; River Aire to Skipton; A65 to Lancashire border; county boundary to Kirkby Lonsdale; River Lune to Tebay; M6 to Carlisle; A69 to Haltwhistle; River South Tyne and River Tyne to South Shields.

Section 35A The Northern Pennines
North of A684 from the River Lune to the A1

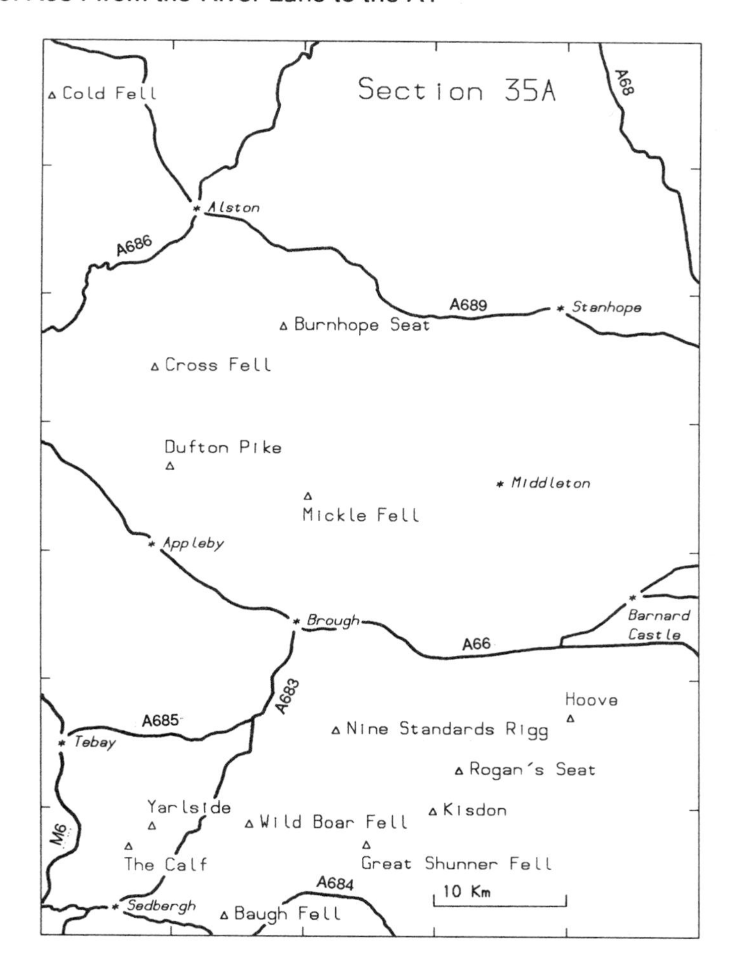

Metres	Feet	Name	Map	Grid Ref	Date
893	2930	Cross Fell	91	NY 687343	______
788	2585	Mickle Fell	91/92	NY 804243	______
747	2450	Burnhope Seat	91	NY 785375	______
716	2349	Great Shunner Fell	98	SD 848973	______
708	2324	Wild Boar Fell	98	SD 758988	______
678	2224	Baugh Fell - Tarn Rigg Hill	98	SD 740916	______
676	2219	The Calf	98	SD 667970	______
672	2205	Rogan's Seat	91/92	NY 919030	______
662	2171	Nine Standards Rigg	91/92	NY 825061	______
639	2096	Yarlside	98	SD 685985	______
621	2037	Cold Fell	86	NY 605556	______
554	1816	Hoove	92	NZ 003071	______
499	1637	Kisdon	98	SD 899998	______
481	1578	Dufton Pike	91	NY 699266	______

Section 35B The Central Pennines
South of A684 from the River Lune to the A1

Metres	Feet	Name	Map	Grid Ref	Date
736	2416	Whernside	98	SD 738814	______
724	2376	Ingleborough	98	SD 740745	______
704	2309	Great Whernside	98	SE 001739	______
702	2302	Buckden Pike	98	SD 960787	______
694	2278	Pen-y-ghent	98	SD 838733	______
687	2255	Great Coum	98	SD 700835	______
672	2205	Great Knoutberry Hill	98	SD 788871	______
668	2192	Dodd Fell Hill	98	SD 840845	______
668	2191	Fountains Fell	98	SD 864715	______
610	2001	Birks Fell	98	SD 918763	______
609	1999	Calf Top	98	SD 664856	______
556	1825	Aye Gill Pike	98	SD 720886	______
506	1660	Thorpe Fell Top	104	SE 008597	______
402	1320	Ilkley Moor	104	SE 114452	______
357	1171	Sharp Haw	103	SD 959552	______

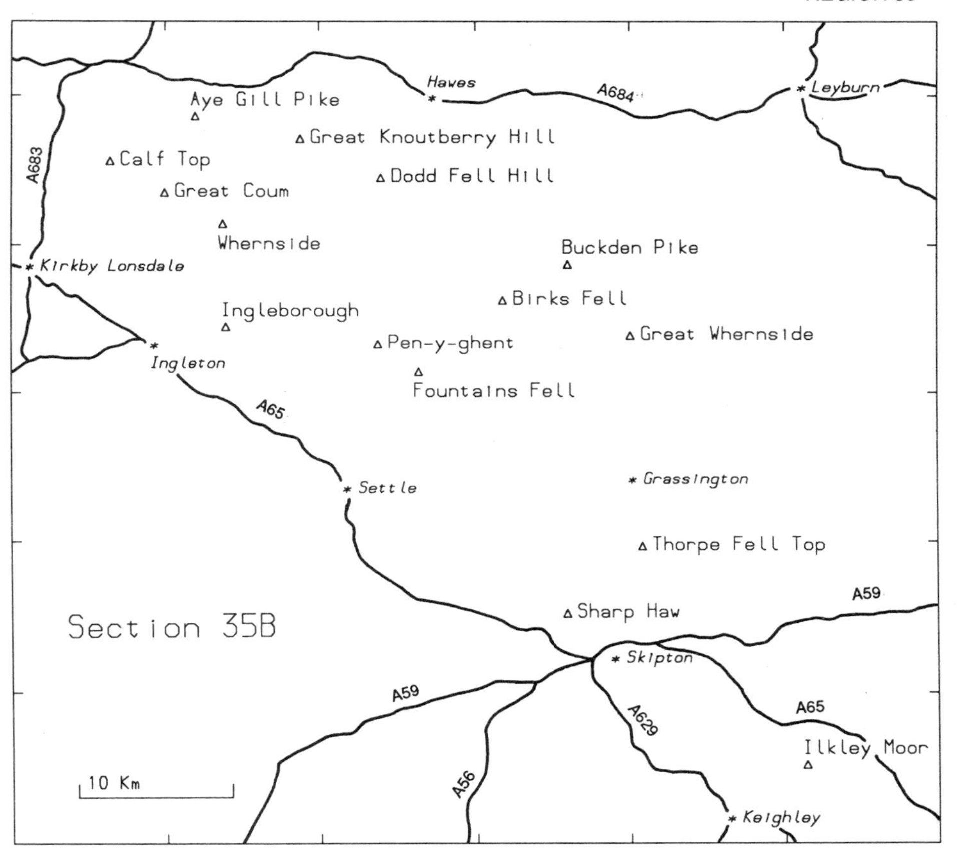
Hawes
A684
Leyburn
Aye Gill Pike
Great Knoutberry Hill
A683
Calf Top
Dodd Fell Hill
Great Coum
Whernside
Buckden Pike
Kirkby Lonsdale
Birks Fell
Ingleborough
Great Whernside
Pen-y-ghent
Ingleton
Fountains Fell
A65
Grassington
Settle
Thorpe Fell Top
A59
Sharp Haw
Section 35B
Skipton
A59
A65
A629
Ilkley Moor
10 Km
A56
Keighley

REGION 36

Lancashire, Cheshire and the Southern Pennines

Kirkby Lonsdale; county boundary and A65 to Skipton; River Aire to Knottingley; A1 to Doncaster; M18 and M1 to Long Eaton; county boundary to Alrewas; A513 to Stafford; A518 to Newport; county boundaries to the River Dee; coast to the Cumbria border; county boundary to Kirkby Lonsdale.

Metres	*Feet*	*Name*	*Map*	*Grid Ref*	*Date*
636	2088	Kinder Scout	110	SK 086875	______
582	1908	Black Hill	110	SE 078047	______
561	1839	Ward's Stone	102	SD 592587	______
559	1834	Shining Tor	118	SJ 994737	______
557	1827	Pendle Hill	103	SD 804414	______
544	1786	White Hill	103	SD 673588	______
520	1707	Fair Snape Fell	102	SD 597472	______
517	1696	Boulsworth Hill - Lad Law	103	SD 929356	______
477	1565	Hail Storm Hill	109	SD 835193	______
456	1497	Winter Hill	109	SD 659149	______
454	1489	Freeholds Top	103	SD 906218	______
396	1300	Easington Fell	103	SD 730487	______
385	1264	Gun	118	SJ 970615	______
350	1148	Longridge Fell	102/103	SD 658410	______
343	1125	The Cloud	118	SJ 904637	______
227	745	Raw Head	117	SJ 508548	______
179	587	Billinge Hill	108	SD 525014	______

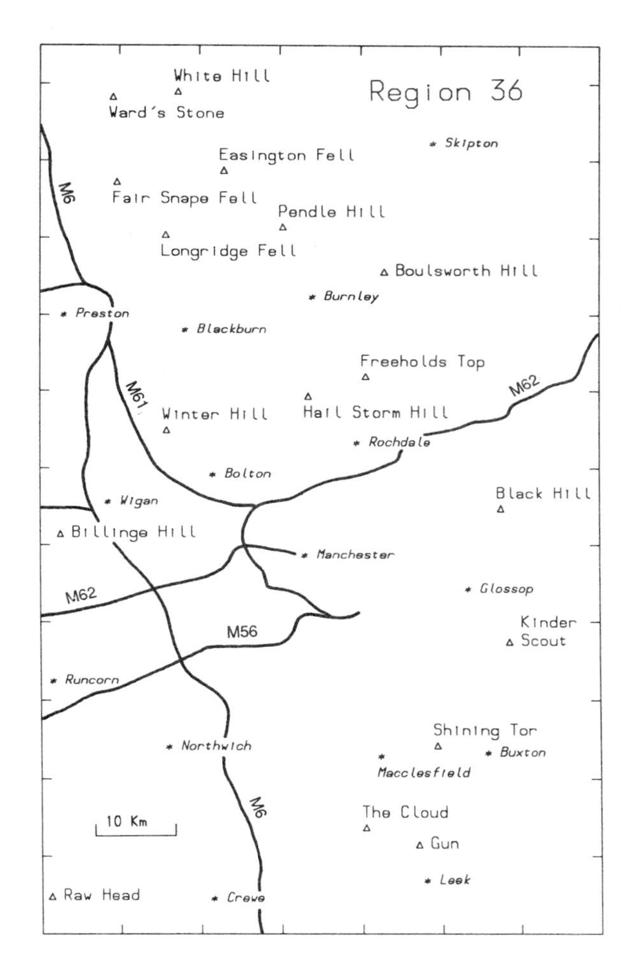
Region 36
White Hill
Ward's Stone
Skipton
Easington Fell
M6
Fair Snape Fell
Pendle Hill
Longridge Fell
Boulsworth Hill
Burnley
Preston
Blackburn
Freeholds Top
M62
M61
Winter Hill
Hail Storm Hill
Rochdale
Bolton
Black Hill
Wigan
Billinge Hill
Manchester
M62
Glossop
Kinder Scout
M56
Runcorn
Shining Tor
Northwich
Buxton
Macclesfield
M6
10 Km
The Cloud
Gun
Leek
Raw Head
Crewe

REGION 37

The River Tees to The Wash

Middlesbrough; coast to The Wash; county boundaries to the River Trent at Long Eaton; M1 and M18 to Doncaster; A1 to Darlington; River Tees to Middlesbrough.

Metres	*Feet*	*Name*	*Map*	*Grid Ref*	*Date*
454	1490	Urra Moor - Round Hill	93	NZ 594016	______
435	1427	Cringle Moor - Drake Howe	93	NZ 537029	______
329	1078	Gisborough Moor	94	NZ 634123	______
246	807	Bishop Wilton Wold	106	SE 821569	______
168	550	The Wolds *	113	TF 121964	______

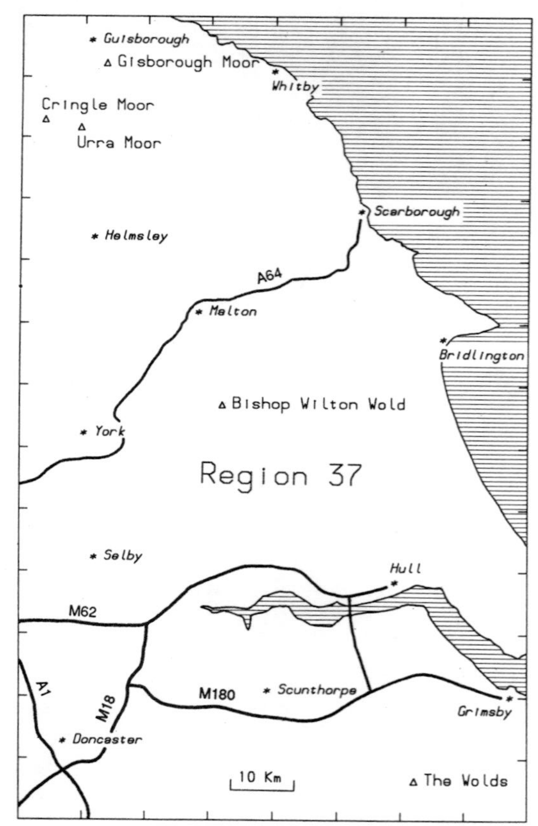

REGION 38
The Welsh Borders

Chirk; Shropshire border to the River Severn south of Bridgnorth; River Severn to Chepstow; Welsh border to Chirk.

Section 38A Shropshire
The county of Shropshire

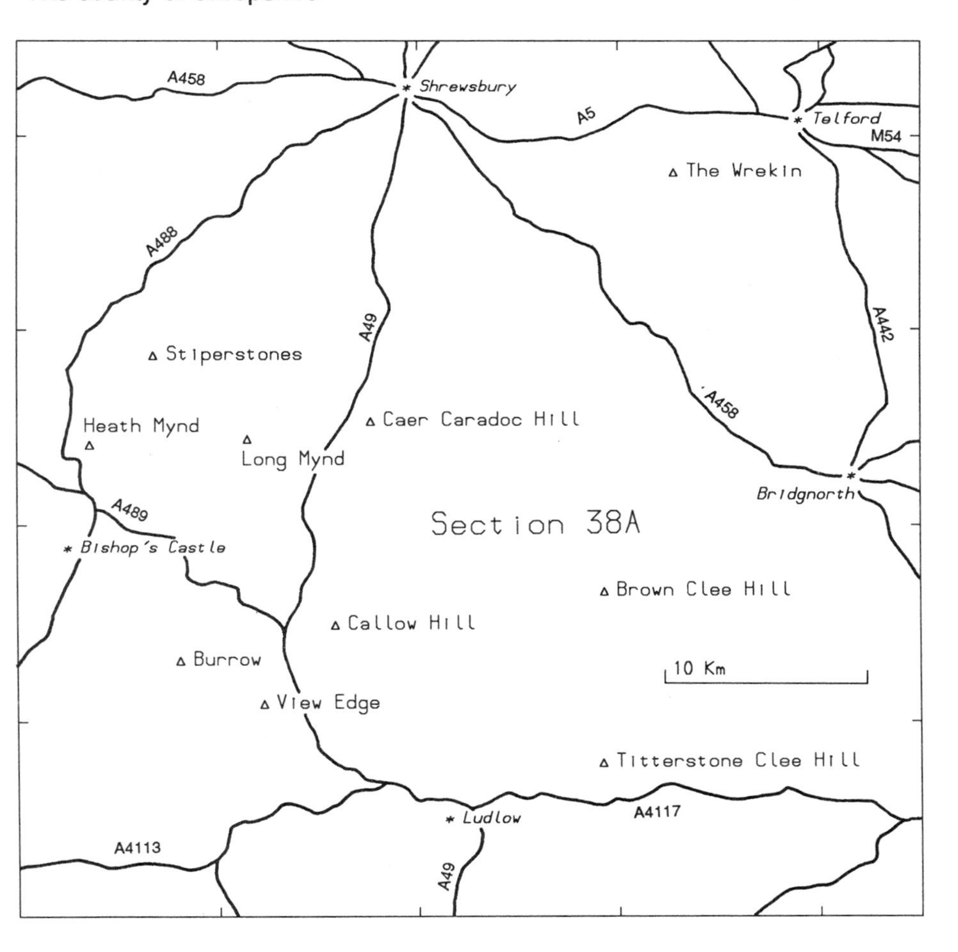

Metres	*Feet*	*Name*	*Map*	*Grid Ref*	*Date*
540	1771	Brown Clee Hill	137/138	SO 593866	______
536	1760	Stiperstones	137	SO 368987	______
533	1750	Titterstone Clee Hill	137/138	SO 592779	______
516	1694	Long Mynd - Pole Bank	137	SO 415944	______
459	1506	Caer Caradoc Hill	137/138	SO 477953	______
452	1483	Heath Mynd	137	SO 336941	______
407	1334	The Wrekin	127	SJ 628081	______
358	1175	Burrow	137	SO 381831	______
334	1096	Callow Hill	137/138	SO 459849	______
321	1053	View Edge	137	SO 423809	______

Section 38B West Gloucestershire and Hereford & Worcester
The counties of Gloucestershire and Hereford & Worcester west of the River Severn

Metres	Feet	Name	Map	Grid Ref	Date
703	2306	Black Mountain *	161	SO 255350	______
426	1397	Hergest Ridge	148	SO 254562	______
425	1394	Worcestershire Beacon	150	SO 768452	______
391	1284	Bradnor Hill	148	SO 282584	______
375	1230	High Vinnalls	137/138/148	SO 478724	______
366	1202	Garway Hill	161	SO 436250	______
329	1080	Wapley Hill	137/148/149	SO 346624	______
326	1070	Shobdon Hill	137/148/149	SO 382641	______
296	971	May Hill	162	SO 695212	______
294	965	Burton Hill	148/149	SO 394488	______
290	951	Ruardean Hill	162	SO 635169	______
269	883	Seager Hill	149	SO 613390	______
252	827	Grendon Green	149	SO 599574	______

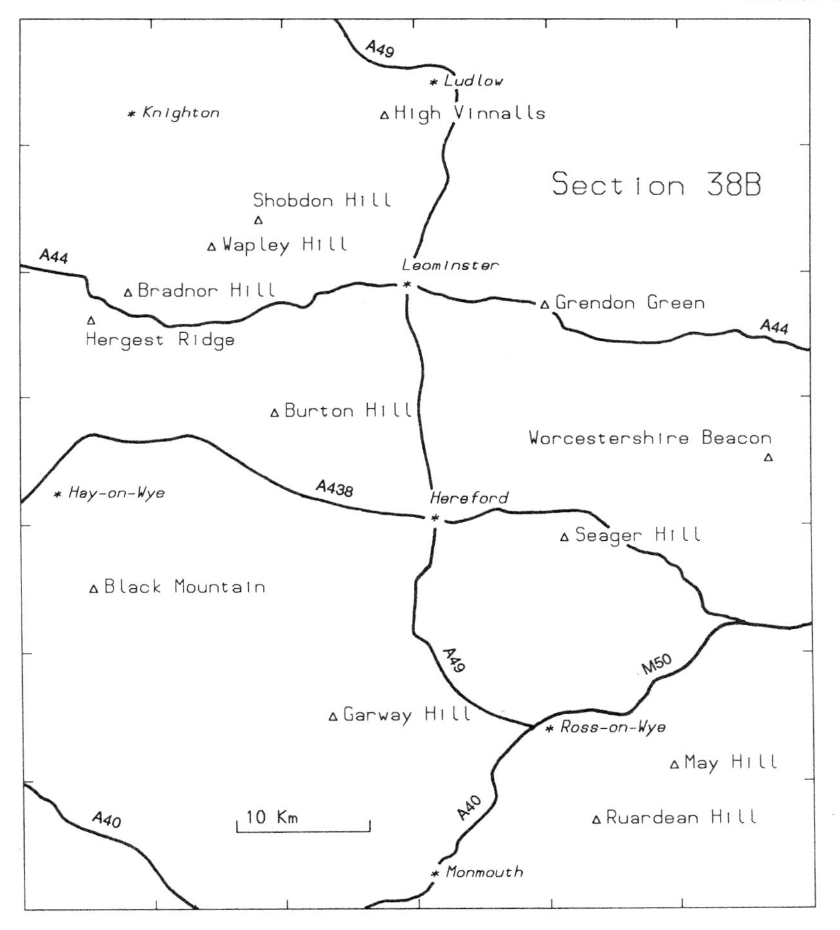
A49
Ludlow
Knighton
High Vinnalls
Section 38B
Shobdon Hill
Wapley Hill
A44
Leominster
Bradnor Hill
Grendon Green
Hergest Ridge
A44
Burton Hill
Worcestershire Beacon
A438
Hay-on-Wye
Hereford
Seager Hill
Black Mountain
A49
M50
Garway Hill
Ross-on-Wye
May Hill
A40
10 Km
A40
Ruardean Hill
Monmouth

REGION 39

Central and Eastern England

Stafford; A513 to Alrewas; county boundaries to the Wash; coast to London; River Thames to Reading; Kennet & Avon Canal and River Avon to the Bristol Channel; River Severn to the Shropshire border; county boundary to Newport; A518 to Stafford. This area includes the counties of West Midlands, Warwickshire, Leicestershire, Northamptonshire, Cambridgeshire, Norfolk, Suffolk, Oxfordshire, Buckinghamshire, Bedfordshire, Hertfordshire and Essex, together with those parts of Staffordshire south of Stafford, Hereford & Worcester and Gloucestershire east of the River Severn, Avon north of the River Avon, Wiltshire and Berkshire north of the Kennet & Avon Canal, and London north of the River Thames.

Metres	*Feet*	*Name*	*Map*	*Grid Ref*	*Date*
330	1083	Cleeve Hill	163	SO 997246	______
315	1034	Walton Hill	139	SO 942798	______
299	980	Bredon Hill	150	SO 958402	______
278	912	Bardon Hill	129	SK 460132	______
267	876	Haddington Hill	165	SP 890089	______

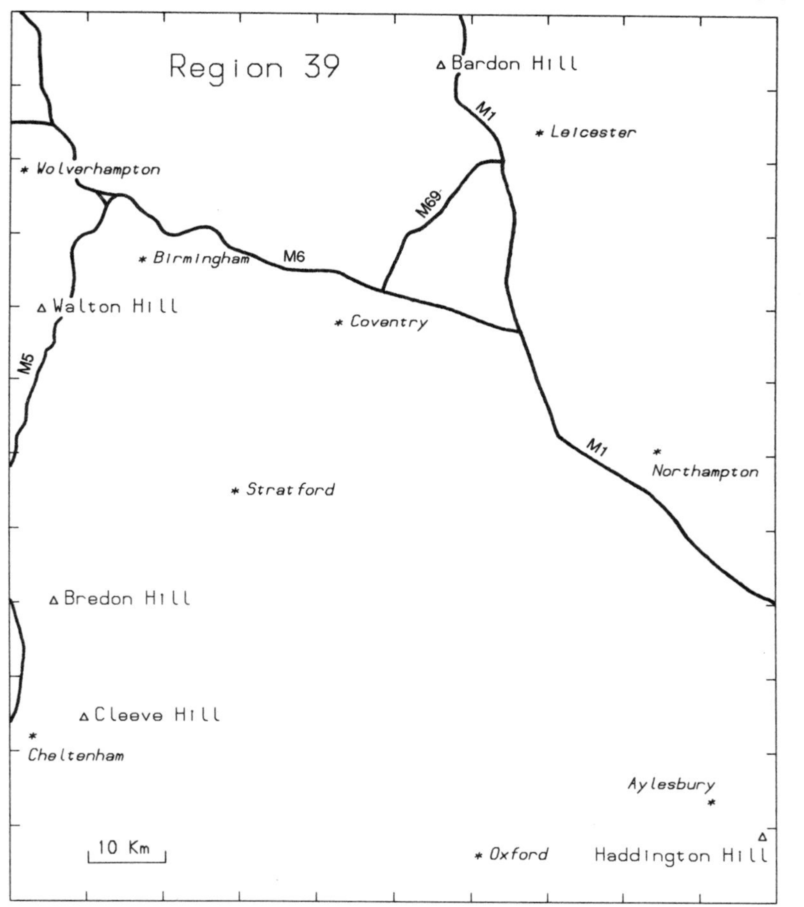
Region 39
Bardon Hill
M1
Leicester
Wolverhampton
M69
Birmingham
M6
Walton Hill
Coventry
M5
M1
Northampton
Stratford
Bredon Hill
Cleeve Hill
Cheltenham
Aylesbury
10 Km
Oxford
Haddington Hill

REGION 40

Cornwall and Devon

Ilfracombe; coast to the Somerset border; county boundaries to Lyme Regis; coast to Ilfracombe.

Metres	*Feet*	*Name*	*Map*	*Grid Ref*	*Date*
621	2038	High Willhays	191	SX 580892	______
420	1377	Brown Willy	201	SX 158800	______
334	1096	Kit Hill	201	SX 375713	______
312	1025	Hensbarrow Beacon *	200	SW 997575	______
261	857	Christ Cross *	192	SS 964052	______
252	828	Carnmenellis	203	SW 696364	______
252	828	White Downs	203	SW 420357	______

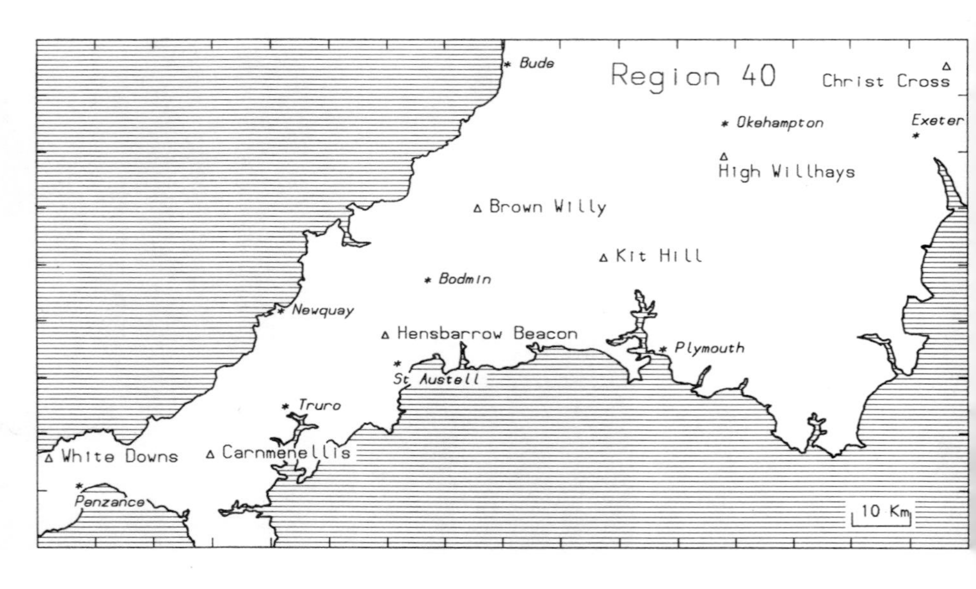

REGION 41
South Central England

Bristol; River Avon and Kennet & Avon Canal to the Berkshire border near Hungerford; county boundaries to the south coast; coast to Lyme Regis; county boundaries to the Bristol Channel; coast and River Avon to Bristol. This area includes the counties of Somerset and Dorset, together with those parts of Avon south of the River Avon and Wiltshire south of the Kennet & Avon Canal.

Metres	*Feet*	*Name*	*Map*	*Grid Ref*	*Date*
519	1704	Dunkery Beacon	181	SS 891416	______
384	1261	Wills Neck	181	ST 165352	______
325	1066	Beacon Batch	172/182	ST 484572	______
315	1035	Staple Hill	193	ST 240167	______
308	1012	Selworthy Beacon	181	SS 919480	______
297	973	Periton Hill	181	SS 946442	______

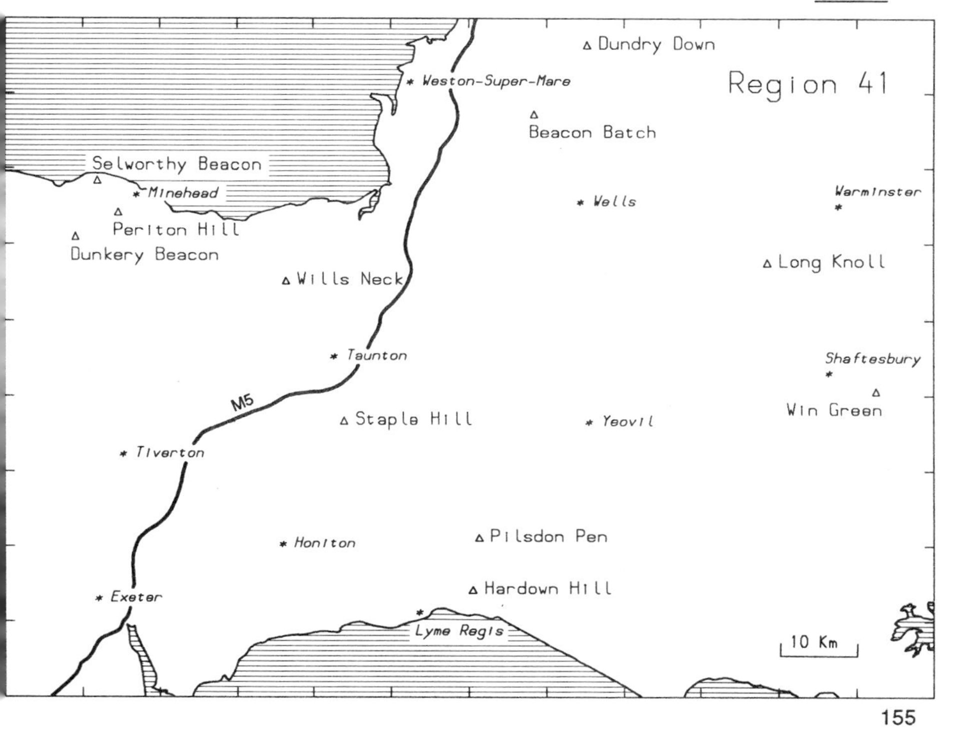

Metres	Feet	Name	Map	Grid Ref	Date
288	945	Long Knoll	183	ST 786376	______
277	910	Win Green	184	ST 925206	______
277	908	Pilsdon Pen	193	ST 413011	______
233	764	Dundry Down *	172/182	ST 553667	______
207	678	Hardown Hill	193	SY 405942	______

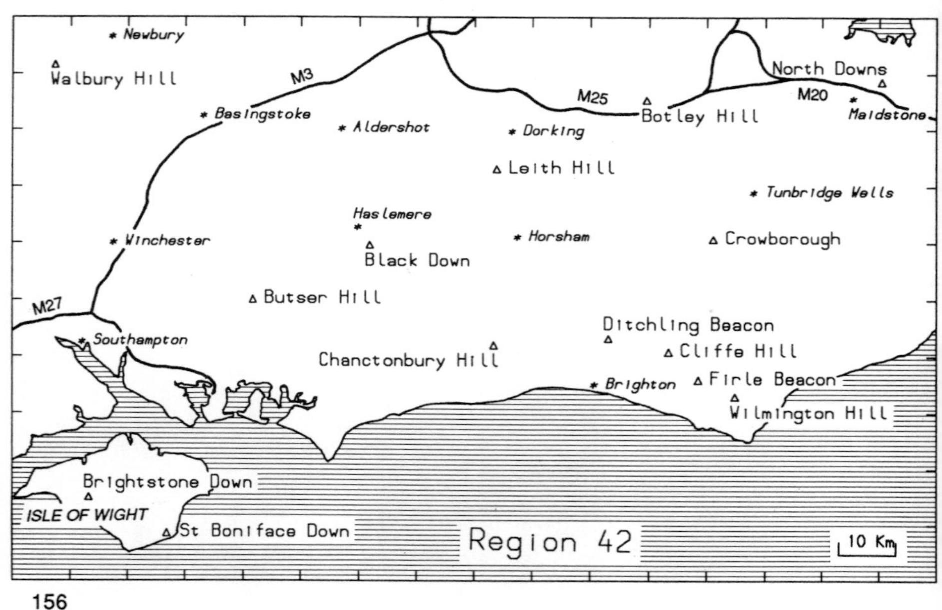

REGION 42
South-East England and the Isle of Wight

Reading; River Thames to London; coast to the Dorset border; county boundaries to the Kennet & Avon Canal near Hungerford; Kennet & Avon Canal to Reading. This area includes the counties of Hampshire, Surrey, Kent, West Sussex, East Sussex, and the Isle of Wight, together with those parts of Berkshire south of the Kennet & Avon Canal and River Thames, and London south of the River Thames.

Metres	*Feet*	*Name*	*Map*	*Grid Ref*	*Date*
297	974	Walbury Hill	174	SU 373616	______
295	968	Leith Hill	187	TQ 139431	______
280	919	Black Down	186/197	SU 919296	______
270	887	Butser Hill	197	SU 717203	______
267	875	Botley Hill	187	TQ 396553	______
248	813	Ditchling Beacon	198	TQ 331130	______
240	788	Crowborough	188	TQ 511307	______
240	786	St Boniface Down	196	SZ 568785	______
238	782	Chanctonbury Hill *	198	TQ 134120	______
217	713	Firle Beacon	198	TQ 485059	______
214	702	Wilmington Hill *	199	TQ 548034	______
214	701	Brightstone Down	196	SZ 432847	______
200	656	North Downs	178/188	TQ 804586	______
164	538	Cliffe Hill	198	TQ 434107	______

Chapter 4
The Marilyns by Height

This chapter lists all the same hills as Chapter 3 but in a different order. The list is believed to include every hill in Britain that rises at least 150 metres above the land around it in any direction, with no higher summit intervening. However, even using the excellent maps produced by the Ordnance Survey, it is impossible to be absolutely certain of the height difference between a summit and a col in all cases. The following strategy has therefore been used to decide whether to include a hill in the list:

- Using the Second Series of the Landranger maps (1:50000 scale) initially, every summit that is surrounded by 16 or more continuous 10-metre contour lines (representing a minimum of 150 metres) is automatically included.
- Any summit that is surrounded by 14 or less 10-metre contour lines (representing a maximum of 149 metres) is automatically excluded.
- Summits that are surrounded by exactly 15 10-metre contour lines have required further investigation. In these cases the relevant Pathfinder or Outdoor Leisure map (1:25000 scale) has been consulted. Some of these maps have contours at 5-metre intervals, which may show clearly whether or not a hill qualifies as a Marilyn. In other cases a spot height indicates the precise height of a col, and if this is 150 or more metres lower than the height of the summit in question then the hill clearly qualifies for inclusion.
- Where spot heights are not shown and the contours are inconclusive, then less precise methods have been used. For example, a hill 549 metres high with exactly 15 contour rings would definitely be included, whereas one 541 metres high would not be included. For those values in between (542 to 548 metres) a reasonable judgement about the probable height difference between hill top and col can usually be made based on both the height of the summit and the distance of the col from the two nearest contour lines. In the few borderline cases where this judgement is difficult to make then I have chosen to include the hill in the list, so it is possible that one or two of the hills listed may in fact have a drop of only 148 or 149 metres on one side, though this would be difficult to prove. By erring on the generous side I have tried to ensure that no eligible hill has been omitted. If anyone finds that a hill qualifying

for inclusion on the basis of the above strategy has been overlooked, then I would be grateful to hear from them.

The 1:25000 maps have also been consulted for every hill to check whether a greater height is given than on the Landranger map. If a metric edition of the 1:25000 map does give a higher figure for the same point, then that figure is given here. In a small number of cases where there is no metric 1:25000 map available, but there is a metric 1:10000 scale map, then the height may have been taken from the 1:10000 map. For example, the summit of Foinaven (Section 16B) is shown as 908 metres on the 1:50000 map but 914 metres on a recently-published 1:10000 map. It is therefore about 2998 feet and very close to being a new Munro!

As the Landranger and Pathfinder maps now show metric heights it is not always possible to give an absolutely precise figure for heights in feet. Summit heights in feet are still shown on Routemaster and one-inch-to-the-mile maps, but these figures are only used if they correspond accurately to the more up-to-date metric figure. In other cases the height in feet has simply been calculated by multiplying the height in metres by 3.2808 and rounding up or down.

The hills are listed below in height order regardless of country or region. The information is laid out as in Chapter 3, except that the section number is given instead of the grid reference and map number. In addition, the hills are numbered in height order from 1 to 1542. As in Chapter 3, a star after a name indicates that the name is not shown on the latest Landranger map. A column has again been provided for you to enter the date of ascent of each hill. This means that you will have to practise double-entry book-keeping if your records are to be complete and consistent with those in Chapter 3!

No.	Metres	Feet	Name	Section	Date
1	1344	4408	Ben Nevis	4A	______
2	1309	4296	Ben Macdui	8	______
3	1296	4252	Braeriach	8	______
4	1293	4242	Cairn Toul	8	______
5	1236	4055	Aonach Beag	4A	______
6	1223	4012	Carn Mor Dearg	4A	______
7	1214	3984	Ben Lawers	2B	______
8	1197	3927	Beinn a'Bhuird - North Top	8	______
9	1183	3880	Carn Eige	11A	______
10	1182	3878	Beinn Mheadhoin	8	______
11	1177	3862	Stob Choire Claurigh	4A	______

No.	Metres	Feet	Name	Section	Date
12	1174	3852	Ben More	1C	______
13	1171	3843	Ben Avon - Leabaidh an Daimh Bhuidhe	8	______
14	1165	3821	Stob Binnein	1C	______
15	1157	3795	Beinn Bhrotain	8	______
16	1155	3790	Lochnagar - Cac Carn Beag	7	______
17	1151	3776	Sgurr nan Ceathreamhnan	11A	______
18	1150	3774	Sgurr na Lapaich	12B	______
19	1150	3773	Bidean nam Bian	3B	______
20	1148	3765	Ben Alder	4B	______
21	1132	3714	Geal-Charn *	4B	______
22	1130	3708	Ben Lui	1D	______
23	1130	3707	Creag Meagaidh	9C	______
24	1130	3706	Binnein Mor	4A	______
25	1129	3704	An Riabhachan	12B	______
26	1129	3704	Beinn a'Ghlo - Carn nan Gabhar	6B	______
27	1126	3695	Ben Cruachan	3C	______
28	1120	3673	A'Chralaig	11B	______
29	1118	3668	Meall Garbh	2B	______
30	1118	3668	Sgor Gaoith	8	______
31	1116	3660	Stob Coire Easain	4A	______
32	1110	3642	Sgurr Mor	14B	______
33	1109	3639	Sgurr nan Conbhairean	11B	______
34	1108	3636	Meall a'Bhuiridh	3C	______
35	1102	3614	Mullach Fraoch-choire	11B	______
36	1100	3609	Creise *	3C	______
37	1099	3606	Sgurr a'Mhaim	4A	______
38	1095	3592	Sgurr Choinnich Mor	4A	______
39	1093	3586	Sgurr nan Clach Geala	14B	______
40	1090	3575	Bynack More	8	______
41	1090	3575	Stob Ghabhar	3C	______
42	1087	3566	Beinn a'Chlachair	4B	______
43	1085	3560	Snowdon - Yr Wyddfa	30B	______
44	1084	3556	Beinn Dearg	15A	______
45	1083	3554	Schiehallion	2A	______

Beinn Chreagach on the island of Ulva (Section 17E), seen across Loch na Keal from the lower slopes of Ben More on Mull.

A windy day on top of Ben Hiant (Section 18A) looking toward Beinn na Seilg, the westernmost Marilyn on the British mainland.

Beinn a'Bhaillidh on Eilean Shona from Beinn Bhreac (Section 18A), which is a mere 240 metres high but provides an excellent walk as well as fine coastal views. The distant island are Eigg and Rhum.

Above: The summit ridge of Goat Fell (Section 20C), the highest point on the island of Arran, with Mullach Mor on Holy Island visible in the middle distance.

Below: Talla Reservoir and a typical landscape in the Southern Uplands of Scotland. The top of Broad Law, the highest point in Region 28, is just out of sight to the right of the picture.

No.	*Metres*	*Feet*	*Name*	*Section*	*Date*
46	1083	3554	Sgurr a'Choire Ghlais	12A	______
47	1082	3550	Beinn a'Chaorainn	8	______
48	1081	3547	Beinn a'Chreachain	2A	______
49	1078	3538	Ben Starav	3C	______
50	1078	3536	Beinn Heasgarnich	2B	______
51	1076	3530	Beinn Dorain	2A	______
52	1070	3510	Braigh Coire Chruinn-bhalgain	6B	______
53	1069	3508	An Socach *	12B	______
54	1069	3507	Meall Corranaich	2B	______
55	1068	3505	Sgurr Fhuaran	11A	______
56	1068	3504	Glas Maol	7	______
57	1064	3490	Carnedd Llewelyn	30B	______
58	1062	3484	An Teallach - Bidein a'Ghlas Thuill	14A	______
59	1055	3460	Liathach - Spidean a'Choire Leith	13A	______
60	1054	3458	Toll Creagach	11A	______
61	1053	3455	Sgurr a'Chaorachain	12A	______
62	1051	3449	Glas Tulaichean	6B	______
63	1050	3445	Beinn a'Chaorainn	9C	______
64	1049	3443	Geal Charn	4B	______
65	1047	3435	Chno Dearg	4B	______
66	1047	3435	Creag Mhor	2B	______
67	1046	3433	Ben Wyvis	15B	______
68	1046	3432	Cruach Ardrain	1C	______
69	1045	3427	Beinn Iutharn Mhor	6B	______
70	1044	3425	Meall nan Tarmachan	2B	______
71	1044	3425	Stob Coir'an Albannaich	3C	______
72	1042	3419	Carn Mairg	2A	______
73	1040	3412	Sgurr na Ciche	10B	______
74	1039	3410	Meall Ghaordaidh	2B	______
75	1038	3404	Beinn Achaladair	2A	______
76	1037	3402	Carn a'Mhaim	8	______
77	1036	3399	Sgurr a'Bhealaich Dheirg	11A	______
78	1035	3394	Gleouraich	10A	______
79	1034	3391	Am Bodach	4A	______

No.	*Metres*	*Feet*	*Name*	*Section*	*Date*
80	1034	3391	Carn Dearg	4B	______
81	1032	3385	Beinn Fhada	11A	______
82	1029	3377	Carn an Righ	6B	______
83	1029	3377	Carn Gorm	2A	______
84	1029	3376	Ben Oss	1D	______
85	1027	3370	Sgurr na Ciste Duibhe	11A	______
86	1027	3369	Sgurr a'Mhaoraich	10A	______
87	1025	3363	Ben Challum	2B	______
88	1024	3361	Beinn a'Bheithir - Sgorr Dhearg	3B	______
89	1023	3356	Liathach - Mullach an Rathain	13A	______
90	1022	3353	Buachaille Etive Mor - Stob Dearg	3B	______
91	1021	3350	Aonach air Chrith	10A	______
92	1020	3345	Ladhar Bheinn	10B	______
93	1019	3343	Beinn Bheoil	4B	______
94	1019	3343	Mullach Coire Mhic Fhearchair	14A	______
95	1013	3323	Garbh Chioch Mhor	10B	______
96	1011	3318	Beinn Ime	1D	______
97	1010	3314	Beinn Udlamain	5	______
98	1010	3314	Sgurr an Doire Leathain	10A	______
99	1010	3314	The Saddle	10A	______
100	1010	3313	Beinn Eighe - Ruadh-stac Mor	13A	______
101	1010	3313	Sgurr Eilde Mor	4A	______
102	1008	3307	Beinn Dearg	6A	______
103	1007	3304	Maoile Lunndaidh	12A	______
104	1006	3300	An Sgarsoch	6A	______
105	1005	3298	Beinn Fhionnlaidh	11A	______
106	1004	3294	Beinn an Dothaidh	2A	______
107	1003	3290	Sgurr Mor	10B	______
108	1001	3284	Aonach Meadhoin *	11A	______
109	1001	3284	Beinn a'Bheithir - Sgorr Dhonuill	3B	______
110	1001	3284	Meall Greigh	2B	______
111	1000	3281	Sgurr Breac	14B	______
112	999	3279	Glyder Fawr	30B	______
113	999	3278	Stob Ban	4A	______

No.	*Metres*	*Feet*	*Name*	*Section*	*Date*
114	999	3276	A'Chailleach	14B	______
115	998	3273	Ben More Assynt	16E	______
116	997	3271	Glas Bheinn Mhor	3C	______
117	996	3268	Spidean Mialach	10A	______
118	995	3264	An Caisteal	1C	______
119	994	3261	Carn an Fhidhleir (Carn Ealar)	6A	______
120	994	3260	Sgor na h-Ulaidh	3B	______
121	993	3258	Beinn Eighe - Spidean Coire nan Clach	13A	______
122	993	3258	Sgurr na Ruaidhe	12A	______
123	993	3257	Sgurr Alasdair	17B	______
124	992	3255	Carn nan Gobhar	12B	______
125	991	3251	Sgairneach Mhor	5	______
126	989	3245	Beinn Eunaich	3C	______
127	989	3245	Sgurr Ban	14A	______
128	987	3238	Gaor Bheinn (Gulvain)	10D	______
129	986	3235	Beinn Alligin - Sgurr Mhor	13A	______
130	986	3234	Lurg Mhor	12A	______
131	986	3234	Sgurr Dearg - Inaccessible Pinnacle	17B	______
132	985	3231	Ben Vorlich	1B	______
133	985	3230	An Gearanach *	4A	______
134	982	3222	Ciste Dhubh	11A	______
135	981	3217	Slioch	14A	______
136	980	3215	Beinn a'Chochuill	3C	______
137	980	3215	Cona' Mheall	15A	______
138	978	3210	Scafell Pike	34B	______
139	978	3209	Beinn Dubhchraig	1D	______
140	977	3205	Stob Ban	4A	______
141	975	3200	Carn Liath	6B	______
142	975	3199	Stuc a'Chroin	1B	______
143	975	3198	Carn a'Gheoidh	6B	______
144	974	3194	Beinn Sgritheall	10A	______
145	974	3194	Ben Lomond	1C	______
146	967	3173	A'Mhaighdean	14A	______
147	967	3173	Aonach Eagach - Sgorr nam Fiannaidh	3A	______

No.	Metres	Feet	Name	Section	Date
148	966	3170	Ben More	17E	______
149	965	3167	Sgurr nan Gillean	17B	______
150	964	3162	Scafell	34B	______
151	963	3160	Sgurr Thuilm	10D	______
152	963	3159	Carn a'Chlamain	6A	______
153	961	3154	Ben Klibreck - Meall nan Con	16D	______
154	960	3150	Beinn nan Aighenan	3C	______
155	960	3150	Sgorr Ruadh	13B	______
156	960	3150	Stuchd an Lochain	2A	______
157	959	3145	Beinn Fhionnlaidh	3B	______
158	959	3145	Meall Glas	2B	______
159	958	3143	Buachaille Etive Beag - Stob Dubh	3B	______
160	956	3136	Sgurr nan Coireachan	10D	______
161	955	3133	Stob Gaibhre	4B	______
162	954	3130	Am Faochagach	15A	______
163	953	3125	Beinn Mhanach	2A	______
164	953	3125	Sgurr nan Coireachan	10B	______
165	951	3120	Meall Chuaich	5	______
166	950	3116	Helvellyn	34C	______
167	948	3111	Beinn Bhuidhe	1D	______
168	947	3107	Stob a'Choire Odhair	3C	______
169	947	3107	Y Garn	30B	______
170	946	3105	Meall Buidhe	10B	______
171	946	3104	Carn Bhac	6B	______
172	946	3104	Sgurr na Sgine	10A	______
173	945	3100	Bidein a'Choire Sheasgaich	12A	______
174	945	3100	Carn Dearg	9B	______
175	944	3097	An Socach	6B	______
176	943	3093	Ben Vorlich	1D	______
177	943	3093	Binnein Beag	4A	______
178	941	3087	Carn na Caim	5	______
179	941	3087	Carn Dearg	4B	______
180	939	3082	Luinne Bheinn	10B	______
181	939	3080	Mount Keen	7	______

No.	Metres	Feet	Name	Section	Date
182	937	3075	Beinn Tarsuinn	14A	______
183	937	3074	Beinn na Lap	4B	______
184	937	3074	Beinn Sgulaird	3B	______
185	935	3066	Sron a'Choire Ghairbh	10C	______
186	933	3062	Fionn Bheinn	14B	______
187	933	3061	Beinn Chabhair	1C	______
188	933	3060	Maol Chean-dearg	13B	______
189	932	3057	Meall Buidhe	2A	______
190	931	3054	Ben Chonzie	1A	______
191	931	3054	Skiddaw	34A	______
192	928	3046	Bla Bheinn (Blaven)	17B	______
193	928	3045	Eididh nan Clach Geala	15A	______
194	928	3045	Meall nan Eun	3C	______
195	928	3045	Moruisg	12A	______
196	927	3040	Ben Hope	16B	______
197	927	3040	Seana Bhraigh	15A	______
198	926	3038	Beinn Narnain	1D	______
199	926	3038	Meall a'Choire Leith	2B	______
200	925	3036	Beinn Liath Mhor	13B	______
201	925	3035	Buachaille Etive Beag - Stob Coire Raineach	3B	______
202	923	3029	Elidir Fawr	30B	______
203	922	3025	Beinn Alligin - Tom na Gruagaich	13A	______
204	921	3021	Sgiath Chuil	2B	______
205	919	3015	Gairich	10B	______
206	918	3012	A'Ghlas-bheinn	11A	______
207	918	3012	Creag nan Damh	10A	______
208	918	3012	Ruadh Stac Mor	14A	______
209	917	3008	Geal-charn	5	______
210	917	3008	Meall na Teanga	10C	______
211	916	3005	Beinn a'Chlaidheimh	14A	______
212	916	3004	Ben Vane	1D	______
213	915	3002	Beinn Teallach	9C	______
214	915	3002	Sgurr nan Ceannaichean	12A	______

No.	Metres	Feet	Name	Section	Date
215	915	3002	Tryfan	30B	______
216	914	2998	Beinn Dearg	13A	______
217	914	2998	Foinaven - Ganu Mor	16B	______
218	913	2994	Sgurr a'Choire-bheithe	10B	______
219	912	2992	Beinn Bhreac	6A	______
220	912	2991	Leathad an Taobhain	6A	______
221	911	2989	The Fara	4B	______
222	910	2985	Beinn Dearg Mor	14A	______
223	910	2985	Meall Buidhe	2A	______
224	909	2982	Beinn nan Oighreag	2B	______
225	909	2982	Streap	10D	______
226	907	2976	Fuar Tholl	13B	______
227	907	2975	Beinn Maol Chaluim	3B	______
228	906	2972	Leum Uilleim	4A	______
229	905	2970	Aran Fawddwy	30E	______
230	903	2962	Ben Vuirich	6B	______
231	902	2959	Beinn Damh	13B	______
232	901	2957	Ben Tee	10C	______
233	901	2956	Beinn an Lochain	19C	______
234	901	2956	Beinn Mheadhonach	6A	______
235	901	2956	Sgurr an Fhuarain	10B	______
236	901	2955	Beinn Odhar	2B	______
237	900	2953	Culardoch	8	______
238	899	2949	Aonach Buidhe	12B	______
239	899	2949	Great Gable	34B	______
240	898	2946	Y Lliwedd	30B	______
241	897	2942	Beinn a'Bhuiridh	3C	______
242	896	2941	Ben Tirran	7	______
243	896	2940	Gairbeinn	9B	______
244	896	2940	Ruadh-stac Beag	13A	______
245	896	2938	Beinn Bhan	13B	______
246	895	2936	Creag Mhor	8	______
247	894	2933	Sgurr nan Eugallt	10B	______
248	893	2930	Cross Fell	35A	______

No.	Metres	Feet	Name	Section	Date
249	893	2929	Cadair Idris - Penygadair	30F	______
250	892	2927	Pillar	34B	______
251	892	2926	An Ruadh-stac	13B	______
252	892	2926	Beinn a'Chuallaich	5	______
253	889	2917	Aonach Shasuinn	11B	______
254	889	2915	Beinn Enaiglair	15A	______
255	888	2914	Sgurr Dhomhnuill	18B	______
256	888	2913	Creagan na Beinne	1A	______
257	887	2910	Ben Aden	10B	______
258	887	2910	Meall a'Ghiubhais	13A	______
259	886	2907	Beinn a'Chaisteil	2B	______
260	886	2906	Pen y Fan	32A	______
261	885	2904	Sgurr a'Bhac Chaolais	10A	______
262	885	2903	Garbh Bheinn	18B	______
263	884	2900	Cam Chreag	2B	______
264	884	2899	The Cobbler (Ben Arthur)	1D	______
265	883	2897	Stob Dubh	3C	______
266	882	2895	Beinn Odhar Bheag	18A	______
267	882	2895	Rois-Bheinn	18A	______
268	880	2887	Beinn Chuirn	1D	______
269	880	2886	Sgurr Mhurlagain	10C	______
270	879	2883	Ben Ledi	1C	______
271	879	2883	Creag Uchdag	1A	______
272	879	2883	Fraochaidh	3B	______
273	879	2883	Sguman Coinntich	12B	______
274	879	2883	Sgurr a'Mhuilinn	12A	______
275	878	2879	Carn an Fhreiceadain	9B	______
276	876	2874	Creag an Loch	6A	______
277	875	2871	Baosbheinn	13A	______
278	874	2868	Goat Fell	20C	______
279	874	2867	Sgurr na Ba Glaise	18A	______
280	873	2863	Ben Hee	16B	______
281	873	2863	Fairfield	34C	______
282	873	2863	Sgorr nan Lochan Uaine	13B	______

No.	*Metres*	*Feet*	*Name*	*Section*	*Date*
283	872	2861	Moel Siabod	30B	______
284	872	2861	Morven	21A	______
285	869	2850	Stob a'Choin	1C	______
286	868	2848	Beinn Pharlagain - Meall na Meoig	4B	______
287	868	2847	Blencathra	34A	______
288	868	2847	Faochaig	12B	______
289	867	2844	Garbh Bheinn	3A	______
290	867	2844	Bidein a'Chabair	10D	______
291	865	2838	Conachcraig	7	______
292	865	2837	Carn a'Choire Ghairbh	11B	______
293	864	2835	Beinn Mhic Chasgaig	3C	______
294	863	2831	Beinn Tharsuinn	12A	______
295	862	2829	Carn Liath	8	______
296	862	2828	Cam Chreag	2A	______
297	862	2828	Meall na h-Aisre	9B	______
298	862	2828	Sgurr na Feartaig	12A	______
299	862	2827	Beinn a'Bha'ach Ard	12A	______
300	860	2821	Beinn Lair	14A	______
301	859	2819	Morrone	6B	______
302	859	2817	Caisteal Abhail	20C	______
303	858	2815	Beinn Luibhean	1D	______
304	858	2815	Fraoch Bheinn	10B	______
305	857	2813	Carn Dearg Mor	6A	______
306	857	2812	Beinn a'Chaisgein Mor	14A	______
307	857	2812	Cruach Innse	4A	______
308	857	2811	Beinn a'Chrulaiste	3A	______
309	855	2805	Beinn an Eoin	13A	______
310	855	2805	Beinn Bhuidhe	10B	______
311	855	2805	Stob an Aonaich Mhoir	5	______
312	854	2801	Arenig Fawr	30D	______
313	853	2798	Creach Bheinn	18C	______
314	852	2795	Grasmoor	34B	______
315	852	2794	Meall an t-Seallaidh	1C	______
316	849	2787	Bac an Eich	12A	______

No.	*Metres*	*Feet*	*Name*	*Section*	*Date*
317	849	2787	Cul Mor	16F	______
318	849	2785	Beinn nan Imirean	2B	______
319	849	2784	Sgurr Ghiubhsachain	18B	______
320	847	2778	Ben Donich	19C	______
321	846	2775	Canisp	16F	______
322	845	2772	Beinn Resipol	18B	______
323	845	2772	Carn Ban	15A	______
324	843	2766	Merrick	27B	______
325	841	2760	St Sunday Crag	34C	______
326	841	2759	Beinn Mholach	5	______
327	841	2759	Ben Vrackie	6B	______
328	841	2759	Sgurr an Airgid	11A	______
329	840	2756	Ben Rinnes	21A	______
330	840	2756	Broad Law	28B	______
331	840	2756	Meallan nan Uan	12A	______
332	840	2755	Beinn Trilleachan	3B	______
333	840	2755	Beinn Udlaidh	3C	______
334	839	2752	Sgurr Gaorsaic	11A	______
335	838	2750	Carn Chuinneag	15B	______
336	838	2749	Meall na h-Eilde	10C	______
337	837	2746	Sron a'Choire Chnapanich *	2A	______
338	835	2739	Sgurr Cos na Breachd-laoidh	10B	______
339	834	2736	Carn Dearg	9C	______
340	834	2736	Creag nan Gabhar	7	______
341	830	2723	Beinn Dearg	2A	______
342	830	2723	Cadair Berwyn	30E	______
343	829	2721	Brown Cow Hill	8	______
344	829	2719	Carn Mor	10D	______
345	828	2718	High Street	34C	______
346	827	2713	An Dun	5	______
347	826	2710	Beinn Tarsuinn	20C	______
348	824	2703	Geal-charn Mor	9B	______
349	822	2696	White Coomb	28B	______
350	821	2694	Benvane	1C	______

No.	Metres	Feet	Name	Section	Date
351	821	2692	Geal Charn	8	______
352	820	2690	Beinn Dearg Bheag	14A	______
353	818	2685	Beinn Chaorach	2B	______
354	818	2685	Carn na Drochaide	8	______
355	818	2684	Sgorr na Diollaid	12B	______
356	817	2680	Binnein an Fhidhleir	1D	______
357	816	2677	Carn a'Chuilinn	9B	______
358	815	2675	Carn Dearg	9B	______
359	815	2674	The Cheviot	33	______
360	814	2671	An Sidhean	12A	______
361	814	2671	An Stac	18A	______
362	814	2670	Breabag	16E	______
363	814	2669	Corserine	27B	______
364	813	2667	Beinn Each	1B	______
365	813	2667	Sgor Mor	8	______
366	812	2663	Askival	17D	______
367	811	2660	Carn na Saobhaidhe	9B	______
368	811	2660	Waun Fach	32A	______
369	810	2657	Meall a'Bhuachaille	8	______
370	810	2656	Creach Bheinn	3B	______
371	809	2654	Creag MacRanaich	1C	______
372	809	2654	Meall na Fearna	1B	______
373	809	2654	Sgurr Innse	4A	______
374	808	2651	Hart Fell	28B	______
375	808	2651	Quinag - Sail Gharbh	16E	______
376	808	2650	Garbh-bheinn	17B	______
377	807	2648	High Stile	34B	______
378	807	2648	Monamenach	7	______
379	807	2647	Creag Rainich	14A	______
380	806	2645	Beinn nam Fuaran	2B	______
381	806	2645	Ben Gulabin	6B	______
382	806	2645	Meall nan Subh	2B	______
383	805	2641	Beinn na h-Eaglaise	10A	______
384	804	2639	Carn Mor	21A	______

No.	Metres	Feet	Name	Section	Date
385	804	2638	Geal Charn	10C	______
386	803	2635	The Old Man of Coniston	34D	______
387	803	2634	The Sow of Atholl	5	______
388	803	2633	Beinn Bhreac-liath	3C	______
389	802	2631	Kirk Fell	34B	______
390	802	2630	Fan Brycheiniog	32A	______
391	801	2627	Meallan Liath Coire Mhic Dhughaill	16B	______
392	800	2625	Beinn Iaruinn	9C	______
393	800	2625	Cranstackie	16B	______
394	799	2622	Clisham	24B	______
395	799	2622	Pen Llithrig y Wrach	30B	______
396	799	2620	Cir Mhor	20C	______
397	798	2618	Am Bathach	11A	______
398	797	2615	Beinn Dronaig	12A	______
399	797	2614	Cairnsmore of Carsphairn	27C	______
400	796	2612	Beinn Bhan	10D	______
401	796	2612	Sgurr Coire Choinnichean	10B	______
402	796	2611	Mam na Gualainn	4A	______
403	796	2610	Beinn Mhic-Mhonaidh	3C	______
404	796	2610	Sgurr an Utha	10D	______
405	792	2600	Carn Ealasaid	8	______
406	792	2599	Beinn Leoid	16E	______
407	792	2598	Sgurr a'Chaorachain	13B	______
408	792	2597	Glas Bheinn	4A	______
409	791	2595	Beinn Airigh Charr	14A	______
410	791	2595	Grisedale Pike	34B	______
411	790	2592	Druim nan Cnamh	10A	______
412	789	2589	Auchnafree Hill	1A	______
413	788	2585	Meall Dubh	10C	______
414	788	2585	Mickle Fell	35A	______
415	787	2582	Arkle	16B	______
416	787	2582	Beinn a'Chaisteil	15B	______
417	787	2582	Meall Tairneachan	2A	______
418	787	2582	The Brack	19C	______

No.	*Metres*	*Feet*	*Name*	*Section*	*Date*
419	786	2579	Carn na Nathrach	18B	______
420	785	2576	Beinn an Oir	20A	______
421	785	2575	Beinn na Caillich	10B	______
422	783	2569	Beinn Mhic Cedidh	18A	______
423	783	2569	Farragon Hill	2A	______
424	782	2566	Moel Hebog	30B	______
425	782	2566	Sgurr Dubh	13B	______
426	781	2562	Ainshval	17D	______
427	781	2561	Corryhabbie Hill	21A	______
428	781	2561	Sgurr Mhic Bharraich	10A	______
429	780	2558	Meall nam Maigheach	2B	______
430	779	2557	Glasgwm	30E	______
431	779	2556	Beinn Bheula	19C	______
432	778	2554	Mount Battock	7	______
433	778	2552	Harter Fell	34C	______
434	777	2548	Meall Horn	16B	______
435	776	2547	Red Screes	34C	______
436	776	2546	Glas Bheinn	16E	______
437	776	2546	Quinag - Sail Gorm	16E	______
438	775	2544	Meall na Leitreach	5	______
439	775	2543	Sgorr Craobh a'Chaorainn	18B	______
440	775	2543	Shalloch on Minnoch	27B	______
441	775	2542	Glamaig - Sgurr Mhairi	17B	______
442	774	2540	Meall a'Phubuill	10D	______
443	774	2539	Beinn nan Caorach	10A	______
444	772	2534	Beinn Spionnaidh	16B	______
445	772	2533	Meall Lighiche	3B	______
446	771	2531	Ceann na Baintighearna	1C	______
447	771	2528	Stob Coire a'Chearcaill	18B	______
448	770	2527	Moelwyn Mawr	30B	______
449	770	2525	Beinn a'Choin	1C	______
450	770	2525	Druim Tarsuinn	18B	______
451	769	2523	Cul Beag	16F	______
452	769	2523	Waun Rydd	32A	______

No.	Metres	Feet	Name	Section	Date
453	769	2522	Meallach Mhor	6A	______
454	768	2520	Carn Dearg	9B	______
455	767	2516	Sail Mhor	14A	______
456	766	2513	Beinn Liath Mhor a'Ghiubhais Li	14B	______
457	766	2512	Dun da Ghaoithe	17E	______
458	766	2512	Fuar Bheinn	18C	______
459	765	2510	Braigh nan Uamhachan	10D	______
460	764	2508	Meall an Fhudair	1D	______
461	764	2507	Little Wyvis	15B	______
462	764	2507	Quinag - Spidean Coinich	16E	______
463	764	2506	Ben Loyal - An Caisteal	16B	______
464	763	2502	Beinn Talaidh	17E	______
465	763	2502	Stony Cove Pike	34C	______
466	762	2500	Beinn na h-Uamha	18B	______
467	762	2500	High Raise	34B	______
468	761	2497	Cnoc Coinnich	19C	______
469	761	2497	Sgurr a'Chaorainn	18B	______
470	759	2490	Beinn a'Chapuill	10A	______
471	759	2490	Carn an Tionail	16B	______
472	759	2490	Ciste Buide a'Claidheimh *	1A	______
473	757	2485	Beinn Shiantaidh	20A	______
474	756	2480	Y Llethr	30D	______
475	756	2479	Cook's Cairn	21A	______
476	756	2479	Creag Dhubh	9B	______
477	753	2470	Dale Head	34B	______
478	753	2470	The Stob	1C	______
479	752	2467	Plynlimon - Pen Pumlumon Fawr	31A	______
480	751	2464	Moel Llyfnant	30D	______
481	750	2461	Meallan a'Chuail	16E	______
482	749	2457	Groban	14B	______
483	749	2457	Sgurr Choinich	10C	______
484	749	2456	Mona Gowan	21A	______
485	748	2455	Culter Fell	28B	______
486	747	2451	Meall Mor	1C	______

No.	Metres	Feet	Name	Section	Date
487	747	2451	Yr Aran	30B	______
488	747	2450	Burnhope Seat	35A	______
489	746	2447	Binnein Shuas	4B	______
490	745	2444	Creag Liath	9B	______
491	745	2444	Meall a'Mhuic	2A	______
492	744	2442	Mount Blair	7	______
493	744	2441	Druim Fada - Stob a'Ghrianain	10D	______
494	743	2438	Ben Mor Coigach	16F	______
495	743	2438	Dun Rig	28B	______
496	743	2438	Geallaig Hill	8	______
497	743	2438	Meall nan Gabhar	1D	______
498	743	2436	Beinn nan Eun	15B	______
499	742	2434	Cnap Cruinn *	4A	______
500	742	2433	Sgorr na Ciche (Pap of Glencoe)	3A	______
501	741	2430	Beinn Mhor	19C	______
502	741	2430	Sgurr Dearg	17E	______
503	740	2428	Badandun Hill	7	______
504	739	2424	Sgurr na Coinnich	17C	______
505	739	2423	Beinn Mheadhoin	18C	______
506	739	2423	Stob na Cruaiche	3A	______
507	738	2421	Meall Mor	15B	______
508	737	2418	Beinn na h-Eaglaise	13B	______
509	737	2417	Robinson	34B	______
510	736	2416	Whernside	35B	______
511	736	2415	Beinn Bheag	18B	______
512	736	2415	Seat Sandal	34C	______
513	736	2414	Marsco	17B	______
514	734	2409	Fan Fawr	32A	______
515	734	2408	Beinn a'Chaolais	20A	______
516	734	2408	Craig Cwm Silyn	30B	______
517	734	2408	Doune Hill	1E	______
518	734	2408	Rhobell Fawr	30D	______
519	734	2407	Druim na Sgriodain *	18B	______
520	733	2405	Beinn na Caillich	17C	______

No.	Metres	Feet	Name	Section	Date
521	732	2403	Beinn na Caillich	17C	______
522	732	2403	Green Lowther	27C	______
523	732	2402	Glas Bheinn	10C	______
524	732	2402	Sgurr a'Gharaidh	13B	______
525	732	2401	Sabhal Beag	16B	______
526	732	2401	Stob an Eas	19C	______
527	731	2399	Suilven - Caisteal Liath	16F	______
528	731	2398	Beinn Dearg Mhor	17B	______
529	730	2395	Beinn na Gainimh	1A	______
530	730	2395	Carnan Cruithneachd	11A	______
531	730	2395	Meall Doire Faid	15A	______
532	729	2392	Uisgnaval Mor	24B	______
533	729	2391	Ben Venue	1C	______
534	727	2385	Mullach Coire nan Geur-oirean	10D	______
535	726	2382	Mam Hael	3B	______
536	726	2382	Moel Eilio	30B	______
537	725	2379	Fan Gyhirych	32A	______
538	725	2378	Beinn a'Chearcaill	13A	______
539	724	2376	Ingleborough	35B	______
540	723	2371	Meall nan Damh	18B	______
541	722	2370	Meall Mheinnidh	14A	______
542	722	2369	Creagan a'Chaise	21A	______
543	721	2366	Beinn Bharrain - Mullach Buidhe	20C	______
544	721	2366	The Buck	21A	______
545	721	2365	Stob Mhic Bheathain	18B	______
546	721	2364	Ben Cleuch	26	______
547	721	2364	Ben Stack	16E	______
548	720	2362	Rhinog Fawr	30D	______
549	719	2359	Meall Buidhe	1A	______
550	719	2358	The Storr	17A	______
551	718	2355	An Stac	10D	______
552	717	2353	Ben Buie	17E	______
553	717	2351	Lamachan Hill	27B	______
554	716	2349	Great Shunner Fell	35A	______

No.	Metres	Feet	Name	Section	Date
555	715	2345	Beinn Mheadhonach	3B	______
556	715	2345	Cnap Chaochan Aitinn	8	______
557	714	2342	Beinn Tharsuinn	15B	______
558	714	2342	Hedgehope Hill	33	______
559	713	2339	Beinn Chaorach	1E	______
560	713	2339	Druim Fada	10A	______
561	713	2338	Creag Mhor	16D	______
562	712	2335	Creag Ruadh *	1A	______
563	711	2334	Tinto	27A	______
564	711	2333	Beinn nan Ramh	14B	______
565	711	2332	Cairnsmore of Fleet	27B	______
566	710	2330	Carn a'Ghille Chearr	21A	______
567	710	2329	Knott	34A	______
568	710	2328	Beinn a'Mhanaich	1E	______
569	710	2328	Meith Bheinn	10D	______
570	709	2327	Beinn nan Lus	3C	______
571	709	2326	Beinn Dearg Mhor	17C	______
572	709	2326	Trum y Ddysgl	30B	______
573	708	2324	Wild Boar Fell	35A	______
574	706	2316	An Cruachan	12B	______
575	706	2316	Beinn Dearg	1B	______
576	706	2315	Carn a'Chaochain	11B	______
577	706	2315	Morven	16C	______
578	705	2313	Hunt Hill	7	______
579	705	2313	Meall a'Chaorainn	14B	______
580	705	2313	Pike of Blisco	34B	______
581	705	2312	Ben Armine - Creag a'Choire Ghlais	16D	______
582	704	2311	Corra-bheinn	17E	______
583	704	2309	Great Whernside	35B	______
584	703	2306	Beinn Lochain	19C	______
585	703	2306	Black Mountain *	38B	______
586	703	2306	Sgurr an Fhidhleir	16F	______
587	703	2305	Beinn Eich	1E	______
588	702	2303	Beinn Fhada	17E	______

No.	*Metres*	*Feet*	*Name*	*Section*	*Date*
589	702	2303	Belig	17B	______
590	702	2303	Trallval	17D	______
591	702	2302	Buckden Pike	35B	______
592	702	2302	Mealna Letter (Duchray Hill)	7	______
593	701	2301	Carn a'Choin Deirg	15A	______
594	701	2300	Meall Garbh	3C	______
595	701	2300	Sgurr nan Cnamh	18B	______
596	700	2298	Blackcraig Hill	27C	______
597	700	2297	Slat Bheinn	10B	______
598	699	2293	Meall Fuar-mhonaidh	11B	______
599	698	2290	Allt Fawr	30B	______
600	698	2290	Carn Loch nan Amhaichean	15B	______
601	698	2290	Creach Beinn	17E	______
602	698	2290	Mynydd Mawr	30B	______
603	698	2290	Windy Standard	27C	______
604	697	2286	Queensberry	27C	______
605	694	2278	Pen-y-ghent	35B	______
606	693	2272	Beinn na Muice	12A	______
607	692	2270	Beinn a'Mhuinidh	14A	______
608	692	2270	Beinn Tharsuinn	15B	______
609	692	2270	Ettrick Pen	28B	______
610	692	2270	Mullwharchar	27B	______
611	692	2270	Seatallan	34B	______
612	691	2268	Ballencleuch Law	27C	______
613	690	2264	Beinn Molurgainn	3B	______
614	690	2264	Meall Dearg	1A	______
615	689	2259	Arenig Fach	30D	______
616	688	2257	Beinn Direach	16B	______
617	688	2257	Gathersnow Hill	28B	______
618	688	2257	Stob Breac	1C	______
619	687	2255	Great Coum	35B	______
620	685	2247	Leana Mhor	9C	______
621	684	2244	Cruach an t-Sidhein	1E	______
622	684	2243	Beinn Damhain	1D	______

No.	Metres	Feet	Name	Section	Date
623	681	2234	Meall Onfhaidh	10D	______
624	681	2233	Beinn Bhreac	1E	______
625	680	2231	Carn Mhic an Toisich	11B	______
626	680	2230	Beinn a'Chaisgein Beag	14A	______
627	680	2230	Meall na Faochaig	12A	______
628	679	2227	Meall a'Chrathaich	11B	______
629	679	2227	Tirga Mor	24B	______
630	678	2224	Baugh Fell - Tarn Rigg Hill	35A	______
631	678	2224	Carn na Breabaig	12B	______
632	678	2224	Cat Law	7	______
633	678	2224	Creigiau Gleision	30B	______
634	678	2224	Hill of Wirren	7	______
635	678	2224	Leana Mhor	9C	______
636	678	2223	Capel Fell	28B	______
637	678	2223	Carn Breac	13B	______
638	677	2222	Andrewhinney Hill	28B	______
639	677	2221	Carn Gorm	12B	______
640	676	2219	The Calf	35A	______
641	676	2218	Beinn Suidhe	3C	______
642	676	2218	Meall Mor	3B	______
643	675	2213	Maesglase - Maen Du	30F	______
644	674	2210	Moel Cynghorion	30B	______
645	673	2209	Carn na Coinnich	12A	______
646	672	2205	An Ruadh-mheallan	13A	______
647	672	2205	Great Knoutberry Hill	35B	______
648	672	2205	Rogan's Seat	35A	______
649	672	2204	Creag Each *	1A	______
650	671	2201	Foel Rhudd	30E	______
651	669	2196	Carnedd y Filiast	30D	______
652	669	2195	Hartaval	17A	______
653	668	2192	Beinn Bheag	14B	______
654	668	2192	Creag Bhalg	8	______
655	668	2192	Dodd Fell Hill	35B	______
656	668	2191	Fountains Fell	35B	______

No.	Metres	Feet	Name	Section	Date
657	667	2189	Tarren y Gesail	30F	______
658	667	2188	Binnein Shios	4B	______
659	667	2188	Cyrniau Nod	30E	______
660	667	2188	Meall nan Eun	10B	______
661	666	2185	Beinn Gaire	18A	______
662	665	2183	Meall Dubh	15A	______
663	665	2181	Meall Tairbh	3C	______
664	665	2181	Uamh Bheag	1B	______
665	664	2178	Beinn Ruadh	19C	______
666	664	2178	Tarn Crag	34C	______
667	663	2175	Aodann Chleireig	10D	______
668	663	2175	Beinn Mheadhoin	12A	______
669	663	2175	Croit Bheinn	18A	______
670	663	2175	Fan Nedd	32A	______
671	663	2175	Sgorr a'Choise	3B	______
672	662	2172	Oreval	24B	______
673	662	2171	Nine Standards Rigg	35A	______
674	661	2168	Manod Mawr	30D	______
675	660	2166	Great Rhos	31B	______
676	659	2163	Windlestraw Law	28A	______
677	659	2162	Carn Glas-choire	9A	______
678	658	2160	Creag Dhubh	9C	______
679	658	2160	Creag Mhor	1C	______
680	658	2159	Creag Ruadh	5	______
681	658	2159	Meall nan Eagan	4B	______
682	658	2159	Stob na Boine Druim-fhinn	19C	______
683	657	2155	Mid Hill	1E	______
684	657	2154	Place Fell	34C	______
685	656	2152	Meall Blair	10C	______
686	656	2152	Meall Odhar	1D	______
687	656	2152	Millfore	27B	______
688	653	2143	Harter Fell	34D	______
689	652	2140	Beinn na Cille	18C	______
690	652	2139	Fiarach	1D	______

No.	*Metres*	*Feet*	*Name*	*Section*	*Date*
691	651	2137	Blackhope Scar	28A	______
692	651	2136	Glas-bheinn Mhor	11B	______
693	650	2133	Sgorr Mhic Eacharna	18B	______
694	649	2128	Beinn Donachain	3C	______
695	646	2120	Beinn na Cloiche	4A	______
696	645	2116	Carn Salachaidh	15B	______
697	645	2116	Craignaw	27B	______
698	645	2116	Sgiath a'Chaise	1B	______
699	645	2115	Drygarn Fawr	31C	______
700	644	2113	Biod an Fhithich	10A	______
701	643	2110	Creag Tharsuinn	19C	______
702	643	2109	Beinn Clachach	10A	______
703	641	2102	Blath Bhalg	6B	______
704	640	2100	Mor Bheinn	1B	______
705	639	2096	Yarlside	35A	______
706	637	2091	Creag Gharbh	1A	______
707	637	2090	Croft Head	28B	______
708	636	2088	Kinder Scout	36	______
709	636	2086	Glas Bheinn	18B	______
710	636	2085	Beinn na Sroine	3C	______
711	636	2085	Beinn Bhalgairean	1D	______
712	635	2082	Beinn Ghobhlach	14A	______
713	634	2080	Tarrenhendre	30F	______
714	633	2077	Cruinn a'Bheinn	1C	______
715	633	2076	Glas-charn	10D	______
716	632	2075	Tullich Hill	1E	______
717	632	2073	Meall a'Chaorainn	15A	______
718	629	2063	Y Garn	30D	______
719	628	2060	Beinn Dhorain	16D	______
720	626	2055	Scaraben	16C	______
721	626	2053	Meall an Doireachain	13B	______
722	625	2050	Beinn na Feusaige	13B	______
723	623	2045	Meall nan Caorach	1A	______
724	623	2044	Moel Ysgyfarnogod	30D	______

No.	Metres	Feet	Name	Section	Date
725	622	2041	Creag Ruadh	9C	______
726	621	2038	High Willhays	40	______
727	621	2037	Cold Fell	35A	______
728	621	2037	Tom Meadhoin	4A	______
729	621	2036	Snaefell	29	______
730	620	2035	Meall Reamhar	1A	______
731	620	2033	Beinn Mhor	24C	______
732	619	2031	Pressendye	21B	______
733	619	2030	Cauldcleuch Head	28B	______
734	618	2029	Beinn Bheag	19C	______
735	618	2028	Beinn an Eoin	16F	______
736	618	2028	Creag Ghuanach	4A	______
737	618	2028	Cruach Choireadail	17E	______
738	618	2027	Carn na h-Easgainn	9B	______
739	617	2024	Cefn yr Ystrad	32A	______
740	616	2022	Beinn na Gucaig	4A	______
741	616	2020	Cushat Law	33	______
742	615	2017	Carn nan Tri-tighearnan	9A	______
743	613	2010	Meall an Fheur Loch	16E	______
744	613	2010	Stac Pollaidh	16F	______
745	612	2008	Creag a'Mhadaidh	5	______
746	612	2008	Creag Dhubh Mhor	12A	______
747	611	2005	Corwharn	7	______
748	611	2005	Cruach nam Mult	19C	______
749	611	2005	Cruach nan Capull	19C	______
750	611	2004	Foel Goch	30D	______
751	610	2002	Beinn a'Mheadhoin	11A	______
752	610	2002	Pen y Garn	31C	______
753	610	2001	Birks Fell	35B	______
754	610	2000	Ben Aslak	17C	______
755	610	2000	Tal y Fan	30B	______
756	609	1999	Calf Top	35B	______
757	609	1998	Illgill Head	34B	______
758	609	1998	Ladylea Hill	21A	______

No.	*Metres*	*Feet*	*Name*	*Section*	*Date*
759	609	1997	Mynydd Troed	32A	______
760	607	1991	Burach	10C	______
761	607	1991	Cruach Neuran	19C	______
762	606	1988	Cruach nam Miseag	19C	______
763	606	1988	Hecla	24C	______
764	606	1987	Well Hill	27C	______
765	603	1977	Beinn a'Chuirn	10A	______
766	602	1975	Peel Fell	33	______
767	601	1972	Leagag	2A	______
768	601	1972	Meallan Odhar Doire nan Gillean	12B	______
769	601	1972	Sgorach Mor	19C	______
770	601	1972	Sidhean Mor	10D	______
771	601	1972	The Coyles of Muick	7	______
772	600	1970	Black Combe	34D	______
773	600	1969	Craig y Llyn	32C	______
774	599	1966	Greatmoor Hill	28B	______
775	598	1963	Colt Hill	27C	______
776	598	1962	Beinn Uamha	1C	______
777	597	1957	Beinn Uird	1C	______
778	596	1955	Sugar Loaf	32A	______
779	595	1953	Wisp Hill	28B	______
780	594	1950	Ward Law	28B	______
781	594	1950	Waun Claerddu	31C	______
782	593	1945	Cairn Table	27C	______
783	592	1942	Beinn Mhealaich	16D	______
784	591	1939	Beinn a'Ghraig	17E	______
785	591	1939	Beinn Dubh an Iaruinn	12B	______
786	591	1939	Cnoc Damh	15A	______
787	590	1936	Ben Griam Mor	16C	______
788	590	1935	Cruban Beag	4B	______
789	589	1933	The Wiss	28B	______
790	589	1932	Beinn Mheadhonach	3B	______
791	589	1932	Cruach Mhor	19A	______
792	589	1932	Moelfre	30D	______

No.	Metres	Feet	Name	Section	Date
793	588	1930	Green Hill *	27C	______
794	588	1928	Sgorr Tuath	16F	______
795	586	1923	Binnean nan Gobhar	1C	______
796	586	1921	Pegwn Mawr	31B	______
797	584	1916	Druim a'Chuirn	10D	______
798	582	1911	Beinn nam Beathrach	18C	______
799	582	1908	Black Hill	36	______
800	581	1905	Coity Mountain	32C	______
801	580	1904	Sgurr Marcasaidh	12A	______
802	580	1903	Beinn nam Ban	14A	______
803	580	1902	Ben Griam Beg	16C	______
804	579	1901	Stulaval	24B	______
805	579	1898	Scald Law	28A	______
806	578	1897	Earl's Seat	26	______
807	578	1896	Moel y Gamelin	30C	______
808	578	1895	Meall an Fhuarain	15A	______
809	576	1890	Druim Leathad nam Fias	18B	______
810	575	1886	Corra Bheinn	20A	______
811	575	1885	Beinn Bhreac	20C	______
812	574	1883	Beinn nan Cabar	10D	______
813	574	1883	Creag na Doire Duibhe	4B	______
814	574	1883	Mealisval	24A	______
815	573	1881	Whitfell	34D	______
816	573	1879	Blake Fell	34B	______
817	572	1878	Ben na Cro	17C	______
818	572	1877	Beinn an t-Sidhein	1C	______
819	572	1877	Beinn Mhor	24A	______
820	572	1877	Dun Coillich	2A	______
821	571	1874	Broughton Heights	28A	______
822	571	1874	Orval	17D	______
823	571	1873	Meikle Conval	21A	______
824	570	1870	Carn Daimh	21A	______
825	570	1870	Glas Bheinn Mhor	17B	______
826	570	1870	Meall nan Damh	20C	______

No.	Metres	Feet	Name	Section	Date
827	570	1870	Meikle Bin	26	______
828	569	1868	Criffel	27C	______
829	569	1866	Beinn a'Chuirn	3C	______
830	569	1866	Hods Hill	27C	______
831	568	1863	Beinn a'Mhonicag	9C	______
832	568	1863	Cruach Bhuidhe	19C	______
833	568	1862	Roan Fell	28B	______
834	567	1860	Beinn Reidh	16F	______
835	567	1859	Minch Moor	28B	______
836	566	1857	Doire Ban	4A	______
837	566	1856	Meall Gainmheich	1C	______
838	565	1854	Ben Newe	21A	______
839	565	1854	Craigenreoch	27B	______
840	565	1853	Cyrn-y-Brain	30C	______
841	564	1850	Pikethaw Hill	28B	______
842	564	1850	Yr Eifl	30A	______
843	563	1848	Tap o'Noth	21A	______
844	563	1846	Creag nam Mial	6B	______
845	562	1845	Glas Bheinn	20A	______
846	562	1844	West Cairn Hill	28A	______
847	562	1843	Stob Odhar	19B	______
848	561	1841	Beinn na Seamraig	17C	______
849	561	1841	Coirc Bheinn	17E	______
850	561	1839	Ward's Stone	36	______
851	560	1837	Banc Llechwedd-mawr	31A	______
852	560	1837	Meall Alvie	8	______
853	559	1835	Beinn Eilideach	15A	______
854	559	1835	Meall a'Bhàinne	18B	______
855	559	1834	Sgaoth Aird	24B	______
856	559	1834	Shining Tor	36	______
857	558	1832	An Cabar	14B	______
858	557	1828	Cnoc nan Cuilean	16B	______
859	557	1827	Pendle Hill	36	______
860	556	1825	Aye Gill Pike	35B	______

No.	Metres	Feet	Name	Section	Date
861	556	1824	Beinn Mheadhoin	9B	______
862	555	1821	Beinn a'Bhacaidh	9B	______
863	555	1821	Beinn Duirinnis	3B	______
864	555	1820	Creag Scalabsdale	16C	______
865	555	1820	Crock	7	______
866	554	1818	Moel Famau	30C	______
867	554	1817	Cairnkinna Hill	27C	______
868	554	1816	Hoove	35A	______
869	553	1814	Creag Dhubh Mhor	16B	______
870	553	1814	Moel-ddu	30B	______
871	552	1812	Ben Dearg	17A	______
872	552	1811	Little Conval	21A	______
873	552	1811	Lord's Seat	34A	______
874	551	1808	Meall Mor	7	______
875	551	1808	Turner Cleuch Law	28B	______
876	551	1807	Sidhean na Raplaich	18C	______
877	551	1807	Tor y Foel	32A	______
878	550	1806	Drosgol	31A	______
879	550	1805	Scaw'd Fell	28B	______
880	550	1804	Beinn Ghlas	1D	______
881	550	1804	Mynydd Carn-y-cefn	32C	______
882	549	1801	Hard Knott	34B	______
883	549	1800	An Grianan	3B	______
884	549	1800	Beinn Churalain	3B	______
885	549	1800	Carn na Loine	9A	______
886	549	1800	Trahenna Hill	28A	______
887	548	1798	Beinn Mhialairigh	10A	______
888	548	1798	Leathad Mor	3A	______
889	548	1798	Meall Liath Choire	15A	______
890	548	1797	Carn a'Ghobhair	10D	______
891	547	1796	Beacon Hill	31B	______
892	545	1788	Carn Garbh	16D	______
893	545	1788	Cnoc a'Bhaid-rallaich	14A	______
894	544	1786	Beinn an Eoin	16E	______

No.	*Metres*	*Feet*	*Name*	*Section*	*Date*
895	544	1786	White Hill	36	______
896	544	1785	Meall Sguman	11A	______
897	543	1781	Meall na Suiramach	17A	______
898	543	1780	Deuchar Law	28B	______
899	542	1777	Gwaunceste Hill	31B	______
900	540	1772	Rhialgwm	30E	______
901	540	1771	Brown Clee Hill	38A	______
902	539	1769	Creag Dhubh	11B	______
903	538	1765	Penvalla	28A	______
904	537	1762	Creag Loch nan Dearcag	12A	______
905	537	1762	Ellson Fell	28B	______
906	537	1761	Great Mell Fell	34C	______
907	536	1760	Stiperstones	38A	______
908	536	1759	Foel Cwmcerwyn	31C	______
909	535	1755	Meikle Says Law	28A	______
910	535	1755	Wether Hill	27C	______
911	535	1754	Ben Hiel	16B	______
912	534	1753	Kerloch	7	______
913	533	1750	Titterstone Clee Hill	38A	______
914	533	1748	Ben Clach	1B	______
915	533	1748	Coiliochbhar Hill	21B	______
916	532	1744	Mwdwl-eithin	30C	______
917	531	1742	Craiglee	27B	______
918	530	1740	Mynydd Nodol	30D	______
919	530	1739	Ben Shieldaig	13B	______
920	529	1735	Bennachie - Oxen Craig	21B	______
921	528	1733	Toddun	24B	______
922	528	1732	Bidein Bad na h-Iolaire	4A	______
923	528	1731	Ben Hiant	18A	______
924	527	1729	Ben Corodale	24C	______
925	527	1728	Beinn Stumanadh	16C	______
926	526	1726	Beinn Bhreac	19A	______
927	523	1716	Cnoc Ceislein	15B	______
928	523	1716	Craiglee	27B	______

No.	*Metres*	*Feet*	*Name*	*Section*	*Date*
929	523	1715	Carnedd Wen	31A	______
930	523	1715	Gyrn Moelfre	30E	______
931	522	1713	Black Craig	19C	______
932	522	1713	West Lomond	26	______
933	522	1712	Gyrn Ddu	30A	______
934	522	1712	Hill of Stake	27A	______
935	522	1712	Nutberry Hill	27A	______
936	521	1710	Beinn na Sreine	17E	______
937	521	1710	Ben Horn	16D	______
938	521	1709	An Lean-charn	16B	______
939	521	1709	Farrmheall	16A	______
940	521	1709	Meall Glac Tigh-fail	14A	______
941	520	1707	Fair Snape Fell	36	______
942	520	1706	Creag a'Chliabhain *	9B	______
943	519	1704	Dunkery Beacon	41	______
944	518	1701	Sighty Crag	33	______
945	518	1699	Druim na Cluain-airighe	10B	______
946	518	1699	Lord Arthur's Hill	21B	______
947	517	1696	Boulsworth Hill - Lad Law	36	______
948	517	1696	Meall Coire an Lochain	15A	______
949	516	1694	Long Mynd - Pole Bank	38A	______
950	516	1693	Hare Cairn	7	______
951	516	1692	Black Mount	28A	______
952	515	1691	Beinn Ghlas	19A	______
953	515	1690	Beinn Chapull	19A	______
954	515	1690	Mynydd Llangorse	32A	______
955	515	1690	Tahaval	24A	______
956	514	1686	Cracaval	24A	______
957	514	1686	Meall Luidh Mor	4B	______
958	514	1685	A'Chruach	20C	______
959	513	1684	An Sleaghach	18C	______
960	513	1683	Corndon Hill	31B	______
961	513	1682	An Staonach	13B	______
962	512	1680	Drumcroy Hill	5	______

No.	*Metres*	*Feet*	*Name*	*Section*	*Date*
963	512	1680	Larriston Fell	28B	______
964	512	1680	Maovally	16E	______
965	512	1680	Mellbreak	34B	______
966	512	1679	Ben Laga	18A	______
967	511	1678	Stronend	26	______
968	511	1676	Deuchary Hill	6B	______
969	511	1676	Foel Fenlli	30C	______
970	511	1676	Sron Smeur	4B	______
971	511	1675	Beinn Dubh	1C	______
972	511	1675	Kirkland Hill	27C	______
973	510	1674	Ben Dreavie	16E	______
974	510	1673	Creag Bhan	10D	______
975	510	1673	Dungavel Hill	27A	______
976	509	1670	Smean	16C	______
977	508	1667	Scrinadle	20A	______
978	508	1666	Beinn Leamhain	18B	______
979	508	1666	Cruach an Lochain	19C	______
980	507	1663	Meall Dheirgidh	15A	______
981	507	1662	Beinn Bhreac	19C	______
982	506	1661	Beinn Dhubh	24B	______
983	506	1660	Thorpe Fell Top	35B	______
984	505	1657	Little Mell Fell	34C	______
985	503	1649	Beinn na Croise	17E	______
986	501	1645	Black Hill	28A	______
987	501	1645	Glas Bheinn	3A	______
988	501	1644	Shillhope Law	33	______
989	501	1643	Carn a'Bhodaich	12B	______
990	499	1637	Kisdon	35A	______
991	499	1636	Garreg Lwyd	31B	______
992	498	1635	Creigh Hill	7	______
993	498	1634	Law Kneis	28B	______
994	497	1631	Griomaval	24A	______
995	497	1631	Sgurr na Stri	17B	______
996	497	1630	Innerdouny Hill	26	______

No.	Metres	Feet	Name	Section	Date
997	494	1621	Benaquhallie	21B	______
998	494	1620	Grayrigg Forest	34C	______
999	493	1619	Ruadh Stac	17B	______
1000	493	1618	Allermuir Hill	28A	______
1001	493	1617	Cairnsmore (Black Craig of Dee)	27B	______
1002	492	1615	Lamington Hill	28B	______
1003	492	1615	Liuthaid	24A	______
1004	492	1615	Meall Mor *	3C	______
1005	492	1615	Meall Mor	9A	______
1006	492	1614	Meall an Tarsaid	9B	______
1007	491	1612	Beinn Bheigier	20B	______
1008	491	1610	Carn Duchara	19A	______
1009	490	1607	Meall nan Each	18A	______
1010	489	1604	Healabhal Bheag	17A	______
1011	489	1603	Husival Mor	24B	______
1012	488	1602	Bryn Amlwg	31A	______
1013	488	1601	Slieau Freoaghane	29	______
1014	488	1600	Common Hill	27A	______
1015	487	1599	Pen y Garn-goch	31C	______
1016	487	1597	Baystones	34C	______
1017	487	1597	Creag Bheag	9B	______
1018	486	1595	Ysgyryd Fawr	32A	______
1019	486	1594	Carn nan Iomairean	12A	______
1020	486	1594	Creag Ghiubhais	7	______
1021	485	1592	Carleatheran	26	______
1022	485	1592	Creag Riabhach	16A	______
1023	485	1592	Steele's Knowe	26	______
1024	485	1590	Dubh Bheinn	20A	______
1025	485	1590	Garreg-hir	31A	______
1026	484	1587	Maiden Pap	16C	______
1027	483	1586	South Barrule	29	______
1028	482	1582	Bryn y Fan	31A	______
1029	481	1578	Dufton Pike	35A	______
1030	481	1578	Hirfynydd	32B	______

No.	Metres	Feet	Name	Section	Date
1031	481	1577	Ward Hill	23	______
1032	479	1572	Beinn Chlaonleud	18C	______
1033	479	1571	Carn na Dubh Choille	14B	______
1034	479	1570	Wether Law	28A	______
1035	478	1568	Mynydd Eppynt	32A	______
1036	477	1566	Gwastedyn Hill	31B	______
1037	477	1565	A'Bheinn Bhan	18B	______
1038	477	1565	Craignell	27B	______
1039	477	1565	Hail Storm Hill	36	______
1040	476	1562	Craiglich	21B	______
1041	476	1561	Beinn Sgeireach	16E	______
1042	473	1553	Beinn Donn	3B	______
1043	473	1552	Meall an Fhuarain	16B	______
1044	472	1550	Mynydd Twyn-glas	32C	______
1045	472	1549	Creag Dhubh Bheag	16B	______
1046	472	1548	Glas Bheinn	20B	______
1047	471	1546	Ben Aigan	21A	______
1048	471	1546	Cacra Hill	28B	______
1049	471	1545	Beinn Mhor	9A	______
1050	471	1545	Hill of Fare	21B	______
1051	471	1544	Healabhal Mhor	17A	______
1052	470	1542	Creachan Dubh	19C	______
1053	470	1542	Fell of Fleet	27B	______
1054	470	1542	Gormol	24A	______
1055	469	1540	Lingmoor Fell	34B	______
1056	469	1538	Mynydd Cwmcelli	30F	______
1057	468	1535	Spartleton	28A	______
1058	467	1532	An Grianan	16A	______
1059	467	1532	Beinn Bhreac	20A	______
1060	467	1531	Hill of Foudland	21B	______
1061	467	1531	Meall an t-Slamain	18B	______
1062	467	1531	Moel Gyw	30C	______
1063	466	1530	Bioda Buidhe	17A	______
1064	466	1530	Cruach Lusach	19B	______

No.	Metres	Feet	Name	Section	Date
1065	466	1530	Middlefield Law	27A	______
1066	466	1529	Beinn Sgluich	3B	______
1067	466	1529	Bidein Clann Raonaild	13B	______
1068	465	1526	Beinn Lagan	19C	______
1069	465	1526	Feinne-bheinn Mhor	16B	______
1070	465	1526	Meall na h-Eilrig	12B	______
1071	465	1525	Beinn na h-Uamha	18C	______
1072	464	1523	Esgair Ddu	31A	______
1073	464	1522	Benbeoch	27C	______
1074	464	1522	Tom Bailgeann	9B	______
1075	462	1516	Breac-Bheinn	15A	______
1076	462	1515	Crugiau Merched	31C	______
1077	461	1512	Beinn a'Bhraghad	17B	______
1078	461	1512	Bishop Hill	26	______
1079	460	1509	Drummond Hill	2B	______
1080	460	1508	Fashven	16A	______
1081	460	1508	Roineabhal	24B	______
1082	459	1506	Beinn Dubh Airigh	19A	______
1083	459	1506	Caer Caradoc Hill	38A	______
1084	458	1503	Cruach nan Caorach	19C	______
1085	458	1503	Tighvein	20C	______
1086	457	1499	Carn nam Bad	12B	______
1087	457	1499	Carn Fiaclach	11B	______
1088	456	1497	Winter Hill	36	______
1089	456	1496	Cairnharrow	27B	______
1090	456	1496	Lendrick Hill	26	______
1091	456	1495	Beinn na Duatharach	17E	______
1092	456	1495	Knock of Braemoray	9A	______
1093	455	1492	Craigowl Hill	26	______
1094	454	1490	Beinn an Tuirc	19B	______
1095	454	1490	Urra Moor - Round Hill	37	______
1096	454	1489	Freeholds Top	36	______
1097	453	1487	Beinn Conchra	12A	______
1098	452	1483	Auchtertyre Hill	12A	______

No.	Metres	Feet	Name	Section	Date
1099	452	1483	Heath Mynd	38A	______
1100	451	1481	Mendick Hill	28A	______
1101	451	1480	Aberedw Hill	31B	______
1102	451	1480	Cairn Hill	27C	______
1103	451	1480	Calkin Rig	28B	______
1104	450	1475	Ronas Hill	22	______
1105	449	1474	Cruach Scarba	20A	______
1106	449	1473	Caiteshal	24A	______
1107	449	1472	Hownam Law	28B	______
1108	448	1471	East Lomond	26	______
1109	448	1469	Cairn William	21B	______
1110	447	1467	Binsey	34A	______
1111	447	1467	Blackwood Hill	28B	______
1112	447	1466	Hill of Persie	6B	______
1113	446	1464	Cnoc Moy	19B	______
1114	446	1463	Beinn Lunndaidh	16D	______
1115	446	1463	Stac na Cathaig	9B	______
1116	445	1460	Beinn Bhreac	17B	______
1117	445	1460	Ben Lee	17A	______
1118	445	1460	Carneddau	31B	______
1119	444	1458	Speinne Mor	17E	______
1120	444	1457	Dun Caan	17A	______
1121	444	1456	Creag Ghlas Laggan	20C	______
1122	442	1450	Rhiw Gwraidd	31B	______
1123	441	1446	Beinn Bhreac	20A	______
1124	440	1444	Sgurr Bhuidhe	10D	______
1125	440	1444	Tosson Hill	33	______
1126	440	1443	Penycloddiau	30C	______
1127	439	1440	Roineval	17A	______
1128	439	1439	Beneraird	27B	______
1129	438	1436	Carn Dearg	19A	______
1130	437	1435	Beinn a'Chaisil	18C	______
1131	437	1435	Seana Mheallan	13B	______
1132	437	1433	Meall nan Con	18A	______

'he rocky summit of Tryfan (Section 30B), one of only six Marilyns in Wales over 3000 feet.

The summit of Stiperstones (Section 38A) is an attractive heathery ridge topped by several quartzite tors. (Photo: R.B.Evans)

Paragliding from near the top of Mynydd Troed (Section 32A). As this hill falls one metre short of 2000 feet, it seems to be more popular with paragliders than walkers. The hill on the far side of the valley is Mynydd Llangorse.

The easiest Marilyn - the summit of Bishop Wilton Wold (Region 37)

No.	Metres	Feet	Name	Section	Date
1133	435	1428	An Cruachan	17B	______
1134	435	1427	Cringle Moor - Drake Howe	37	______
1135	435	1427	Cuilags	23	______
1136	435	1427	Goseland Hill	28B	______
1137	434	1423	Cnoc an Liath-bhaid Mhoir	16D	______
1138	432	1417	Bogrie Hill	27C	______
1139	432	1416	Cruach nan Cuilean	19C	______
1140	430	1412	Knock Hill	21A	______
1141	430	1411	Conachair	25	______
1142	430	1411	Stac Gorm	9B	______
1143	429	1407	Sgorr nam Faoileann	20B	______
1144	429	1407	Suainaval	24A	______
1145	428	1404	Beinn na Lice	19B	______
1146	428	1404	Ord Ban	8	______
1147	427	1402	White Meldon	28A	______
1148	427	1400	Beinn Dearg	1C	______
1149	426	1399	Broomy Law	28A	______
1150	426	1397	Hergest Ridge	38B	______
1151	425	1394	Worcestershire Beacon	38B	______
1152	424	1392	Beinn na Drise	17E	______
1153	424	1391	Muaithabhal	24A	______
1154	424	1391	Rubers Law	28B	______
1155	423	1389	Edmund's Tump *	32A	______
1156	423	1389	Meigle Hill	28A	______
1157	423	1388	Low Fell	34B	______
1158	422	1385	Braigh na h-Eaglaise	16C	______
1159	422	1385	Eildon Mid Hill *	28B	______
1160	422	1385	Meall Meadhonach	16B	______
1161	422	1383	Cnoc a'Bhaile-shios	19B	______
1162	420	1378	Beinn Ghlas	19A	______
1163	420	1378	Meall an Doirein	13A	______
1164	420	1377	Brown Willy	40	______
1165	418	1373	Dumyat	26	______
1166	418	1373	The Sneug	22	______

No.	Metres	Feet	Name	Section	Date
1167	418	1370	Mynydd Marchywel	32B	______
1168	417	1368	Beinn Dubhain	16C	______
1169	417	1368	Fell Hill	27C	______
1170	417	1367	Beinn na Greine	17A	______
1171	416	1364	Meadie Ridge	16B	______
1172	415	1363	The Begwns	31B	______
1173	415	1362	Cademuir Hill	28B	______
1174	415	1362	Cruach Tairbeirt	1D	______
1175	415	1360	Trichrug	32B	______
1176	414	1358	Beinn a'Mheadhoin	11A	______
1177	414	1358	Strathfinella Hill	7	______
1178	413	1355	Beinn Bhuidhe	17E	______
1179	413	1355	Ben Tianavaig	17A	______
1180	412	1353	Creag Loisgte	15A	______
1181	410	1345	Beinn a'Chaoinich	10A	______
1182	410	1345	Mile Hill	7	______
1183	409	1342	Millstone Hill	21B	______
1184	409	1341	Beinn Bhac-ghlais	17A	______
1185	408	1338	Ben Hutig	16B	______
1186	408	1338	Long Mountain - Beacon Ring	31B	______
1187	407	1336	Creag nan Clag	9B	______
1188	407	1335	Blaeloch Hill	27A	______
1189	407	1335	Creag Mhor	12A	______
1190	407	1334	The Wrekin	38A	______
1191	406	1332	Guainemol	24A	______
1192	405	1329	Creag Thoraraidh	16C	______
1193	405	1329	Druim Fada	17E	______
1194	405	1329	Foel Offrwm	30D	______
1195	404	1324	Birnam Hill - King's Seat	1A	______
1196	404	1324	Moel y Golfa	31B	______
1197	403	1322	Meall Lochan a'Chleirich	13A	______
1198	402	1320	Ilkley Moor	35B	______
1199	402	1319	Cnoc na Maoile	16C	______
1200	402	1319	Craigendarroch	21A	______

No.	Metres	Feet	Name	Section	Date
1201	401	1316	Duncolm	26	______
1202	400	1312	Craig of Monievreckie *	1C	______
1203	399	1310	Knap of Trowieglen	23	______
1204	398	1307	Dirrington Great Law	28A	______
1205	398	1306	Bennan	27C	______
1206	398	1305	Bleaval	24B	______
1207	397	1303	Beinn Mheadhonach	24A	______
1208	397	1302	Sgreadan Hill	19B	______
1209	397	1301	Cnoc Corr Guinie	15B	______
1210	397	1301	Glas Bheinn	10A	______
1211	396	1300	Easington Fell	36	______
1212	396	1298	Mullach na Carn	17C	______
1213	395	1296	Bad a'Chreamha	13B	______
1214	395	1295	Frenni Fawr	31C	______
1215	393	1290	Allt yr Esgair	32A	______
1216	393	1290	An Sgurr	17D	______
1217	393	1290	Torlum	1B	______
1218	392	1287	Sithean Bhealaich Chumhaing	17A	______
1219	392	1286	An Sgurr	13B	______
1220	392	1285	Bishop Forest Hill	27C	______
1221	391	1284	Bradnor Hill	38B	______
1222	391	1283	Bengairn	27C	______
1223	390	1280	Meall Innis an Loichel	12B	______
1224	389	1276	An Coileach	24B	______
1225	388	1273	Hallin Fell	34C	______
1226	387	1271	Creag nam Fiadh	16D	______
1227	385	1264	Gun	36	______
1228	385	1264	Mynydd y Lan	32C	______
1229	385	1263	The Slate	19B	______
1230	384	1261	Wills Neck	41	______
1231	384	1260	Heileasbhal Mor	24B	______
1232	384	1259	Mullach an Eilein *	25	______
1233	383	1257	Biod Mor	17B	______
1234	383	1257	Deadh Choimhead	19A	______

No.	*Metres*	*Feet*	*Name*	*Section*	*Date*
1235	383	1257	Pibble Hill	27B	______
1236	383	1255	Heaval	24D	______
1237	382	1254	Moel y Dyniewyd	30B	______
1238	382	1253	Cefn Eglwysilan	32C	______
1239	381	1250	Bryn Arw	32A	______
1240	381	1250	Mynydd y Glyn	32C	______
1241	381	1249	Hill of Tillymorgan	21B	______
1242	380	1247	Cruach na Seilcheig	19A	______
1243	380	1246	Cnoc an t-Sabhail	15B	______
1244	380	1246	Foel Cae'rberllan	30F	______
1245	379	1243	Dumglow	26	______
1246	378	1241	Cairn-mon-earn	7	______
1247	378	1240	Kearnaval	24A	______
1248	378	1239	Cnoc Glas	25	______
1249	377	1236	Beinn Chreagach	17E	______
1250	377	1236	King's Seat	26	______
1251	376	1232	Corse Hill	27A	______
1252	376	1232	Cruachan Min	17E	______
1253	375	1230	High Vinnalls	38B	______
1254	374	1228	Stulaval	24C	______
1255	374	1227	Uisenis	24A	______
1256	374	1226	Mynydd y Betws	32B	______
1257	373	1225	Struie	15B	______
1258	372	1220	Knockan	21A	______
1259	371	1218	Carn Fadryn	30A	______
1260	371	1217	Ben Garrisdale	20A	______
1261	371	1216	Sgribhis-bheinn	16A	______
1262	370	1215	Carn Faire nan Con	12A	______
1263	370	1214	Foel Fynyddau	32C	______
1264	370	1214	Meall a'Chaise	16D	______
1265	369	1210	Arnaval	17B	______
1266	368	1208	A'Chruach	19A	______
1267	368	1207	Chaipaval	24B	______
1268	366	1202	Bengray	27B	______

No.	Metres	Feet	Name	Section	Date
1269	366	1202	Garway Hill	38B	______
1270	366	1200	Meikle Balloch Hill	21A	______
1271	364	1195	Sgarbh Breac	20B	______
1272	362	1188	Mynydd Machen	32C	______
1273	362	1187	An Socach	16A	______
1274	361	1185	Conic Hill	1C	______
1275	361	1183	Hafod Ithel	31C	______
1276	361	1183	The Fruin *	1E	______
1277	359	1179	Dun Leacainn	19A	______
1278	358	1175	Burrow	38A	______
1279	358	1175	Stingwern Hill	31A	______
1280	358	1173	Mynydd Uchaf	32B	______
1281	357	1172	Wauk Hill	27C	______
1282	357	1171	Sharp Haw	35B	______
1283	357	1170	High Rigg	34C	______
1284	357	1170	Triuirebheinn	24C	______
1285	356	1169	Allt y Main	30E	______
1286	356	1168	Benarty Hill	26	______
1287	356	1167	Cnoc an Daimh Mor	16B	______
1288	355	1164	Caeliber Isaf	31B	______
1289	354	1161	Belling Hill	28B	______
1290	354	1160	Beinn Ghuilean	19B	______
1291	352	1155	Long Barrow	34B	______
1292	352	1155	Upper Park *	31A	______
1293	350	1148	Longridge Fell	36	______
1294	350	1147	Na Maoilean	3B	______
1295	349	1144	Beinn Domhnaill	16D	______
1296	347	1139	Eaval	24C	______
1297	347	1138	Mynydd Carningli	31C	______
1298	346	1135	Ben Meabost	17B	______
1299	346	1135	Creag a'Ghobhair	16D	______
1300	344	1130	Beinn na Seilg	18A	______
1301	344	1130	White Top of Culreoch	27B	______
1302	344	1128	Fourman Hill	21A	______

No.	Metres	Feet	Name	Section	Date
1303	343	1125	The Cloud	36	______
1304	341	1119	Mynydd-y-briw	30E	______
1305	341	1119	Y Golfa	30E	______
1306	340	1115	Sgorr an Fharaidh	17D	______
1307	339	1113	Mynydd Allt-y-grug	32B	______
1308	339	1111	Brown Muir	9A	______
1309	338	1109	Ailsa Craig	27B	______
1310	338	1109	Lambrigg Fell	34D	______
1311	338	1109	Maol Ban	17E	______
1312	336	1102	Cipeagil Bheag	24A	______
1313	336	1102	Meall nan Clach Ruadha	16C	______
1314	335	1100	Loughrigg Fell	34B	______
1315	335	1100	Top o'Selside	34D	______
1316	334	1096	Callow Hill	38A	______
1317	334	1096	Kit Hill	40	______
1318	333	1093	Ben Tangaval	24D	______
1319	333	1092	Lowick High Common	34D	______
1320	332	1089	Cruach nam Fearna	19A	______
1321	332	1089	Ghlas-bheinn	16A	______
1322	331	1086	Creachan Mor	17E	______
1323	330	1083	Cleeve Hill	39	______
1324	330	1083	Hope Mountain	30C	______
1325	329	1080	Wapley Hill	38B	______
1326	329	1079	Mynydd Cynros	31C	______
1327	329	1078	Gisborough Moor	37	______
1328	328	1075	Beinn Chreagach	17A	______
1329	327	1074	Beinn Bhreac	17A	______
1330	327	1073	Feirihisval	24A	______
1331	327	1073	Rhos Ymryson	31C	______
1332	326	1070	Pen-crug-melyn *	31C	______
1333	326	1070	Shobdon Hill	38B	______
1334	325	1066	Beacon Batch	41	______
1335	323	1059	Meall Dola	16D	______
1336	321	1054	Cnoc an t-Sabhail	15B	______

No.	Metres	Feet	Name	Section	Date
1337	321	1054	Gummer's How	34D	______
1338	321	1053	View Edge	38A	______
1339	320	1051	Bin of Cullen	21A	______
1340	319	1048	Beinn Bhan	19A	______
1341	319	1047	Grange Fell	28B	______
1342	319	1047	Long Crag	33	______
1343	319	1046	Hill of the Wangie	9A	______
1344	317	1041	Newtyle Hill	6B	______
1345	317	1040	Holm Fell	34D	______
1346	317	1040	Mochrum Fell	27C	______
1347	315	1035	Staple Hill	41	______
1348	315	1034	Ros Hill	33	______
1349	315	1034	Walton Hill	39	______
1350	314	1031	Cnoc nam Broighleag	19A	______
1351	314	1030	Black Hill	28A	______
1352	314	1030	Mullach Mor	20C	______
1353	314	1029	Ben Bowie	1E	______
1354	313	1028	Biod an Athair	17A	______
1355	313	1027	Ffridd Cocyn	30F	______
1356	313	1026	Beinn Chreagach	17E	______
1357	312	1025	Hensbarrow Beacon *	40	______
1358	312	1023	Cairnpapple Hill	28A	______
1359	309	1013	Wentwood	32C	______
1360	308	1012	Selworthy Beacon	41	______
1361	308	1012	Sron Romul	24B	______
1362	308	1010	Beinn Lora	3B	______
1363	307	1007	Garth Hill	32C	______
1364	304	999	Mynydd Rhiw	30A	______
1365	304	997	Mullach Mor	17D	______
1366	303	994	Cnoc an Ime	20A	______
1367	303	993	Tom an t-Saighdeir	19A	______
1368	301	988	Beinn nan Carn	17C	______
1369	299	981	Sgorach Breac	17C	______
1370	299	980	Bredon Hill	39	______

No.	Metres	Feet	Name	Section	Date
1371	297	975	Grey Hill	27B	______
1372	297	974	Walbury Hill	42	______
1373	297	973	Periton Hill	41	______
1374	296	972	An Cuaidh	13A	______
1375	296	971	Cruach na Seilcheig	20A	______
1376	296	971	May Hill	38B	______
1377	296	971	Troweir Hill	27B	______
1378	295	969	Cruachan-Glen Vic Askill	17A	______
1379	295	968	'S Airde Beinn	17E	______
1380	295	968	Leith Hill	42	______
1381	294	965	Burton Hill	38B	______
1382	294	965	Gamallt	30F	______
1383	294	965	Meall an Fhithich *	19A	______
1384	293	962	Royl Field	22	______
1385	292	959	Myarth	32A	______
1386	292	959	Sgurr na h-Iolaire	17C	______
1387	292	958	Beinn Mholach	24A	______
1388	292	958	Cruach Doir'an Raoigh *	10D	______
1389	290	952	Largo Law	26	______
1390	290	951	Ruardean Hill	38B	______
1391	288	945	Long Knoll	41	______
1392	288	944	Beinn Akie	16A	______
1393	288	944	Druim na h-Earba *	4A	______
1394	287	943	Brown Carrick Hill	27A	______
1395	287	942	Bainloch Hill	27C	______
1396	285	936	Norman's Law	26	______
1397	285	935	Saxa Vord	22	______
1398	284	933	Mynydd Sylen	32B	______
1399	284	932	Meall a'Mhaoil	17B	______
1400	284	931	Ben Geary	17A	______
1401	283	930	Fitful Head	22	______
1402	282	926	Linton Hill	28B	______
1403	281	922	Roineval	24A	______
1404	281	922	Scalla Field	22	______

No.	Metres	Feet	Name	Section	Date
1405	281	922	South Lee	24C	______
1406	280	920	Beinn Ruigh Choinnich	24C	______
1407	280	920	Greabhal	24B	______
1408	280	920	Sgurr nan Caorach	17C	______
1409	280	919	Black Down	42	______
1410	279	915	Garn Boduan	30A	______
1411	279	915	Knock of Crieff	1A	______
1412	278	913	Windy Hill	19C	______
1413	278	912	Bardon Hill	39	______
1414	277	910	Hill of Garvock	7	______
1415	277	910	Win Green	41	______
1416	277	908	Pilsdon Pen	41	______
1417	275	901	Mid Hill	23	______
1418	275	901	Tom nam Fitheach	17E	______
1419	274	899	Craig yr Allt	32C	______
1420	274	899	Hutton Roof Crags	34D	______
1421	273	896	Carnan	24D	______
1422	272	893	Mynydd Drumau	32B	______
1423	270	887	Butser Hill	42	______
1424	270	885	Claife Heights	34D	______
1425	269	883	Cnoc Mor	15B	______
1426	269	883	Seager Hill	38B	______
1427	267	877	Ben Raah	24B	______
1428	267	877	Housedon Hill	33	______
1429	267	876	Haddington Hill	39	______
1430	267	875	Botley Hill	42	______
1431	266	874	Brimmond Hill	21B	______
1432	265	871	Knockdolian	27B	______
1433	265	870	Cnoc Reamhar	19B	______
1434	265	869	Beinn a'Bhaillidh	18A	______
1435	263	864	Ardsheal Hill	3B	______
1436	263	863	Ward of Scousburgh	22	______
1437	262	861	Mynydd Llangyndeyrn	32B	______
1438	262	860	North Lee	24C	______

No.	Metres	Feet	Name	Section	Date
1439	262	858	Moel-y-gest	30A	______
1440	261	857	Christ Cross *	40	______
1441	258	846	Woodhead Hill	27C	______
1442	256	841	Mount Eagle	15B	______
1443	256	840	Arnaval	24C	______
1444	256	840	Conostom	24A	______
1445	256	840	Torr Achilty	12A	______
1446	254	833	Beinn na h-Iolaire	17A	______
1447	254	833	Watch Hill	34A	______
1448	254	832	Burgiehill	9A	______
1449	252	828	Carnmenellis	40	______
1450	252	828	White Downs	40	______
1451	252	827	Cruach Lerags	19A	______
1452	252	827	Dalescord Hill	22	______
1453	252	827	Grendon Green	38B	______
1454	252	826	Turin Hill	26	______
1455	251	822	Arthur's Seat	28A	______
1456	250	821	Blotchnie Fiold	23	______
1457	250	820	Hightown Hill	27C	______
1458	249	817	Sandness Hill	22	______
1459	248	814	Sleiteachal Mhor	24A	______
1460	248	814	The Noup	22	______
1461	248	813	Ditchling Beacon	42	______
1462	248	813	Muirneag	24A	______
1463	248	812	Carn Ban	17E	______
1464	246	807	Bishop Wilton Wold	37	______
1465	243	797	Easaval	24C	______
1466	240	788	Crowborough	42	______
1467	240	787	Beinn Bhreac	18A	______
1468	240	787	See Morris Hill	27C	______
1469	240	786	St Boniface Down	42	______
1470	238	782	Chanctonbury Hill *	42	______
1471	235	770	Carneddol	30A	______
1472	234	768	Waughton Hill	21B	______

No.	Metres	Feet	Name	Section	Date
1473	233	764	Dundry Down *	41	______
1474	232	760	Beinn Tart a'Mhill	20B	______
1475	231	758	Muncaster Fell	34D	______
1476	230	756	Bradda Hill	29	______
1477	230	756	Marrival	24C	______
1478	228	749	Cairnie Hill *	26	______
1479	228	748	Caultrashal Mor	24A	______
1480	227	745	Raw Head	36	______
1481	226	740	Ward of Bressay	22	______
1482	225	738	Wideford Hill	23	______
1483	224	735	Milldoe - Mid Tooin	23	______
1484	223	732	Moncreiffe Hill	26	______
1485	221	726	Mount Hill	26	______
1486	221	724	Keelylang Hill	23	______
1487	220	722	Holyhead Mountain	30A	______
1488	217	713	Firle Beacon	42	______
1489	217	713	Seaforth Island	24A	______
1490	217	712	Ward Hill	22	______
1491	216	709	Scrae Field	22	______
1492	216	708	Valla Field	22	______
1493	215	706	Whitbarrow	34D	______
1494	214	702	Wilmington Hill *	42	______
1495	214	701	Brightstone Down	42	______
1496	210	690	Carn a'Ghaill	17D	______
1497	210	690	Hill of Arisdale	22	______
1498	207	679	Great Orme	30C	______
1499	207	678	Cairn Galtar	24D	______
1500	207	678	Hardown Hill	41	______
1501	206	676	Ben Cliad	24D	______
1502	205	673	Brandy Hill	31C	______
1503	205	673	Forsnaval	24A	______
1504	203	667	Meall an Fheadain	16F	______
1505	203	665	Hill of Nigg *	15B	______
1506	202	662	Beinn Mhor	20B	______

No.	*Metres*	*Feet*	*Name*	*Section*	*Date*
1507	201	661	Roneval	24C	______
1508	200	656	North Downs	42	______
1509	197	646	Sgurr na Dubh-chreige *	10D	______
1510	196	644	Stac an Armin	25	______
1511	196	642	Beinn a'Charnain	24C	______
1512	194	637	Beinn Mhor	19A	______
1513	193	633	Sotan *	24D	______
1514	191	627	Beinn Bhreac	24A	______
1515	190	624	Beinn Mhor	24C	______
1516	190	624	Heishival Mor	24D	______
1517	189	620	Carn Breugach	19A	______
1518	187	613	North Berwick Law	28A	______
1519	185	607	Ben Scrien	24C	______
1520	182	596	Cairn Pat	27B	______
1521	181	594	Noss Head	22	______
1522	181	593	Airds Hill	3B	______
1523	180	590	Crogary Mor	24C	______
1524	179	587	Billinge Hill	36	______
1525	178	584	Yr Arwydd *	30A	______
1526	178	583	Bioda Mor *	25	______
1527	176	577	Cunnigill Hill	22	______
1528	173	567	White Grunafirth	22	______
1529	172	565	Mid Ward	22	______
1530	172	564	Stac Lee	25	______
1531	171	561	The Hoe	24D	______
1532	170	558	Cruachan Charna	18C	______
1533	169	555	Fitty Hill	23	______
1534	169	554	Mull Hill	29	______
1535	168	550	The Wolds *	37	______
1536	167	548	Mynydd Enlli	30A	______
1537	164	538	Cliffe Hill	42	______
1538	160	525	Mullach Buidhe *	24A	______
1539	159	522	Vord Hill	22	______
1540	155	509	Gometra	17E	______

No.	*Metres*	*Feet*	*Name*	*Section*	*Date*
1541	154	504	Crogary na Hoe	24C	______
1542	153	503	Muldoanich	24D	______

Chapter 5

The Absolute Summits of England and Wales

This chapter is a concession to those walkers who are still resolutely attached to the concept of absolute height rather than relative height. It lists all the summits in England and Wales that are over 2000 feet high (610 metres) and have a drop of at least thirty metres (about one hundred feet) on all sides. There are 319 of these summits, 107 of which are also Marilyns. This list was originally compiled because none of the existing lists of this kind were wholly satisfactory, as discussed in Chapter 1. The recent publication of the books by Nuttall & Nuttall has improved matters, but they still include a large number of relatively boring tops which in my opinion do not merit a detour from a path or ridge. By using a measure of thirty metres, most of these insignificant tops have been excluded. Some of the summits that are listed here may also be regarded as insignificant, but as they are all at least 2000 feet above sea level they should have the terrain and weather conditions associated with high ground, even if they do not necessarily provide interesting walks or good viewpoints.

No attempt has been made to compile a similar list of hills in Scotland. The Donalds (see Chapter 1) cover Southern Scotland, but in the Scottish highlands there is such a large area of land above 2000 feet that the measure of a mere 100 feet of re-ascent is just not appropriate. By contrast, England and Wales contain relatively small areas of land over 2000 feet high, so it is not surprising that many writers and walkers try to make the most of them.

Another problem with the 2000-foot summits in England and Wales is their lack of a convincing and commonly accepted collective name. It sounds pretty silly to try to apply the term 'Bridges' or 'Marshes' to a set of hills. In the computer industry the usual method of inventing a new name is to construct a word from the initial letters of the description of a product (an acronym). Applying this tactic to the Summits in Wales and England Above Two-thousand FEET seems to give an appropriate result, which can be conveniently abbreviated to 'Sweats'. This new terminology will be used in the rest of this chapter.

In order to determine which hills to include in the list of Sweats, a similar strategy to that used for the Marilyns has been applied. Any summit surrounded by four or more ten-metre contour lines is automatically included, any summit with only one or two ten-metre contours is excluded, while summits with exactly three ten-metre contours have been studied in more detail, and are included if there is a reasonable doubt about whether they should qualify for inclusion. In practice this means that a few of the summits may have only twenty-five to twenty-nine metres of re-ascent, but it seems best to include them in case the Ordnance Survey manage to find an extra metre or two on future editions of the relevant maps!

The hills are listed in the same style used for the Marilyns in Chapters 3 and 4, by region and then by height. The number refers to the Marilyn number (if any), a star indicates that a name is not marked on the Landranger map, and a blank column has again been included for entering the date of each ascent.

The same region and section numbers are used as for the Marilyns. There are two slight anomalies in the allocation of summits to these regions: Gragareth is geographically part of the Northern Pennines (Region 35), but is included in Region 36 because it is the highest point in Lancashire and therefore qualifies as a County Top (see Chapter 6). Similarly, it would be more natural to list the summit known as Black Mountain in Region 32 (South Wales) along with other summits in the Black Mountains, but it is assigned to Region 38 because it is the highest point in the county of Hereford & Worcester. The summit of Snaefell (Region 29) has been omitted because the Isle of Man does not appear to be part of England or Wales.

The Sweats by Region

REGION 30
North Wales

Section 30B Snowdonia

No.	Metres	Feet	Name	Map	Grid Ref		Date
43	1085	3560	Snowdon - Yr Wyddfa	115	SH	609544	______
-	1065	3495	Crib-y-Ddysgl	115	SH	611552	______
57	1064	3490	Carnedd Llewelyn	115	SH	684644	______
-	1044	3424	Carnedd Dafydd	115	SH	663631	______
112	999	3279	Glyder Fawr	115	SH	642579	______
-	994	3262	Glyder Fach	115	SH	656583	______
-	978	3210	Pen yr Ole Wen	115	SH	656619	______
-	976	3202	Foel Grach	115	SH	689659	______
-	962	3156	Yr Elen	115	SH	674651	______
169	947	3107	Y Garn	115	SH	631596	______
-	942	3091	Foel-fras	115	SH	696682	______
-	926	3037	Garnedd Uchaf	115	SH	687669	______
202	923	3029	Elidir Fawr	115	SH	612613	______
-	923	3027	Crib Goch	115	SH	624552	______
215	915	3002	Tryfan	115	SH	664594	______
240	898	2946	Y Lliwedd	115	SH	622533	______
283	872	2861	Moel Siabod	115	SH	705546	______
-	849	2785	Llwytmor	115	SH	689692	______
-	833	2733	Pen yr Helgi Du	115	SH	698630	______
-	831	2727	Foel-goch	115	SH	628612	______
-	822	2696	Carnedd y Filiast	115	SH	620628	______
-	805	2642	Y Foel Goch	115	SH	678582	______
395	799	2622	Pen Llithrig y Wrach	115	SH	716623	______
-	794	2604	Bera Mawr	115	SH	675683	______
424	782	2566	Moel Hebog	115	SH	565469	______
448	770	2527	Moelwyn Mawr	124	SH	658449	______
-	770	2526	Drum	115	SH	708696	______
-	763	2503	Gallt yr Ogof	115	SH	685586	______

No.	Metres	Feet	Name	Map	Grid Ref		Date
-	758	2487	Drosgl	115	SH	664680	______
487	747	2451	Yr Aran	115	SH	604515	______
516	734	2408	Craig Cwm Silyn	115	SH	525503	______
536	726	2382	Moel Eilio	115	SH	556577	______
-	711	2333	Moelwyn Bach	124	SH	660437	______
572	709	2326	Trum y Ddysgl	115	SH	545516	______
599	698	2290	Allt Fawr	115	SH	682475	______
602	698	2290	Mynydd Mawr	115	SH	539547	______
-	695	2280	Mynydd Drws-y-coed	115	SH	549518	______
-	689	2262	Cnicht	115	SH	645466	______
633	678	2224	Creigiau Gleision	115	SH	729615	______
-	676	2217	Moel Druman	115	SH	671476	______
644	674	2210	Moel Cynghorion	115	SH	586564	______
-	672	2204	Ysgafell Wen	115	SH	667481	______
-	669	2195	Ysgafell Wen - North Top	115	SH	663485	______
-	655	2148	Moel yr Ogof	115	SH	556478	______
-	653	2142	Mynydd Tal-y-mignedd	115	SH	535514	______
-	648	2125	Moel-yr-hydd	115	SH	672454	______
-	638	2094	Moel Lefn	115	SH	553485	______
-	634	2080	Creigiau Gleision - North Top	115	SH	734622	______
-	629	2063	Foel Gron	115	SH	560569	______
755	610	2000	Tal y Fan	115	SH	729727	______

Section 30D Barmouth to Betws-y-Coed and Bala

No.	Metres	Feet	Name	Map	Grid Ref		Date
312	854	2801	Arenig Fawr	124/125	SH	827369	______
474	756	2480	Y Llethr	124	SH	661258	______
480	751	2464	Moel Llyfnant	124/125	SH	808352	______
-	750	2462	Diffwys	124	SH	661234	______
518	734	2408	Rhobell Fawr	124	SH	787257	______
548	720	2362	Rhinog Fawr	124	SH	657290	______
-	712	2335	Rhinog Fach	124	SH	665270	______
615	689	2259	Arenig Fach	124/125	SH	821416	______
651	669	2196	Carnedd y Filiast	124/125	SH	871446	______
-	662	2172	Dduallt	124/125	SH	811274	______
674	661	2168	Manod Mawr	124	SH	724447	______

No.	Metres	Feet	Name	Map	Grid Ref		Date
-	658	2158	Manod Mawr - North Top	115	SH	727458	______
-	643	2109	Llechwedd-llyfn	124/125	SH	857445	______
718	629	2063	Y Garn	124	SH	702230	______
-	623	2044	Moel Penamnen	115	SH	716483	______
724	623	2044	Moel Ysgyfarnogod	124	SH	658346	______
-	619	2031	Foel Boeth - Gallt y Daren	124	SH	779345	______
-	614	2014	Foel Penolau	124	SH	661348	______
750	611	2004	Foel Goch	125	SH	953423	______

Section 30E Bala to Welshpool

No.	Metres	Feet	Name	Map	Grid Ref		Date
229	905	2970	Aran Fawddwy	124/125	SH	863224	______
-	885	2904	Aran Benllyn	124/125	SH	867243	______
-	872	2860	Erw y Ddafad-ddu *	124/125	SH	865234	______
342	830	2723	Cadair Berwyn	125	SJ	071323	______
-	827	2712	Moel Sych	125	SJ	066318	______
-	785	2575	Cadair Bronwen	125	SJ	077346	______
430	779	2557	Glasgwm	124/125	SH	837194	______
-	691	2266	Foel Wen	125	SJ	099334	______
-	689	2260	Foel Hafod-fynydd *	124/125	SH	877227	______
-	685	2248	Gwaun y Llwyni *	124/125	SH	857205	______
-	685	2247	Pen y Brynfforchog *	124/125	SH	818179	______
-	681	2233	Mynydd Tarw	125	SJ	113324	______
650	671	2201	Foel Rhudd - Esgeiriau Gwynion	124/125	SH	889236	______
659	667	2188	Cyrniau Nod	125	SH	988279	______
-	665	2181	Post Gwyn	125	SJ	048294	______
-	648	2125	Foel Cwm Sian Llwyd	125	SH	996314	______
-	646	2120	Pen y Boncyn Trefeilw	125	SH	963283	______
-	630	2066	Moel Fferna	125	SJ	116398	______
-	626	2054	Foel y Geifr	125	SH	937275	______
-	625	2049	Moel y Cerrig Duon	125	SH	923242	______
-	621	2037	Pen Bwlch Llandrillo Top *	125	SJ	089369	______
-	620	2034	Pen yr Allt Uchaf *	124/125	SH	871197	______
-	614	2013	Llechwedd Du *	124/125	SH	894224	______
-	613	2010	Foel Goch	125	SH	943291	______

Section 30F Dolgellau to Machynlleth

No.	Metres	Feet	Name	Map	Grid Ref		Date
249	893	2929	Cadair Idris - Penygadair	124	SH	711130	______
-	863	2830	Mynydd Moel	124	SH	727137	______
-	811	2660	Cyfrwy *	124	SH	704133	______
-	791	2595	Craig Cwm Amarch	124	SH	711121	______
-	683	2240	Gau Graig	124	SH	744141	______
643	675	2213	Maesglase - Maen Du	124/125	SH	823152	______
-	670	2197	Waun-oer	124	SH	786148	______
657	667	2189	Tarren y Gesail	124	SH	711059	______
-	661	2168	Craig-las (Tyrrau Mawr)	124	SH	677135	______
-	659	2161	Cribin Fawr	124	SH	795153	______
713	634	2080	Tarrenhendre	135	SH	683041	______
-	622	2040	Craig-y-llyn	124	SH	665119	______

REGION 31
Mid Wales and Pembrokeshire

Section 31A Aberystwyth to Welshpool

No.	Metres	Feet	Name	Map	Grid Ref		Date
479	752	2467	Plynlimon - Pen Pumlumon Fawr	135	SN	789869	______
-	741	2430	Pen Pumlumon Arwystli	135/136	SN	815877	______
-	727	2385	Plynlimon - East Top	135	SN	799872	______
-	684	2245	Y Garn	135	SN	776852	______

Section 31B Welshpool to Hay-on-Wye

No.	Metres	Feet	Name	Map	Grid Ref		Date
675	660	2166	Great Rhos	148	SO	182639	______
-	650	2132	Black Mixen	148	SO	196644	______
-	610	2001	Bache Hill	148	SO	214636	______

Section 31C South-West Wales

No.	Metres	Feet	Name	Map	Grid Ref		Date
699	645	2115	Drygarn Fawr	147	SN	862584	______
-	613	2010	Gorllwyn	147	SN	918591	______
752	610	2002	Pen y Garn	135	SN	798771	______

REGION 32
South Wales

Section 32A Llandovery to Monmouth

No.	Metres	Feet	Name	Map	Grid Ref		Date
260	886	2906	Pen y Fan	160	SO	012216	______
-	873	2863	Corn Du	160	SO	007213	______
368	811	2660	Waun Fach	161	SO	215300	______
390	802	2630	Fan Brycheiniog	160	SN	825218	______
-	800	2624	Pen y Gadair Fawr	161	SO	229287	______
-	795	2608	Cribyn	160	SO	024213	______
452	769	2523	Waun Rydd	160	SO	062206	______
-	761	2496	Fan Hir	160	SN	831209	______
-	749	2457	Bannau Sir Gaer (Picws Du)	160	SN	812218	______
514	734	2409	Fan Fawr	160	SN	970193	______
537	725	2379	Fan Gyhirych	160	SN	881191	______
-	719	2360	Pen Allt-mawr	161	SO	207243	______
-	719	2358	Fan y Big	160	SO	036207	______
-	701	2300	Pen Cerrig-calch	161	SO	217223	______
-	690	2263	Twmpa	161	SO	225350	______
-	679	2228	Chwarel y Fan	161	SO	258294	______
670	663	2175	Fan Nedd	160	SN	913184	______
-	663	2174	Mynydd Llysiau	161	SO	207279	______
-	654	2145	Allt Lwyd	160	SO	079189	______
-	635	2083	Garreg Las	160	SN	777203	______
-	632	2072	Fan Llia	160	SN	938186	______
-	629	2065	Craig Cerrig-gleisiad	160	SN	961218	______
-	629	2063	Fan Frynych	160	SN	958228	______
-	619	2030	Moel Gornach (Garreg Lwyd)	160	SN	741179	______
739	617	2024	Cefn yr Ystrad	160	SO	087137	______

REGION 33
The Scottish Border to the River Tyne

No.	Metres	Feet	Name	Map	Grid Ref		Date
359	815	2674	The Cheviot	74/75	NT	909205	______
558	714	2342	Hedgehope Hill	80	NT	943197	______
-	652	2138	Comb Fell	80	NT	924187	______
-	619	2032	Windy Gyle	80	NT	855152	______
741	616	2020	Cushat Law	80	NT	928137	______
-	610	2001	Bloodybush Edge	80	NT	902143	______

REGION 34
The Lake District

Section 34A Northern Fells

No.	Metres	Feet	Name	Map	Grid Ref		Date
191	931	3054	Skiddaw	89/90	NY	260290	______
287	868	2847	Blencathra	90	NY	323277	______
-	865	2837	Little Man	89/90	NY	266278	______
-	746	2446	Carl Side	89/90	NY	254280	______
-	734	2408	Long Side	89/90	NY	248284	______
-	715	2345	Lonscale Fell	89/90	NY	285271	______
567	710	2329	Knott	89/90	NY	296329	______
-	702	2303	Bowscale Fell	90	NY	333305	______
-	690	2265	Great Calva	89/90	NY	290311	______
-	683	2240	Bannerdale Crags	90	NY	335290	______
-	660	2165	Carrock Fell	90	NY	341336	______
-	658	2159	High Pike	90	NY	318350	______

Section 34B Central and Western Fells

No.	Metres	Feet	Name	Map	Grid Ref		Date
138	978	3210	Scafell Pike	89/90	NY	215072	______
150	964	3162	Scafell	89/90	NY	206064	______
-	935	3067	Ill Crag	89/90	NY	223073	______
-	934	3063	Broad Crag	89/90	NY	218075	______
-	910	2984	Great End	89/90	NY	226084	______

No.	Metres	Feet	Name	Map	Grid Ref		Date
-	902	2960	Bowfell	89/90	NY	244064	______
239	899	2949	Great Gable	89/90	NY	211103	______
250	892	2927	Pillar	89/90	NY	171120	______
-	885	2903	Esk Pike	89/90	NY	236075	______
-	859	2817	Crinkle Crags - Long Top	89/90	NY	248048	______
314	852	2795	Grasmoor	89/90	NY	174203	______
-	841	2760	Little Scoat Fell *	89	NY	159113	______
-	839	2753	Crag Hill	89/90	NY	192203	______
-	834	2735	Crinkle Crags - South Top	89/90	NY	249045	______
-	828	2716	Pillar - South-west Top	89	NY	166117	______
-	826	2710	Red Pike	89	NY	165106	______
-	815	2673	Shelter Crags	89/90	NY	249053	______
-	807	2649	Lingmell	89/90	NY	209081	______
377	807	2648	High Stile	89	NY	170148	______
389	802	2631	Kirk Fell	89/90	NY	194104	______
-	801	2628	Green Gable	89/90	NY	214107	______
-	797	2615	Haycock	89	NY	144107	______
410	791	2595	Grisedale Pike	89/90	NY	198225	______
-	787	2582	Kirk Fell - East Top	89/90	NY	199106	______
-	785	2575	Allen Crags	89/90	NY	236085	______
-	783	2570	Glaramara	89/90	NY	246104	______
-	773	2535	Sail	89/90	NY	198202	______
-	770	2525	Hopegill Head	89/90	NY	185221	______
467	762	2500	High Raise	89/90	NY	280095	______
-	755	2478	Red Pike	89	NY	160154	______
477	753	2470	Dale Head	89/90	NY	223153	______
-	744	2442	High Crag	89/90	NY	180140	______
-	739	2424	Grisedale Pike - South-west Top	89/90	NY	194220	______
509	737	2417	Robinson	89/90	NY	201168	______
-	736	2415	Harrison Stickle	89/90	NY	281073	______
-	727	2385	Hindscarth	89/90	NY	215165	______
-	726	2381	Ullscarf	89/90	NY	291121	______
-	721	2365	Glaramara - South Top	89/90	NY	242097	______
-	719	2360	Whiteside	89/90	NY	175221	______

No.	Metres	Feet	Name	Map	Grid Ref		Date
-	715	2345	Brandreth	89/90	NY	214119	______
-	709	2325	Pike of Stickle	89/90	NY	273073	______
580	705	2313	Pike of Blisco	89/90	NY	271042	______
-	703	2306	Ladyside Pike	89/90	NY	184227	______
-	701	2300	Cold Pike	89/90	NY	262035	______
611	692	2270	Seatallan	89	NY	139083	______
-	672	2205	Scar Crags	89/90	NY	208206	______
-	660	2165	Whiteless Pike	89/90	NY	180189	______
-	653	2143	High Spy	89/90	NY	234162	______
-	651	2135	Rossett Pike	89/90	NY	249075	______
-	648	2126	Fleetwith Pike	89/90	NY	205141	______
-	646	2120	Base Brown	89/90	NY	225114	______
-	642	2105	Iron Crag	89	NY	123119	______
-	637	2089	Causey Pike	89/90	NY	218208	______
-	633	2076	Starling Dodd	89	NY	141157	______
-	632	2073	Seathwaite Fell	89/90	NY	227096	______
-	632	2072	Rosthwaite Fell	89/90	NY	256113	______
-	628	2060	Yewbarrow	89/90	NY	173084	______
-	616	2020	Great Borne	89	NY	123163	______
-	616	2020	Yewbarrow - North Top	89/90	NY	176092	______

Section 34C Eastern Fells

No.	Metres	Feet	Name	Map	Grid Ref		Date
166	950	3116	Helvellyn	90	NY	341151	______
-	890	2920	Catstye Cam	90	NY	348158	______
-	883	2896	Raise	90	NY	342174	______
281	873	2863	Fairfield	90	NY	358117	______
-	863	2832	White Side	90	NY	337166	______
-	858	2815	Dollywaggon Pike	90	NY	345130	______
-	857	2811	Great Dodd	90	NY	342206	______
-	843	2765	Stybarrow Dodd	90	NY	343189	______
325	841	2760	St Sunday Crag	90	NY	369134	______
345	828	2718	High Street	90	NY	440110	______
-	822	2698	Hart Crag	90	NY	368112	______
-	802	2630	High Raise	90	NY	448134	______

No.	Metres	Feet	Name	Map	Grid Ref		Date
-	795	2608	Green Side	90	NY	352187	______
-	792	2600	Dove Crag	90	NY	374104	______
-	792	2598	Rampsgill Head	90	NY	442127	______
-	784	2572	Thornthwaite Crag	90	NY	431100	______
433	778	2552	Harter Fell	90	NY	459092	______
435	776	2547	Red Screes	90	NY	396087	______
-	766	2513	Great Rigg	90	NY	355104	______
465	763	2502	Stony Cove Pike	90	NY	417100	______
-	757	2485	Ill Bell	90	NY	436077	______
512	736	2415	Seat Sandal	90	NY	343115	______
-	730	2396	Kentmere Pike	90	NY	465077	______
-	726	2382	Clough Head	90	NY	333225	______
-	720	2362	Froswick	90	NY	435085	______
-	713	2340	Branstree	90	NY	477100	______
-	706	2315	Yoke	90	NY	437067	______
-	696	2283	Rest Dodd	90	NY	432136	______
-	675	2215	Sheffield Pike	90	NY	369181	______
-	671	2200	Loadpot Hill	90	NY	456181	______
666	664	2178	Tarn Crag	90	NY	488078	______
684	657	2154	Place Fell	90	NY	405169	______
-	655	2150	Selside Pike	90	NY	490111	______
-	638	2093	Grey Crag	90	NY	496072	______
-	637	2091	Little Hart Crag	90	NY	387100	______
-	628	2060	Rough Crag	90	NY	454112	______

Section 34D Southern Cumbria

No.	Metres	Feet	Name	Map	Grid Ref		Date
386	803	2635	The Old Man of Coniston	96/97	SD	272978	______
-	802	2630	Swirl How	89/90	NY	272005	______
-	779	2555	Dow Crag	96/97	SD	262978	______
-	773	2536	Grey Friar	89/90	NY	259003	______
-	763	2502	Wetherlam	89/90	NY	288011	______
-	745	2443	Black Sails	89/90	NY	282007	______
688	653	2143	Harter Fell	96	SD	218997	______

REGION 35
The Northern and Central Pennines

Section 35A The Northern Pennines

No.	Metres	Feet	Name	Map	Grid Ref		Date
248	893	2930	Cross Fell	91	NY	687343	______
-	848	2781	Great Dun Fell	91	NY	710321	______
-	842	2761	Little Dun Fell	91	NY	704330	______
-	794	2604	Knock Fell	91	NY	721302	______
414	788	2585	Mickle Fell	91/92	NY	804243	______
-	767	2517	Meldon Hill	91	NY	771290	______
-	748	2455	Little Fell	91	NY	781224	______
488	747	2450	Burnhope Seat	91	NY	785375	______
554	716	2349	Great Shunner Fell	98	SD	848973	______
-	710	2329	Dead Stones	91	NY	793399	______
-	709	2327	High Seat	91/92	NY	802012	______
-	709	2326	Melmerby Fell	91	NY	652380	______
573	708	2324	Wild Boar Fell	98	SD	758988	______
-	708	2322	Great Stony Hill	91/92	NY	823359	______
-	703	2305	Chapelfell Top	91/92	NY	875346	______
-	686	2250	Round Hill	91	NY	744361	______
-	681	2235	Swarth Fell	98	SD	755966	______
630	678	2224	Baugh Fell - Tarn Rigg Hill	98	SD	740916	______
640	676	2219	The Calf	98	SD	667970	______
-	675	2216	James's Hill *	91/92	NY	923325	______
-	675	2215	Murton Fell	91	NY	753246	______
-	675	2213	Lovely Seat	98	SD	879950	______
-	674	2211	Calders	98	SD	671960	______
-	673	2207	Killhope Law	86	NY	819448	______
648	672	2205	Rogan's Seat	91/92	NY	919030	______
-	667	2188	Sails	98	SD	808971	______
-	664	2179	Black Fell	86	NY	648444	______
673	662	2171	Nine Standards Rigg	91/92	NY	825061	______

No.	*Metres*	*Feet*	*Name*	*Map*	*Grid Ref*		*Date*
-	656	2153	Grey Nag	86	NY	664476	______
-	651	2135	Three Pikes	91/92	NY	833343	______
-	649	2130	Viewing Hill	91	NY	788332	______
-	640	2100	Fell Head	97	SD	649981	______
705	639	2096	Yarlside	98	SD	685985	______
-	634	2079	Fiend's Fell	86	NY	643406	______
-	624	2047	Randygill Top	91	NY	686000	______
727	621	2037	Cold Fell	86	NY	605556	______
-	619	2030	Bink Moss	91/92	NY	875243	______
-	614	2013	Flinty Fell	86/87	NY	771419	______
-	612	2007	Burtree Fell	87	NY	862432	______

Section 35B The Central Pennines

No.	Metres	Feet	Name	Map	Grid Ref		Date
510	736	2416	Whernside	98	SD	738814	______
539	724	2376	Ingleborough	98	SD	740745	______
583	704	2309	Great Whernside	98	SE	001739	______
591	702	2302	Buckden Pike	98	SD	960787	______
605	694	2278	Pen-y-ghent	98	SD	838733	______
619	687	2255	Great Coum	98	SD	700835	______
-	680	2231	Plover Hill	98	SD	848752	______
647	672	2205	Great Knoutberry Hill	98	SD	788871	______
655	668	2192	Dodd Fell Hill	98	SD	840845	______
656	668	2191	Fountains Fell	98	SD	864715	______
-	650	2132	Simon Fell	98	SD	754751	______
-	643	2109	Yockenthwaite Moor	98	SD	909810	______
-	624	2048	Darnbrook Fell	98	SD	884727	______
-	614	2015	Drumaldrace	98	SD	873866	______
753	610	2001	Birks Fell	98	SD	918763	______

REGION 36
Lancashire, Cheshire and the Southern Pennines

No.	Metres	Feet	Name	Map	Grid Ref		Date
708	636	2088	Kinder Scout	110	SK	086875	______
-	633	2077	Bleaklow Head	110	SK	092959	______
-	627	2057	Gragareth	98	SD	687792	______

REGION 38
The Welsh Borders

Section 38B West Gloucestershire and Hereford & Worcester

No.	Metres	Feet	Name	Map	Grid Ref		Date
585	703	2306	Black Mountain *	161	SO	255350	______

REGION 40
Cornwall and Devon

No.	Metres	Feet	Name	Map	Grid Ref		Date
726	621	2038	High Willhays	191	SX	580892	______

The Sweats by Height

No.	Metres	Feet	Name	Section	Date
43	1085	3560	Snowdon - Yr Wyddfa	30B	______
-	1065	3495	Crib-y-Ddysgl	30B	______
57	1064	3490	Carnedd Llewelyn	30B	______
-	1044	3424	Carnedd Dafydd	30B	______
112	999	3279	Glyder Fawr	30B	______
-	994	3262	Glyder Fach	30B	______
-	978	3210	Pen yr Ole Wen	30B	______
138	978	3210	Scafell Pike	34B	______
-	976	3202	Foel Grach	30B	______
150	964	3162	Scafell	34B	______
-	962	3156	Yr Elen	30B	______
166	950	3116	Helvellyn	34C	______
169	947	3107	Y Garn	30B	______
-	942	3091	Foel-fras	30B	______
-	935	3067	Ill Crag	34B	______
-	934	3063	Broad Crag	34B	______
191	931	3054	Skiddaw	34A	______
-	926	3037	Garnedd Uchaf	30B	______
202	923	3029	Elidir Fawr	30B	______
-	923	3027	Crib Goch	30B	______
215	915	3002	Tryfan	30B	______
-	910	2984	Great End	34B	______
229	905	2970	Aran Fawddwy	30E	______
-	902	2960	Bowfell	34B	______
239	899	2949	Great Gable	34B	______
240	898	2946	Y Lliwedd	30B	______
248	893	2930	Cross Fell	35A	______
249	893	2929	Cadair Idris - Penygadair	30F	______
250	892	2927	Pillar	34B	______
-	890	2920	Catstye Cam	34C	______
260	886	2906	Pen y Fan	32A	______

No.	Metres	Feet	Name	Section	Date
-	885	2904	Aran Benllyn	30E	______
-	885	2903	Esk Pike	34B	______
-	883	2896	Raise	34C	______
-	873	2863	Corn Du	32A	______
281	873	2863	Fairfield	34C	______
283	872	2861	Moel Siabod	30B	______
-	872	2860	Erw y Ddafad-ddu *	30E	______
287	868	2847	Blencathra	34A	______
-	865	2837	Little Man	34A	______
-	863	2832	White Side	34C	______
-	863	2830	Mynydd Moel	30F	______
-	859	2817	Crinkle Crags - Long Top	34B	______
-	858	2815	Dollywaggon Pike	34C	______
-	857	2811	Great Dodd	34C	______
312	854	2801	Arenig Fawr	30D	______
314	852	2795	Grasmoor	34B	______
-	849	2785	Llwytmor	30B	______
-	848	2781	Great Dun Fell	35A	______
-	843	2765	Stybarrow Dodd	34C	______
-	842	2761	Little Dun Fell	35A	______
-	841	2760	Little Scoat Fell *	34B	______
325	841	2760	St Sunday Crag	34C	______
-	839	2753	Crag Hill	34B	______
-	834	2735	Crinkle Crags - South Top	34B	______
-	833	2733	Pen yr Helgi Du	30B	______
-	831	2727	Foel-goch	30B	______
342	830	2723	Cadair Berwyn	30E	______
345	828	2718	High Street	34C	______
-	828	2716	Pillar - South-west Top	34B	______
-	827	2712	Moel Sych	30E	______
-	826	2710	Red Pike	34B	______
-	822	2698	Hart Crag	34C	______
-	822	2696	Carnedd y Filiast	30B	______
359	815	2674	The Cheviot	33	______

No.	Metres	Feet	Name	Section	Date
-	815	2673	Shelter Crags	34B	______
-	811	2660	Cyfrwy *	30F	______
368	811	2660	Waun Fach	32A	______
-	807	2649	Lingmell	34B	______
377	807	2648	High Stile	34B	______
-	805	2642	Y Foel Goch	30B	______
386	803	2635	The Old Man of Coniston	34D	______
389	802	2631	Kirk Fell	34B	______
390	802	2630	Fan Brycheiniog	32A	______
-	802	2630	High Raise	34C	______
-	802	2630	Swirl How	34D	______
-	801	2628	Green Gable	34B	______
-	800	2624	Pen y Gadair Fawr	32A	______
395	799	2622	Pen Llithrig y Wrach	30B	______
-	797	2615	Haycock	34B	______
-	795	2608	Cribyn	32A	______
-	795	2608	Green Side	34C	______
-	794	2604	Bera Mawr	30B	______
-	794	2604	Knock Fell	35A	______
-	792	2600	Dove Crag	34C	______
-	792	2598	Rampsgill Head	34C	______
-	791	2595	Craig Cwm Amarch	30F	______
410	791	2595	Grisedale Pike	34B	______
414	788	2585	Mickle Fell	35A	______
-	787	2582	Kirk Fell - East Top	34B	______
-	785	2575	Allen Crags	34B	______
-	785	2575	Cadair Bronwen	30E	______
-	784	2572	Thornthwaite Crag	34C	______
-	783	2570	Glaramara	34B	______
424	782	2566	Moel Hebog	30B	______
430	779	2557	Glasgwm	30E	______
-	779	2555	Dow Crag	34D	______
433	778	2552	Harter Fell	34C	______
435	776	2547	Red Screes	34C	______

No.	Metres	Feet	Name	Section	Date
-	773	2536	Grey Friar	34D	______
-	773	2535	Sail	34B	______
448	770	2527	Moelwyn Mawr	30B	______
-	770	2526	Drum	30B	______
-	770	2525	Hopegill Head	34B	______
452	769	2523	Waun Rydd	32A	______
-	767	2517	Meldon Hill	35A	______
-	766	2513	Great Rigg	34C	______
-	763	2503	Gallt yr Ogof	30B	______
465	763	2502	Stony Cove Pike	34C	______
-	763	2502	Wetherlam	34D	______
467	762	2500	High Raise	34B	______
-	761	2496	Fan Hir	32A	______
-	758	2487	Drosgl	30B	______
-	757	2485	Ill Bell	34C	______
474	756	2480	Y Llethr	30D	______
-	755	2478	Red Pike	34B	______
477	753	2470	Dale Head	34B	______
479	752	2467	Plynlimon - Pen Pumlumon Fawr	31A	______
480	751	2464	Moel Llyfnant	30D	______
-	750	2462	Diffwys	30D	______
-	749	2457	Bannau Sir Gaer (Picws Du)	32A	______
-	748	2455	Little Fell	35A	______
487	747	2451	Yr Aran	30B	______
488	747	2450	Burnhope Seat	35A	______
-	746	2446	Carl Side	34A	______
-	745	2443	Black Sails	34D	______
-	744	2442	High Crag	34B	______
-	741	2430	Pen Pumlumon Arwystli	31A	______
-	739	2424	Grisedale Pike - South-west Top	34B	______
509	737	2417	Robinson	34B	______
510	736	2416	Whernside	35B	______
-	736	2415	Harrison Stickle	34B	______
512	736	2415	Seat Sandal	34C	______

No.	*Metres*	*Feet*	*Name*	*Section*	*Date*
514	734	2409	Fan Fawr	32A	______
516	734	2408	Craig Cwm Silyn	30B	______
-	734	2408	Long Side	34A	______
518	734	2408	Rhobell Fawr	30D	______
-	730	2396	Kentmere Pike	34C	______
-	727	2385	Hindscarth	34B	______
-	727	2385	Plynlimon - East Top	31A	______
-	726	2382	Clough Head	34C	______
536	726	2382	Moel Eilio	30B	______
-	726	2381	Ullscarf	34B	______
537	725	2379	Fan Gyhirych	32A	______
539	724	2376	Ingleborough	35B	______
-	721	2365	Glaramara - South Top	34B	______
-	720	2362	Froswick	34C	______
548	720	2362	Rhinog Fawr	30D	______
-	719	2360	Pen Allt-mawr	32A	______
-	719	2360	Whiteside	34B	______
-	719	2358	Fan y Big	32A	______
554	716	2349	Great Shunner Fell	35A	______
-	715	2345	Brandreth	34B	______
-	715	2345	Lonscale Fell	34A	______
558	714	2342	Hedgehope Hill	33	______
-	713	2340	Branstree	34C	______
-	712	2335	Rhinog Fach	30D	______
-	711	2333	Moelwyn Bach	30B	______
-	710	2329	Dead Stones	35A	______
567	710	2329	Knott	34A	______
-	709	2327	High Seat	35A	______
-	709	2326	Melmerby Fell	35A	______
572	709	2326	Trum y Ddysgl	30B	______
-	709	2325	Pike of Stickle	34B	______
573	708	2324	Wild Boar Fell	35A	______
-	708	2322	Great Stony Hill	35A	______
-	706	2315	Yoke	34C	______

No.	Metres	Feet	Name	Section	Date
580	705	2313	Pike of Blisco	34B	______
583	704	2309	Great Whernside	35B	______
585	703	2306	Black Mountain *	38B	______
-	703	2306	Ladyside Pike	34B	______
-	703	2305	Chapelfell Top	35A	______
-	702	2303	Bowscale Fell	34A	______
591	702	2302	Buckden Pike	35B	______
-	701	2300	Cold Pike	34B	______
-	701	2300	Pen Cerrig-calch	32A	______
599	698	2290	Allt Fawr	30B	______
602	698	2290	Mynydd Mawr	30B	______
-	696	2283	Rest Dodd	34C	______
-	695	2280	Mynydd Drws-y-coed	30B	______
605	694	2278	Pen-y-ghent	35B	______
611	692	2270	Seatallan	34B	______
-	691	2266	Foel Wen	30E	______
-	690	2265	Great Calva	34A	______
-	690	2263	Twmpa	32A	______
-	689	2262	Cnicht	30B	______
-	689	2260	Foel Hafod-fynydd *	30E	______
615	689	2259	Arenig Fach	30D	______
619	687	2255	Great Coum	35B	______
-	686	2250	Round Hill	35A	______
-	685	2248	Gwaun y Llwyni *	30E	______
-	685	2247	Pen y Brynfforchog *	30E	______
-	684	2245	Y Garn	31A	______
-	683	2240	Bannerdale Crags	34A	______
-	683	2240	Gau Graig	30F	______
-	681	2235	Swarth Fell	35A	______
-	681	2233	Mynydd Tarw	30E	______
-	680	2231	Plover Hill	35B	______
	679	2228	Chwarel y Fan	32A	______
630	678	2224	Baugh Fell - Tarn Rigg Hill	35A	______
633	678	2224	Creigiau Gleision	30B	______

No.	Metres	Feet	Name	Section	Date
640	676	2219	The Calf	35A	______
-	676	2217	Moel Druman	30B	______
-	675	2216	James's Hill *	35A	______
-	675	2215	Murton Fell	35A	______
-	675	2215	Sheffield Pike	34C	______
-	675	2213	Lovely Seat	35A	______
643	675	2213	Maesglase - Maen Du	30F	______
-	674	2211	Calders	35A	______
644	674	2210	Moel Cynghorion	30B	______
-	673	2207	Killhope Law	35A	______
647	672	2205	Great Knoutberry Hill	35B	______
648	672	2205	Rogan's Seat	35A	______
-	672	2205	Scar Crags	34B	______
-	672	2204	Ysgafell Wen	30B	______
650	671	2201	Foel Rhudd - Esgeiriau Gwynion	30E	______
-	671	2200	Loadpot Hill	34C	______
-	670	2197	Waun-oer	30F	______
651	669	2196	Carnedd y Filiast	30D	______
-	669	2195	Ysgafell Wen - North Top	30B	______
655	668	2192	Dodd Fell Hill	35B	______
656	668	2191	Fountains Fell	35B	______
657	667	2189	Tarren y Gesail	30F	______
659	667	2188	Cyrniau Nod	30E	______
-	667	2188	Sails	35A	______
-	665	2181	Post Gwyn	30E	______
-	664	2179	Black Fell	35A	______
666	664	2178	Tarn Crag	34C	______
670	663	2175	Fan Nedd	32A	______
-	663	2174	Mynydd Llysiau	32A	______
-	662	2172	Dduallt	30D	______
673	662	2171	Nine Standards Rigg	35A	______
-	661	2168	Craig-las (Tyrrau Mawr)	30F	______
674	661	2168	Manod Mawr	30D	______
675	660	2166	Great Rhos	31B	______

No.	*Metres*	*Feet*	*Name*	*Section*	*Date*
-	660	2165	Carrock Fell	34A	______
-	660	2165	Whiteless Pike	34B	______
-	659	2161	Cribin Fawr	30F	______
-	658	2159	High Pike	34A	______
-	658	2158	Manod Mawr - North Top	30D	______
684	657	2154	Place Fell	34C	______
-	656	2153	Grey Nag	35A	______
-	655	2150	Selside Pike	34C	______
-	655	2148	Moel yr Ogof	30B	______
-	654	2145	Allt Lwyd	32A	______
688	653	2143	Harter Fell	34D	______
-	653	2143	High Spy	34B	______
-	653	2142	Mynydd Tal-y-mignedd	30B	______
-	652	2138	Comb Fell	33	______
-	651	2135	Rossett Pike	34B	______
-	651	2135	Three Pikes	35A	______
-	650	2132	Black Mixen	31B	______
-	650	2132	Simon Fell	35B	______
-	649	2130	Viewing Hill	35A	______
-	648	2126	Fleetwith Pike	34B	______
-	648	2125	Foel Cwm Sian Llwyd	30E	______
-	648	2125	Moel-yr-hydd	30B	______
-	646	2120	Base Brown	34B	______
-	646	2120	Pen y Boncyn Trefeilw	30E	______
699	645	2115	Drygarn Fawr	31C	______
-	643	2109	Llechwedd-llyfn	30D	______
-	643	2109	Yockenthwaite Moor	35B	______
-	642	2105	Iron Crag	34B	______
-	640	2100	Fell Head	35A	______
705	639	2096	Yarlside	35A	______
-	638	2094	Moel Lefn	30B	______
-	638	2093	Grey Crag	34C	______
-	637	2091	Little Hart Crag	34C	______
-	637	2089	Causey Pike	34B	______

No.	Metres	Feet	Name	Section	Date
708	636	2088	Kinder Scout	36	______
-	635	2083	Garreg Las	32A	______
-	634	2080	Creigiau Gleision - North Top	30B	______
713	634	2080	Tarrenhendre	30F	______
-	634	2079	Fiend's Fell	35A	______
-	633	2077	Bleaklow Head	36	______
-	633	2076	Starling Dodd	34B	______
-	632	2073	Seathwaite Fell	34B	______
-	632	2072	Fan Llia	32A	______
-	632	2072	Rosthwaite Fell	34B	______
-	630	2066	Moel Fferna	30E	______
-	629	2065	Craig Cerrig-gleisiad	32A	______
-	629	2063	Fan Frynych	32A	______
-	629	2063	Foel Gron	30B	______
718	629	2063	Y Garn	30D	______
-	628	2060	Rough Crag	34C	______
-	628	2060	Yewbarrow	34B	______
-	627	2057	Gragareth	36	______
-	626	2054	Foel y Geifr	30E	______
-	625	2049	Moel y Cerrig Duon	30E	______
-	624	2048	Darnbrook Fell	35B	______
-	624	2047	Randygill Top	35A	______
-	623	2044	Moel Penamnen	30D	______
724	623	2044	Moel Ysgyfarnogod	30D	______
-	622	2040	Craig-y-llyn	30F	______
726	621	2038	High Willhays	40	______
727	621	2037	Cold Fell	35A	______
-	621	2037	Pen Bwlch Llandrillo Top *	30E	______
-	620	2034	Pen yr Allt Uchaf *	30E	______
-	619	2032	Windy Gyle	33	______
-	619	2031	Foel Boeth - Gallt y Daren	30D	______
-	619	2030	Bink Moss	35A	______
-	619	2030	Moel Gornach (Garreg Lwyd)	32A	______
739	617	2024	Cefn yr Ystrad	32A	______

No.	Metres	Feet	Name	Section	Date
741	616	2020	Cushat Law	33	______
-	616	2020	Great Borne	34B	______
-	616	2020	Yewbarrow - North Top	34B	______
-	614	2015	Drumaldrace	35B	______
-	614	2014	Foel Penolau	30D	______
-	614	2013	Flinty Fell	35A	______
-	614	2013	Llechwedd Du *	30E	______
-	613	2010	Foel Goch	30E	______
-	613	2010	Gorllwyn	31C	______
-	612	2007	Burtree Fell	35A	______
750	611	2004	Foel Goch	30D	______
752	610	2002	Pen y Garn	31C	______
-	610	2001	Bache Hill	31B	______
753	610	2001	Birks Fell	35B	______
-	610	2001	Bloodybush Edge	33	______
755	610	2000	Tal y Fan	30B	______

Chapter 6
The County Tops

County boundaries often follow a watershed or ridge of high ground, and therefore they tend to be unsuitable for dividing groups of hills into different regions. For this reason the division of the country into forty-two regions in Chapter 3 is based more on geographical features such as rivers and passes than on county boundaries. However, counties are well-known and well-established, and so a list of the highest point in each county is likely to be more meaningful than the highest points of forty-two arbitrary regions. The county tops were listed by George Bridge in his book *The Mountains of England and Wales,* but publication of this was soon followed by the reorganisation of local government, as well as the reorganisation of Ordnance Survey maps, so the list is doubly out of date.

In most counties the highest point is also a Marilyn, but not all the county tops can be regarded as summits. Some are indeterminate points along a county boundary on the slope of a hill, while others are wholly within a county but have no clearly identifiable highest point. The appeal of this type of top is fairly limited, though some walkers might relish the challenge of locating and standing on the highest point in each county.

The details of the county tops are set out below in the same format used for the Marilyns in Chapters 3 and 4, with the Marilyn number given where relevant. In counties where the highest point is not a Marilyn, then both the highest point and the highest Marilyn are listed. If there is no Marilyn in the county, then just the highest point is given. The list is given first in alphabetical order of county and then in height order.

The County Tops by Country

Scotland

No.	Metres	Feet	Name	Map	Grid Ref		Date
Borders							
330	840	2756	Broad Law	72	NT	146235	______
Central							
12	1174	3852	Ben More	51	NN	432244	______
Dumfries & Galloway							
324	843	2766	Merrick	77	NX	428855	______
Fife							
932	522	1713	West Lomond	58	NO	197066	______
Grampian							
2	1309	4296	Ben Macdui	36/43	NN	989989	______
Highland							
1	1344	4408	Ben Nevis	41	NN	166713	______
Lothian							
691	651	2137	Blackhope Scar	73	NT	315483	______
Strathclyde							
27	1126	3695	Ben Cruachan	50	NN	069304	______
Tayside							
7	1214	3984	Ben Lawers	51	NN	636414	______
Orkney							
1031	481	1577	Ward Hill	6/7	HY	229022	______
Shetland							
1104	450	1475	Ronas Hill	3	HU	305835	______
Western Isles							
394	799	2622	Clisham	13/14	NB	155073	______

Wales

No.	*Metres*	*Feet*	*Name*	*Map*	*Grid Ref*		*Date*
Clwyd							
342	830	2723	Cadair Berwyn	125	SJ	071323	______
Dyfed							
Highest Marilyn:							
479	752	2467	Plynlimon - Pen Pumlumon Fawr	135	SN	789869	______
Highest Point:							
-	781	2561	Fan Foel	160	SN	821223	______
Gwent							
Highest Marilyn:							
778	596	1955	Sugar Loaf	161	SO	272188	______
Highest Point:							
-	679	2228	Chwarel y Fan	161	SO	258294	______
Gwynedd							
43	1085	3560	Snowdon - Yr Wyddfa	115	SH	609544	______
Mid Glamorgan							
Highest Marilyn:							
1238	382	1253	Cefn Eglwysilan	171	ST	097905	______
Highest Point:							
-	588	1929	Craig y Llyn	170	SN	909031	______
Powys							
260	886	2906	Pen y Fan	160	SO	012216	______
South Glamorgan							
No Marilyn. Highest Point:							
-	264	866	*Craig Llysfaen	171	ST	190851	______
West Glamorgan							
773	600	1969	Craig y Llyn	170	SN	907032	______

England

No.	Metres	Feet	Name	Map	Grid Ref		Date
Avon							
Highest Marilyn:							
1473	233	764	*Dundry Down	172/182	ST	553667	______
Highest Point:							
-	264	866	Niver Hill	182	ST	565539	______
Bedfordshire							
No Marilyn. Highest Point:							
-	243	798	Dunstable Downs	166	TL	009194	______
Berkshire							
1372	297	974	Walbury Hill	174	SU	373616	______
Buckinghamshire							
1429	267	876	Haddington Hill	165	SP	890089	______
Cambridgeshire							
No Marilyn. Highest Point:							
-	146	480	Great Chishill	154	TL	428384	______
Cheshire							
856	559	1834	Shining Tor	118	SJ	994737	______
Cleveland							
1327	329	1078	Gisborough Moor	94	NZ	634123	______
Cornwall							
1164	420	1377	Brown Willy	201	SX	158800	______
Cumbria							
138	978	3210	Scafell Pike	89/90	NY	215072	______
Derbyshire							
708	636	2088	Kinder Scout	110	SK	086875	______
Devon							
726	621	2038	High Willhays	191	SX	580892	______
Dorset							
1416	277	908	Pilsdon Pen	193	ST	413011	______
Durham							
414	788	2585	Mickle Fell	91/92	NY	804243	______
East Sussex							
1461	248	813	Ditchling Beacon	198	TQ	331130	______

No.	Metres	Feet	Name	Map	Grid Ref		Date
Essex							
No Marilyn. Highest Point:							
-	147	482	Chrishall Common	154	TL	443362	______
Gloucestershire							
1323	330	1083	Cleeve Hill	163	SO	997246	______
Greater Manchester							
No Marilyn. Highest Point:							
-	542	1778	Black Chew Head	110	SE	056020	______
Hampshire							
Highest Marilyn:							
1423	270	887	Butser Hill	197	SU	717203	______
Highest Point:							
-	286	937	Pilot Hill	174	SU	398601	______
Hereford & Worcester							
585	703	2306	*Black Mountain	161	SO	255350	______
Hertfordshire							
No Marilyn. Highest Point:							
-	244	802	*Pavis Wood	165	SP	914092	______
Humberside							
1464	246	807	Bishop Wilton Wold	106	SE	821569	______
Isle of Wight							
1469	240	786	St Boniface Down	196	SZ	568785	______
Kent							
Highest Marilyn:							
1508	200	656	North Downs	178/188	TQ	804586	______
Highest Point:							
-	251	823	Betsom's Hill	187	TQ	436563	______
Lancashire							
Highest Marilyn:							
850	561	1839	Ward's Stone	102	SD	592587	______
Highest Point:							
-	627	2057	Gragareth	98	SD	687792	______
Leicestershire							
1413	278	912	Bardon Hill	129	SK	460132	______
Lincolnshire							
1535	168	550	*The Wolds	113	TF	121964	______

No.	Metres	Feet	Name	Map	Grid Ref	Date
London						
No Marilyn. Highest Point:						
-	250	820	Botley Hill	187	TQ 407563	______
Merseyside						
1524	179	587	Billinge Hill	108	SD 525014	______
Norfolk						
No Marilyn. Highest Point:						
-	102	336	Beacon Hill	133	TG 186413	______
Northamptonshire						
No Marilyn. Highest Point:						
-	225	737	Arbury Hill	152	SP 540587	______
Northumberland						
359	815	2674	The Cheviot	74/75	NT 909205	______
North Yorkshire						
510	736	2416	Whernside	98	SD 738814	______
Nottinghamshire						
No Marilyn. Highest Point:						
-	203	666	*Newtonwood Lane	120	SK 457605	______
Oxfordshire						
No Marilyn. Highest Point:						
-	261	855	Whitehorse Hill	174	SU 301864	______
Shropshire						
901	540	1771	Brown Clee Hill	137/138	SO 593866	______
Somerset						
943	519	1704	Dunkery Beacon	181	SS 891416	______
South Yorkshire						
No Marilyn. Highest Point:						
-	546	1791	Margery Hill	110	SK 189957	______
Staffordshire						
Highest Marilyn:						
1227	385	1264	Gun	118	SJ 970615	______
Highest Point:						
-	520	1705	Cheeks Hill	119	SK 026699	______
Suffolk						
No Marilyn. Highest Point:						
-	128	419	Great Wood	155	TL 786559	______

No.	Metres	Feet	Name	Map	Grid Ref	Date
Surrey						
1380	295	968	Leith Hill	187	TQ 139431	______
Tyne & Wear						
No Marilyn. Highest Point:						
-	259	850	Currock Hill	88	NZ 107592	______
Warwickshire						
No Marilyn. Highest Point:						
-	261	855	Ebrington Hill	151	SP 187426	______
West Midlands						
No Marilyn. Highest Point:						
-	271	889	Turner's Hill	139	SO 967887	______
West Sussex						
1409	280	919	Black Down	186/197	SU 919296	______
West Yorkshire						
799	582	1908	Black Hill	110	SE 078047	______
Wiltshire						
Highest Marilyn:						
1391	288	945	Long Knoll	183	ST 786376	______
Highest Point:						
-	295	968	Milk Hill	173	SU 104643	______

The County Tops by Height

County	*No.*	*Metres*	*Feet*	*Name*	*Section*	*Date*
Highland	1	1344	4408	Ben Nevis	4A	
Grampian	2	1309	4296	Ben Macdui	8	
Tayside	7	1214	3984	Ben Lawers	2B	
Central	12	1174	3852	Ben More	1C	
Strathclyde	27	1126	3695	Ben Cruachan	3C	
Gwynedd	43	1085	3560	Snowdon - Yr Wyddfa	30B	
Cumbria	138	978	3210	Scafell Pike	34B	
Powys	260	886	2906	Pen y Fan	32A	
Dumfries & Galloway	324	843	2766	Merrick	27B	
Borders	330	840	2756	Broad Law	28B	
Clwyd	342	830	2723	Cadair Berwyn	30E	
Northumberland	359	815	2674	The Cheviot	33	
Western Isles	394	799	2622	Clisham	24B	
Durham	414	788	2585	Mickle Fell	35A	
Dyfed	-	781	2561	Fan Foel	32A	
North Yorkshire	510	736	2416	Whernside	35B	
Hereford & Worcester	585	703	2306	Black Mountain *	38B	
Gwent	-	679	2228	Chwarel y Fan	32A	
Lothian	691	651	2137	Blackhope Scar	28A	
Derbyshire	708	636	2088	Kinder Scout	36	
Lancashire	-	627	2057	Gragareth	36	
Devon	726	621	2038	High Willhays	40	
West Glamorgan	773	600	1969	Craig y Llyn	32C	
Mid Glamorgan	-	588	1929	Craig y Llyn	32C	
West Yorkshire	799	582	1908	Black Hill	36	
Cheshire	856	559	1834	Shining Tor	36	
South Yorkshire	-	546	1791	Margery Hill	36	
Greater Manchester	-	542	1778	Black Chew Head	36	
Shropshire	901	540	1771	Brown Clee Hill	38A	
Fife	932	522	1713	West Lomond	26	
Staffordshire	-	520	1705	Cheeks Hill	36	

County	No.	Metres	Feet	Name	Section	Date
Somerset	943	519	1704	Dunkery Beacon	41	______
Orkney	1031	481	1577	Ward Hill	23	______
Shetland	1104	450	1475	Ronas Hill	22	______
Cornwall	1164	420	1377	Brown Willy	40	______
Gloucestershire	1323	330	1083	Cleeve Hill	39	______
Cleveland	1327	329	1078	Gisborough Moor	37	______
Berkshire	1372	297	974	Walbury Hill	42	______
Surrey	1380	295	968	Leith Hill	42	______
Wiltshire	-	295	968	Milk Hill	39	______
Hampshire	-	286	937	Pilot Hill	42	______
West Sussex	1409	280	919	Black Down	42	______
Leicestershire	1413	278	912	Bardon Hill	39	______
Dorset	1416	277	908	Pilsdon Pen	41	______
West Midlands	-	271	889	Turner's Hill	39	______
Buckinghamshire	1429	267	876	Haddington Hill	39	______
Avon	-	264	866	Niver Hill	41	______
South Glamorgan	-	264	866	Craig Llysfaen *	32C	______
Oxfordshire	-	261	855	Whitehorse Hill	39	______
Warwickshire	-	261	855	Ebrington Hill	39	______
Tyne & Wear	-	259	850	Currock Hill	35A	______
Kent	-	251	823	Betsom's Hill	42	______
London	-	250	820	Botley Hill	42	______
East Sussex	1461	248	813	Ditchling Beacon	42	______
Humberside	1464	246	807	Bishop Wilton Wold	37	______
Hertfordshire	-	244	802	Pavis Wood *	39	______
Bedfordshire	-	243	798	Dunstable Downs	39	______
Isle of Wight	1469	240	786	St Boniface Down	42	______
Northamptonshire	-	225	737	Arbury Hill	39	______
Nottinghamshire	-	203	666	Newtonwood Lane *	37	______
Merseyside	1524	179	587	Billinge Hill	36	______
Lincolnshire	1535	168	550	The Wolds *	37	______
Essex	-	147	482	Chrishall Common	39	______
Cambridgeshire	-	146	480	Great Chishill	39	______
Suffolk	-	128	419	Great Wood	39	______
Norfolk	-	102	336	Beacon Hill	39	______

Chapter 7
Hill Walking by Numbers

I owe the title of this chapter to a magazine article by John Perriment in which he argued convincingly in defence of the practice of peak bagging. The basic case was stated with honest simplicity:

> Many people indulge in pointless leisure activities like collecting stamps, coins, old bottles, cigarette cards - whatever.
> I just happen to collect hills.

He has since claimed to have given up collecting hills in favour of 'view bagging' but, significantly, only after he had achieved his goal of climbing all 408 hills listed in Bridge's book.

There is a clear parallel between collecting objects of a certain type and the practice of climbing all the hills in a given list or category. Most hill walkers would argue that there's a bit more to it than that - the views, the open air, the solitude, the scenery, the wildlife, the exercise, the escape from the pressure or routine of everyday life, and so on. All are reasons why so many of us enjoy hill walking, but the fact remains that people climb the Munros because there is a well-publicised list of them, and not because the Munros always offer a better walk than slightly lower hills, which are visited much less often. This doesn't mean that collecting hills is competitive. There are no prizes for completing a list or medals for the fastest finish. In most cases there is just great personal satisfaction at achieving a long-held ambition, and doing so in a harmless, healthy and enjoyable manner.

This chapter unashamedly caters for the hill walker who admits to being a collector, or at least an enthusiast. It contains a collection of statistics and other less serious information about the 1542 Marilyns (the Sweats and County Tops are ignored). The obvious place to start is with a comparison of Marilyns and Munros.

Munros

There are currently 277 Scottish mountains that have been granted Munro status. 202 of these qualify as Marilyns. However, there are 205 Marilyns in Scotland over 3000 feet, which is explained by the fact that three Marilyns are categorised only as Munro tops. These three are:

> Buachaille Etive Beag - Stob Coire Raineach (Section 3B)
> Beinn Alligin - Tom na Gruagaich (Section 13A)
> Beinn Eighe - Spidean Coire nan Clach (Section 13A)

In the 1981 edition of *Munro's Tables*, the third of the Torridon giants, Liathach, was elevated to two-Munro status, yet for some reason Beinn Alligin and Beinn Eighe did not receive the same treatment. In fact, the drop between the two Marilyns on Beinn Alligin and Beinn Eighe is much greater than that on Liathach, which only has two Marilyns by virtue of a generous application of the 15-contour rule (explained in Chapter 4).

The 75 Munros that do not qualify as Marilyns are listed below.

Region	*Metres*	*Munro*	*Nearest Marilyn*
1	946	Beinn Tulaichean	Cruach Ardrain
1	940	Beinn a'Chroin	An Caisteal
1	916	Beinn a'Chleibh	Ben Lui
2	981	Creag Mhor	Carn Mairg
2	968	Meall Garbh	Carn Mairg
2	1103	Beinn Ghlas	Ben Lawers
3	953	Meall Dearg	Aonach Eagach - Sgorr nam Fiannaidh
3	998	Stob Diamh	Ben Cruachan
4	1221	Aonach Mor	Aonach Beag
4	1116	Stob Coire an Laoigh	Stob Choire Claurigh
4	1106	Stob a'Choire Mheadhoin	Stob Coire Easain
4	1056	Na Gruagaichean	Binnein Mor
4	1001	Sgor an Iubhair	Sgurr a'Mhaim
4	981	Stob Coire a'Chairn	An Gearanach
4	939	Mullach nan Coirean	Stob Ban
4	977	Stob Coire Sgriodain	Chno Dearg
4	1114	Aonach Beag	Geal-charn
4	1100	Beinn Eibhinn	Geal-charn
4	924	Creag Pitridh	Geal Charn
5	975	A'Mharconaich	Beinn Udlamain
5	936	A'Bhuidheanach Bheag	Carn na Caim
6	933	The Cairnwell	Carn a'Gheoidh
6	917	Carn Aosda	Carn a'Gheoidh
7	1064	Cairn of Claise	Glas Maol
7	1019	Carn an Tuirc	Glas Maol
7	987	Creag Leacach	Glas Maol
7	958	Tolmount	Glas Maol
7	957	Tom Buidhe	Glas Maol
7	947	Driesh	Glas Maol
7	928	Mayar	Glas Maol
7	1118	White Mounth	Lochnagar
7	1047	Carn an t-Sagairt Mor	Lochnagar

Region	Metres	Munro	Nearest Marilyn
7	1012	Cairn Bannoch	Lochnagar
7	998	Broad Cairn	Lochnagar
8	1019	Mullach Clach a'Bhlair	Sgor Gaoith
8	1113	Monadh Mor	Beinn Bhrotain
8	1004	The Devil's Point	Cairn Toul
8	1245	Cairn Gorm	Ben Macdui
8	1155	Derry Cairngorm	Ben Macdui
8	931	Beinn Bhreac	Beinn a'Chaorainn
9	930	A'Chailleach	Carn Dearg
9	926	Geal Charn	Carn Dearg
9	920	Carn Sgulain	Carn Dearg
9	1006	Carn Liath	Creag Meagaidh
9	1053	Stob Poite Coire Ardair	Creag Meagaidh
10	1004	Sgurr an Lochain	Sgurr an Doire Leathain
10	987	Druim Shionnach	Aonach air Chrith
10	981	Maol Chinn-dearg	Aonach air Chrith
10	947	Creag a'Mhaim	Aonach air Chrith
11	1181	Mam Sodhail	Carn Eige
11	1112	Tom a'Choinich	Carn Eige
11	982	Mullach na Dheiragain	Sgurr nan Ceathreamhnan
11	921	An Socach	Sgurr nan Ceathreamhnan
11	959	Saileag	Sgurr a'Bhealaich Dheirg
11	1002	Sail Chaorainn	Sgurr nan Conbhaireann
11	957	Carn Ghluasaid	Sgurr nan Conbhaireann
12	1049	Sgurr Fhuar-thuill	Sgurr a'Choire Ghlais
12	992	Carn nan Gobhar	Sgurr a'Choire Ghlais
12	999	Sgurr Choinnich	Sgurr a'Chaorachain
14	1060	Sgurr Fiona	An Teallach - Bidean a'Ghlas Thuill
14	954	Beinn Liath Mhor Fannaich	Sgurr Mor
14	949	Meall Gorm	Sgurr Mor
14	923	An Coileachan	Sgurr Mor
14	934	Meall a'Chrasgaidh	Sgurr nan Clach Geala
14	923	Sgurr nan Each	Sgurr nan Clach Geala
15	977	Meall nan Ceapraichean	Beinn Dearg
16	987	Conival	Ben More Assynt
17	958	Bruach na Frithe	Sgurr nan Gillean
17	934	Am Basteir	Sgurr nan Gillean
17	973	Sgurr a'Ghreadaidh	Sgurr Dearg - Inaccessible Pinnacle
17	918	Sgurr a'Mhadaidh	Sgurr Dearg - Inaccessible Pinnacle
17	965	Sgurr na Banachdich	Sgurr Dearg - Inaccessible Pinnacle

Region	Metres	Munro	Nearest Marilyn
17	948	Sgurr Mhic Choinnich	Sgurr Alasdair
17	944	Sgurr Dubh Mor	Sgurr Alasdair
17	924	Sgurr nan Eag	Sgurr Alasdair

The numbers in each region are roughly proportional to the number of Munros, with the exception of Region 7 (fourteen Munros, only three Marilyns over 3000 feet) and Region 17 (thirteen Munros, only five Marilyns over 3000 feet). These two regions are worth further comment. The Munros in Region 7 are spread over an extensive high plateau, so presumably Sir Hugh was fairly generous with separate mountain status because of the large distances between summits, even though there is little height difference. In contrast, eleven of the thirteen Munros in Region 17 are along the Black Cuillin Ridge of Skye. These summits are not far apart in terms of distance or height, but because of the steepness and difficulty of the terrain they are well separated by time, ie. the time it takes most walkers to get from one summit to the next. These two regions illustrate that measures such as distance and time may be as relevant as height when assessing mountains. The Marilyns, though, are judged strictly by relative height, and the numbers of them in Regions 7 and 17 simply reflect this.

Corbetts

The definition of Corbetts is the same as that of Marilyns, over a limited height range, so there is an almost perfect correlation between the 220 Scottish Marilyns in the 2500-2999 feet band and the 221 Corbetts listed in the 1990 edition of *Munro's Tables.* The only discrepancy concerns the treatment of Gairbeinn and Corrieyairack Hill (Section 9B), which are both 896 metres high but are not separated by the required 150-metre drop. These are listed as one Marilyn (Gairbeinn) but two Corbetts.

Some of the mountains in this category appear to be less stable than we might imagine, and are liable to soar or diminish in the time it takes to produce a new map. For example, Sron a'Choire Chnapanich (Section 2A) appeared from nowhere to leap into the Corbett chart at 837 metres in 1984, while Cook's Cairn (Section 21A) dropped out shortly afterwards when a new map showed that it had slumped from 774 to 756 metres, though it still qualifies as a Marilyn. By contrast, Beinn Teallach (Section 9C) was quite a slow mover when it rose by only two metres in 1984, but this was sufficient to promote it from Corbett to Munro status and thereby ensure that it became host to a vast increase in footprints. And even at the time of writing it seems that further orogenesis may have taken place, as the status of Foinaven (Section 16B) is still unclear; its newly-discovered height of 914 metres puts it firmly on the Corbett/Munro boundary, and the Ordnance Survey seem unwilling to commit themselves as to whether it has actually risen above the magic 914.4-metre mark. All aspiring Munroists are advised to climb it just in case.

There are a further thirty-two Marilyns of Corbett height located in England and Wales, but these seem to be in a relatively stable condition, with little recent height change recorded as a result of metrication, re-surveying or geological upheaval.

Lesser Corbetts

It seems strange that with all the attention paid to the 2000-foot summits in England, Wales and Southern Scotland, there is no tradition of climbing all the equivalent summits in the rest of Scotland. Perhaps it has been generally assumed that there are too many of them to make it a feasible proposition. This proves not to be the case. Remarkably, there are almost exactly the same number of Scottish Marilyns (222) between 2000 and 2499 feet as there are Corbetts. This group of hills may be referred to as the Lesser Corbetts, which can be conveniently abbreviated to Elsies. They include some of the finest and most distinctive peaks in the country, such as Stac Pollaidh, Suilven, The Storr and Ben Stack, as well as popular hills like Tinto and Ben Venue. A few of these are described in the Scottish Mountaineering Club guidebook *The Corbetts and Other Scottish Hills,* but many of the others are in remote settings and must have been very rarely visited. Certainly the Elsies will present a worthwhile challenge to Munroists and Corbetteers, and will provide a good incentive to head off into relatively uncharted territory, with few paths and fewer people. A concise list can be easily abstracted from Chapter 4 (610 to 761 metres) though committed Scots will probably ignore those in Regions 29 to 42. Most of the sixty-five Elsies in England and Wales are well-documented and fairly well-worn but are still capable of providing enjoyable and worthwhile excursions.

Regions

The tables below show the number of Marilyns in each of the forty-two regions, subdivided into different height categories; first in metres and then in feet.

Region	*150-499 Metres*	*500-999 Metres*	*1000+ Metres*	*Total*
1	9	68	6	83
2	1	24	16	41
3	7	45	10	62
4	1	28	17	46

Region	*150-499 Metres*	*500-999 Metres*	*1000+ Metres*	*Total*
5	0	13	1	14
6	2	19	7	28
7	6	18	2	26
8	1	13	11	25
9	12	26	2	40
10	5	64	9	78
11	2	16	12	30
12	9	31	6	46
13	7	27	3	37
14	1	28	5	34
15	9	26	2	37
16	29	54	0	83
17	48	38	0	86
18	11	36	0	47
19	30	26	0	56
20	16	14	0	30
21	16	19	0	35
22	20	0	0	20
23	9	0	0	9
24	55	15	0	70
25	6	0	0	6
26	18	5	0	23
27	31	30	0	61
28	25	33	0	58
29	4	1	0	5
30	21	50	2	73
31	24	13	0	37
32	24	15	0	39
33	4	6	0	10
34	19	37	0	56
35	4	25	0	29
36	9	8	0	17
37	5	0	0	5
38	18	5	0	23

Region	150-499 Metres	500-999 Metres	1000+ Metres	Total
39	5	0	0	5
40	6	1	0	7
41	10	1	0	11
42	14	0	0	14
Total	553	878	111	1542
Scotland	386	716	109	1211
Isle of Man	4	1	0	5
Wales	69	78	2	149
England	94	83	0	177

Region	500-999 Feet	1000-1999 Feet	2000-2999 Feet	3000+ Feet	Total
1	1	16	49	17	83
2	0	3	16	22	41
3	2	12	26	22	62
4	1	6	15	24	46
5	0	1	8	5	14
6	0	4	11	13	28
7	1	10	12	3	26
8	0	2	12	11	25
9	1	16	19	4	40
10	2	12	42	22	78
11	0	4	12	14	30
12	1	13	20	12	46
13	1	8	19	9	37
14	0	5	16	13	34
15	3	13	15	6	37
16	2	45	33	3	83
17	14	44	23	5	86
18	3	16	28	0	47
19	7	35	14	0	56
20	4	18	8	0	30
21	2	23	10	0	35
22	18	2	0	0	20

Region	500-999 Feet	1000-1999 Feet	2000-2999 Feet	3000+ Feet	Total
23	6	3	0	0	9
24	31	34	5	0	70
25	3	3	0	0	6
26	6	16	1	0	23
27	9	37	15	0	61
28	3	42	13	0	58
29	2	2	1	0	5
30	9	24	34	6	73
31	1	32	4	0	37
32	5	26	8	0	39
33	1	6	3	0	10
34	5	23	24	4	56
35	0	8	21	0	29
36	2	14	1	0	17
37	2	3	0	0	5
38	5	17	1	0	23
39	3	2	0	0	5
40	3	3	1	0	7
41	6	5	0	0	11
42	14	0	0	0	14
Total	179	608	540	215	1542
Scotland	121	443	442	205	1211
Isle of Man	2	2	1	0	5
Wales	15	82	46	6	149
England	41	81	51	4	177

Islands

The mainland of Britain contains 1306 Marilyns, which leaves 236 distributed as follows among 58 other islands:

Region	Island	Marilyns	Region	Island	Marilyns
17	Skye	48	18	Eilean Shona	1
24	Lewis/Harris	39	24	Eriskay	1
17	Mull	25	22	Fair Isle	1
20	Jura	12	22	Fetlar	1

Region	Island	Marilyns	Region	Island	Marilyns
22	Mainland Shetland	11	24	Garbh Eilean	1
20	Arran	10	17	Gometra	1
24	South Uist	9	25	Hirta	1
24	North Uist	7	30	Holy Island (Anglesey)	1
20	Islay	6	20	Holy Island (Arran)	1
29	Isle of Man	5	22	Isle of Noss	1
17	Rhum	5	19	Kerrera	1
23	Mainland Orkney	4	24	Mingulay	1
24	Barra	3	24	Muldoanich	1
23	Hoy	3	24	Pabbay (North)	1
17	Eigg	2	24	Pabbay (South)	1
22	Foula	2	23	Rousay	1
42	Isle of Wight	2	24	Sandray	1
17	Raasay	2	17	Scalpay	1
22	Unst	2	20	Scarba	1
27	Ailsa Craig	1	24	Scarp	1
30	Anglesey	1	24	Seaforth Island	1
30	Bardsey Island	1	25	Soay	1
24	Berneray	1	25	Stac an Armin	1
25	Boreray	1	25	Stac Lee	1
22	Bressay	1	24	Taransay	1
19	Bute	1	17	Ulva	1
17	Canna	1	24	Vatersay	1
18	Carna	1	23	Westray	1
25	Dun	1	22	Yell	1

A few of these islands are connected by road; Anglesey and Holy Island are linked to each other and to the mainland by two bridges, while North Uist and South Uist are connected to each other by road causeway (via the island of Benbecula). By the end of the century it seems probable that Skye will also have a road link to the Scottish mainland. This still leaves a lot of boat travel for anyone planning to visit all the islands. Many of the small islands in the Outer Hebrides (Region 24) are completely uninhabited, and so of course have no ferry service.

The island with the highest single peak is Scarba (Section 20A), on which

Cruach Scarba rises 449 metres above the sea. The smallest island peak is Muldoanich (Section 24D), which at 153 metres is the smallest of all the Marilyns.

Names

It seems common knowledge that in the Inuit (Eskimo) language there are supposed to be over thirty different words for snow, though I have never heard this confirmed by an Inuit. It is less well-known that the British have over seventy different words for a hill, though not all derive from the same language. The most common of these is 'Beinn', which applies to 234 of the Marilyns. A count of all the words for a hill that appear more than once in the list of Marilyns is shown below.

Name	Count	Name	Count
Beinn	234	Biod	5
Hill	165	Carnedd	5
Meall	88	Crag	5
Ben	73	Cruachan	5
Carn	64	Field	5
Sgurr	64	Mount	5
Creag	45	Mountain	5
Bheinn	41	Rig	5
Fell	41	Tom	5
-val	32	Garn	4
Mynydd	23	Knock	4
Stob	23	Meallan	4
Cruach	21	Spidean	4
Law	21	Sron	4
Cnoc	18	Top	4
Moel	16	Tor	4
Craig	14	Braigh	3
Stac	13	Bryn	3
Cairn	12	Maol	3
Pen	12	Sail	3
Sgorr	12	Sgor	3
Druim	10	Sidhean	3
Mullach	9	Barrow	2
Seat	8	Carnan	2
Charn	8	Cefn	2
Aonach	7	Chreag	2
Beacon	7	Cnap	2
Foel	7	Creachan	2

Head	7	Heights	2
Pike	7	Knott	2
-bhal	7	Mam	2
Down	6	Mheall	2
Dun	6	Mheallan	2
Fan	6	Rhos	2
Moor	6	Ridge	2
Bidein	5	Sgorach	2
Binnein	5	Stuc	2
		Wold	2

This leaves 276 Marilyns that have some other kind of name. An elementary knowledge of the meaning of some of these Gaelic words can give a good indication of the character of a hill. For example, a 'Meall' or 'Meallan' will probably be a rounded, relatively featureless shape, whereas a 'Sgurr' or 'Sgorr' is likely to be a distinctive peak. Several of the books about Scottish mountains (see Chapter 8) give a translation of the common Gaelic hill names.

The full name that appears most often in the list of Marilyns is Beinn Bhreac, which means speckled hill. There are 11 of them, plus one Beinn Bhreac-liath (speckled grey hill). The ten most common names of Marilyns are as follows:

11	Beinn Bhreac	(speckled hill)
8	Glas Bheinn	(greenish-grey hill)
7	Beinn Mhor	(big hill)
7	Carn Dearg	(red hill)
6	Beinn Dearg	(red hill)
6	Meall Mor	(big hill)
5	Creag Mhor	(big rock)
4	Beinn Mheadhoin	(middle hill)
4	Beinn Mheadhonach	(middle hill)
4	Meall Buidhe	(yellow hill)

There are three Geal Charn, one Geal-charn and one Geal-Charn (all meaning 'white hill'), so maybe these should also be included in the top ten. The most common English name is Black Hill, which occurs three times, though as it happens two of them are in Southern Scotland (Section 28A). The Gaelic names may pose severe pronunciation problems, but we should be grateful for them, as the above hills would sound much less interesting if the English translations were in common use.

Many of the Gaelic names include a word which describes the colour of the hill. There are twenty-six Marilyns with the word 'Dearg' in their name (plus two 'Dheirg' and one 'Dhearg'), which suggests that there are more red hills than any other colour. However, adding together all the 'Black', 'Dubh' and 'Dhubh' Marilyns gives a total of thirty-four, so black is the most commonly named colour. As most hills tend to look brownish or greenish in colour, it might seem surprising that so few of them are named accordingly. A little further thought reveals why - most hills were originally named to distinguish them from other nearby hills, so calling them 'brown hill' or 'green hill' would not have been terribly helpful.

The Marilyn with the longest name is Meallan Liath Coire Mhic Dhughaill, in the far north of Scotland (Section 16B), which translates as 'Grey Hill of McDougall's Corrie'. The shortest name is Gun (Region 36), which is the highest point of the Staffordshire hills known as The Roaches - a popular rock-climbing area.

Most Remote Hills

There are several candidates for the title of most remote Marilyn but no clear winner, as there are different ways of defining remoteness. The St Kilda group of islands (Region 25) are so far away from the rest of Scotland (about forty miles from North Uist) that they are rarely included in a map of the British Isles. Of the six Marilyns of St Kilda, Cnoc Glas on the island of Soay is the farthest away from the mainland or any civilian habitation, though it is not far from the other five Marilyns in the group.

By contrast, the Marilyns in Central and Eastern England are close to civilisation but remote from each other. Both Bardon Hill and Haddington Hill (Region 39) are over thirty miles from any other Marilyn, but the honour of being the most isolated hill goes to the highest point in the Lincolnshire Wolds (Region 37), which does not appear to have a specific name, and is therefore listed as 'The Wolds'. The summit is over forty miles from the nearest Marilyn (Bishop Wilton Wold), and over sixty miles from the next nearest.

The most commonly-accepted meaning of remoteness is that of distance from the nearest road. On the Scottish mainland there are a number of hills that are about ten miles from a public road in any direction. It is often reckoned that the most remote Munros are A'Mhaighdean and Ruadh Stac Mor (Section 14A). Most of the Knoydart mountains (Section 10B) are even more distant from the road network, but can be made more accessible by taking a ferry from Mallaig to Inverie. Similarly, some of the remote hills in the Ben Alder group (Section 4B) can be approached more easily by using the railway over Rannoch Moor to Corrour Station. In his *Handbook of the Scottish Hills,* Eric Yeaman rates Caiteshal (Section 24A) as the toughest hill in Scotland, based on a combination of height and inaccessibility. This peak is also about ten miles from the nearest public road but is conveniently near the coast for anyone with their own boat.

The summits which appear to be most remote from access by road, rail or boat are Beinn Bhreac (Section 6A), An Cruachan (Section 12B), Carn Ban (Section 15A) and Creag Mhor (Section 16D), with Beinn Bhreac possibly top of the list. However, distance does not always correspond exactly with time or difficulty of access, as a good track or path can make some of these very remote hills more easily accessible than those in more rugged areas such as Knoydart.

Another possible measure of remoteness is that of relative height. The hills of the far north of Scotland (Region 16) are not among the highest in the country, but many of them rise quite individually from the surrounding land and so have an impressively monolithic appearance. For example, Cul Mor (Section 16F) has a drop of over 600 metres on all sides before the terrain rises towards the next nearest Marilyns, while Ben Hope (Section 16B) has a drop of over 660 metres all round. This gives Ben Hope a second claim to fame, as it is also the most northerly 3000-foot Marilyn (though Foinaven is running it very close). In England and Wales the summit with the greatest drop all round seems to be Moel Siabod (Section 30B), which is about 490 metres clear of the slopes of any other Marilyn.

The question of what is remote obviously depends on what criteria you use and where you start from. For a resident of Lerwick, the Cornish Marilyns are the most remote. The four Marilyns at the extremes of the country are:

Northernmost:	Saxa Vord (Region 22)
Southernmost:	White Downs (Region 40)
Westernmost:	Cnoc Glas (Region 25)
Easternmost:	North Downs (Region 42)

On mainland Britain, Sgribhis-bheinn (Section 16A) is the most northerly Marilyn, while Beinn na Seilg (Section 18A) is the most westerly. It is also worth mentioning Beinn na Lice (Section 19B) which is at the southern tip of the Kintyre peninsula, near the Mull of Kintyre, and is about one hundred miles by road from the nearest hills in any other mainland region.

Easiest Summits

Yeaman's *Handbook of the Scottish Hills* gives an energy rating of 0.00 to Wideford Hill on Orkney Mainland, which is supposed to mean that it requires no energy at all to ascend, as a road leads all the way to the summit. However, this only makes it easy if you happen to be on Orkney Mainland in the first place. Yeaman's book covers only Scotland, of course, but some of the most easily attained Marilyns are in England and Wales. My own nomination for the easiest summit goes to Bishop Wilton Wold (Region 37) which is the highest point in the Yorkshire Wolds and the endangered county of Humberside. The triangulation point on the summit is on exactly the same level as the main A166 road from York to Bridlington. However, there are two mounds belonging to the local water company that are a few feet higher than both the triangulation point and the road (even the smallest hills seem to have two tops). This means that anyone driving past on the A166 has not reached the highest point, whereas someone sitting upstairs on a passing 841 bus can reasonably claim to have bagged the summit!

Boggiest Summits

Most hills over 1000 feet high have boggy areas at some point on their slopes, but it is only popular hills with flattish tops that manage to maintain their bogginess all the way to the summit. I have only once been prevented from standing on the highest point of a hill by the depth of bog surrounding it. This dubious honour belongs to Waun Fach, which is the highest point in the Black Mountains of south Wales (Section 32A). When I visited this summit it had no triangulation point, just a little concrete platform set in the middle of a sea of very deep ooze (I still regard the summit as bagged, as my head was higher than the highest point). I have heard great tales of the quagmire on the summit of The Cheviot (Region 33) but have not yet managed to inspect it personally. The highest point in Region 36, which is on the summit plateau of Kinder Scout (not the triangulation point), is also highly regarded for being both difficult to locate and adrift in a sea of peat hags, though when I managed to find it during a very dry spell some years ago my feet emerged dusty but dry. The best tactic seems to be to catch this type of summit in winter when the bog is either frozen or snow-covered.

Most Boring Hills

Boringness is quite distinct from bogginess, as a boggy summit may have superb views, whereas the only satisfaction provided by a truly boring hill is that of ticking it off a list. There are several strong contenders for the title of Britain's most boring hill.

In his continuous journey over all the Munros (described in *Hamish's Mountain Walk),* Hamish Brown reckoned that the area he called 'The Grey Wasteland' was probably the 'least notable of all'. This is in Section 6B, and includes the Marilyns (and Munros) of Carn Bhac, Beinn Iutharn Mhor, Carn an Righ and Glas Tulaichean. Irvine Butterfield, in *The High Mountains of Britain and Ireland,* agrees that these hills 'lack topographical interest and stimulating views' and have 'long plods between the summits'.

However, Butterfield seems to take greater exception to parts of Region 2, for he unfairly describes Beinn Mhanach as a 'tedious lump' and Meall

Ghaordaidh as 'quite the dullest hill in the Southern Highlands'. He is also contemptuous of Meall Chuaich (Region 5), which is described as 'a boring hill with an equally drab outlook' and all of the Monadh Liath Hills (Section 9B), which he rates as 'unrelentingly tedious' (is he trying to prevent erosion by putting people off?). The good news is that only one of the Monadh Liath Munros qualifies as a Marilyn; the bad news is that there are several Corbetts and lower Marilyns in this area that may be equally tedious. W. H. Murray, in *Scotland's Mountains,* switches attention to Section 16D, where he describes Ben Klibreck and Ben Armine as 'dull mountains in a dreary bog.

Some walkers would argue that all of the Scottish hills are full of interest compared to parts of the English Pennines. There are certainly plenty of boring summits in England, but fortunately not many of them qualify as Marilyns (beware of Section 35A in Chapter 5). In *Classic Walks in the Yorkshire Dales*, Walt Unsworth claims that Rogan's Seat (which *is* a Marilyn) is the worst of all; it has been described as 'so bad it just has to be collected'.

In Wales there is the featureless flat top of Cyrniau Nod (Section 30E) to be reckoned with. It is one of the Berwyn Hills that Terry Marsh (in *The Mountains of Wales*) believes would be immensely popular were it not for the heather, which is so thick that 'a considerable portion of them fall at best into the category of "sheer purgatory"'. This description does not apply to the highest peak in the range, Cadair Berwyn, which can offer an excellent walk over easy terrain with fine views, but few of the lesser summits in this area are interesting enough to justify thrashing through the heather jungle to reach them.

All these candidates for being the most boring hill in Britain are over 2000 feet high, so it would seem that there must be some lower Marilyns with outstandingly uninteresting qualities that have yet to be recognised. Of course, the lack of merit has to be balanced against the effort involved in reaching the summit. To be significantly boring a hill should be at least a couple of hours walk from the nearest road, so that a full sense of anti-climax can be experienced on reaching the top.

Best Viewpoints

One of the provisional titles for this book was 'The Viewpoints of Britain', as the majority of Marilyns provide splendid views in favourable weather (there aren't really all that many boring ones). But this title would have been a little misleading, as many fine viewpoints are not on the summits of Marilyns. For those more interested in views than hills, well-known viewpoints are identified on recent Ordnance Survey maps by a small blue sun symbol.

The quality of any view is entirely subjective and weather-dependent, so there can be no consensus of opinion about which is the best. The man who has probably climbed more Scottish hills more often than anyone else is Hamish Brown, and so his opinion must be respected when he rates the summit of A'Mhaighdean (Section 14A) as providing the finest view of any among the Munros. He also considers it to be the least easily reached Munro, so there is an admitted elitism in his judgement, but Irvine Butterfield agrees that A'Mhaighdean and neighbouring Ruadh Stac Mor provide 'outstanding vantage points'.

Different views have contrasting qualities. W.H.Murray asserts that the view from the top of Foinaven (Section 16B) is 'unmatched in scale for its kind - glittering desolation', while for a 'vast spread of sea and mountains' he recommends the summits of Garbh Bheinn and Ben Resipol (Section 18B). Then of course there are the very well-known but still magnificent peaks of Glencoe such as Buachaille Etive Mor and Bidean nam Bian (Section 3B), which in good conditions provide dramatic mountain skylines in all directions. Beinn Sgritheall (Section 10A) has also received great acclaim as a viewpoint from those fortunate enough to reach the top in good visibility.

There are a host of superb viewpoints in the Lake District, Snowdonia and other parts of England and Wales, but it is generally agreed that they can not compare in scale or grandeur with the best that Scotland has to offer. My personal nomination for best viewpoint goes to Bla Bheinn on Skye (Section 17B), with its 360-degree panorama of jagged ridges, green valleys, shimmering seas, scattered islands, extensive coastlines and countless distant peaks. This judgement was naturally influenced by a rare combination of cloudless sky, haze-free horizon and wind-free warmth. Such days make up for dozens of damp and chilly expeditions to lesser summits. They can provide unforgettable memories to treasure for all time, and if you are in the right frame of mind they can even help to put the rest of your life into some sort of perspective.

Chapter 8
Further Reading

There is a great wealth of literature available about hill walking in Britain, both in general and in specific areas of the country. The brief, selective bibliography below includes details of books referred to in the preceding text together with other recent publications that are particularly relevant to a large number of the relative hills of Britain.

Lists

Scottish Mountaineering Club. *Munro's Tables.* Scottish Mountaineering Trust, 1990.
Lists all the Munros, Munro Tops, Corbetts and Donalds, plus the names of all known Munroists (those known to have climbed all the Munros) and a brief Gaelic guide.

Bridge,G. *The Mountains of England and Wales.* Gaston's Alpine Books and West Col Productions, 1973.
An old but much-used list of the 2000-foot tops in England and Wales. Now out of print and out of date, it is mainly of historical interest.

Buxton,C. & Lewis,G. *The Mountain Summits of England and Wales.* Red Dial Publications, 1986.
A brief, inexpensive booklet which updates and enlarges on the list of summits in Bridge's book. Includes some very insignificant tops.

Yeaman,E.J. *Handbook of the Scottish Hills.* Wafaida, 1989.
Lists all the hills in Scotland over one hundred metres high, and includes meticulous codes and notes about many of them.

Hackenthorpe,R., Hackenthorpe,D., Hackenthorpe,J. & Hackenthorpe,L.V. *The Hackenthorpe Book of Lies.* Slater-Methuen, 1973.
Mythical collection of miscellaneous misinformation. Contains over sixty million untrue facts and figures.

Guides

Bennet,D. (ed). *The Munros.* Scottish Mountaineering Trust, 1985.
Well-illustrated guide to the main ascent routes on every Munro, conveniently grouped into walks of reasonable length. Does not include the Munro Tops.

Butterfield,I. *The High Mountains of Britain and Ireland.* Diadem Books, 1986.
Coffee-table guide to all the Munros, Munro Tops, deleted Munros, deleted Tops, and 3000-foot summits in England, Wales and Ireland. The mountains are divided into non-standard sections and some mammoth expeditions. Also available in a more portable edition without the photographs.

Johnstone,S., Brown,H. & Bennet,D. (ed). *The Corbetts and Other Scottish Hills.* Scottish Mountaineering Trust, 1990.
Companion guide to *The Munros* in the same format, covering the main ascent routes on a few selected Lesser Corbetts and even lower hills, as well as all the Corbetts.

Marsh,T.

The Mountains of Wales. Hodder & Stoughton, 1985.
The Lake Mountains One. Hodder & Stoughton, 1987.
The Lake Mountains Two. Hodder & Stoughton, 1987.
The Pennine Mountains. Hodder & Stoughton, 1989.
Series of guides that together cover almost all the 600-metre summits of England and Wales. Several routes are described on the more popular hills.

Nuttall,J. & Nuttall,A.

The Mountains of England and Wales. Volume 1: Wales. Cicerone Press, 1989.
The Mountains of England and Wales. Volume 2: England. Cicerone Press, 1990
A pair of guides intended specifically for walkers aiming to bag all the 2000-foot summits outside Scotland. Most of the suggested walks are designed to include as many tops as possible in a circuit of reasonable length.

Poucher,W.A.

The Scottish Peaks. Constable, 1988.
The Welsh Peaks. Constable, 1987.
The Lakeland Peaks. Constable, 1983.
The Peak and Pennines. Constable, 1983.
A relatively old series of guides that describe routes on the more popular summits in a country or area. The books were first published in the 1950's and 60's but have been regularly revised since. Each one contains a multitude of black-and-white photographs.

Wainwright,A.

The Eastern Fells. Westmorland Gazette, 1955.
The Far Eastern Fells. Westmorland Gazette, 1957.
The Central Fells. Westmorland Gazette, 1958.
The Southern Fells. Westmorland Gazette, 1960.
The Northern Fells. Westmorland Gazette, 1962.
The North Western Fells. Westmorland Gazette, 1964.
The Western Fells. Westmorland Gazette, 1966.
A set of hand-written and hand-drawn books, often considered to be the definitive guides to the hills of the Lake District. They have not been revised since first publication, so details of some routes have become out of date.

True Stories

Brown,H.

Hamish's Mountain Walk. Paladin, 1980.
Climbing the Corbetts. Gollancz, 1988.
Enthusiastic accounts of the ascent of all the Munros (in one continuous journey) and all the Corbetts (over several years).

Moran,M. *The Munros in Winter.* David & Charles, 1985.
Detailed account of the first continuous journey over all the Munros in winter.

Caldwell,C. *Climb Every Mountain.* MacDonald, 1990.
Description of the first (and possibly the last) continuous self-propelled journey over all the Munros and all the Corbetts.

Symonds,H. *Running High.* 1991.
The book of the first run over and between all the 3000-foot summits in Scotland, England, Wales and Ireland.

Colour printed by Carnmor Print & Design, Preston
Text printed by Martins of Berwick